The EVERYTHING®
Guide to Writing a Book Proposal

Dear Reader:

The first time I saw my name—*my* name!—on the cover of a book, I feared I was hallucinating. Writers are notoriously loopy, and it seemed quite probable that I had fallen victim to some delusional disease in which all my senses conspired to deceive me into believing that I had joined the ranks of published book authors.

Since that first book, which was as much Barb's doing as mine, we have spent many hours discussing ways to share that incredible "newly published" sensation with more writers. The problem with most books about writing, we agreed, is that they're written by writers who, besides being loopy, tend to suffer from severe tunnel vision when it comes to the business of writing.

Our mission here, then, is to give you a more balanced view of the art and business of getting published. The more you know about how the publishing industry works, the better equipped you are to build a proposal that will knock the breath out of an editor and make him scramble for the telephone. And someday you, too, may wake up to find you aren't hallucinating after all.

Meg Schneider   *Barbara Doyen*

The EVERYTHING® Series

Editorial

Publishing Director	Gary M. Krebs
Managing Editor	Kate McBride
Copy Chief	Laura M. Daly
Acquisitions Editor	Gina Marzilli
Development Editor	Julie Gutin
Production Editors	Jamie Wielgus

Production

Production Director	Susan Beale
Production Manager	Michelle Roy Kelly
Series Designers	Daria Perreault
	Colleen Cunningham
	John Paulhus
Cover Design	Paul Beatrice
	Matt LeBlanc
Layout and Graphics	Colleen Cunningham
	Rachael Eiben
	John Paulhus
	Daria Perreault
	Monica Rhines
	Erin Ring
Series Cover Artist	Barry Littmann

Visit the entire Everything® Series at *www.everything.com*

THE

EVERYTHING®

GUIDE TO
WRITING A
BOOK PROPOSAL

Insider advice on how to
get your work published

Meg Schneider and Barbara Doyen

Adams Media
Avon, Massachusetts

*For authors everywhere, we offer these tools to help you in your
pursuit of publication. May success attend your quest!*

An Everything® Series Book.
Everything® and everything.com® are registered trademarks of F+W Publications, Inc.

Published by Adams Media, an F+W Publications Company
57 Littlefield Street, Avon, MA 02322 U.S.A.
www.adamsmedia.com

ISBN: 1-59337-313-9
Printed in the United States of America.

J I H G F E D C B A

Library of Congress Cataloging-in-Publication Data
Schneider, Meg Elaine.
The everything guide to writing a book proposal / Meg Schneider and Barbara Doyen.
p.   cm.
ISBN 1-59337-313-9
1. Book proposals. 2. Authorship. I. Doyen, Barbara. II. Title.
PN161.S36   2005
808'.02--dc22   2004026532

This publication is designed to provide accurate and authoritative information with regard
to the subject matter covered. It is sold with the understanding that the publisher is not
engaged in rendering legal, accounting, or other professional advice. If legal advice or other expert assistance is required, the services of a competent professional person should
be sought.
—From a *Declaration of Principles* jointly adopted by a Committee of the
American Bar Association and a Committee of Publishers and Associations

Many of the designations used by manufacturers and sellers to distinguish their products
are claimed as trademarks. Where those designations appear in this book and Adams
Media was aware of a trademark claim, the designations have been printed with initial
capital letters.

*This book is available at quantity discounts for bulk purchases.
For information, call 1-800-872-5627.*

Contents

Acknowledgments

Life experiences shape an author's work and message. The information in this book comes from helping my clients prepare all types of book proposals and from the feedback I've received from the many editors who have considered these proposals through the years. For these experiences, I am truly grateful.

—Barb Doyen

So many people have had a hand in this work: my parents, who taught me the joys of reading and encouraged my own writing; the myriad authors who inspired me, from Dr. Seuss onward; the teachers who prodded me to expand my abilities; and the countless professionals who helped me turn an avocation into a vocation. There are no words sufficient to describe their influence, nor how dear they are to me.

—Meg Schneider

Top Ten Things You Should Know
about Book Publishing

1. Agents and editors are always looking for great new talent.

2. Nonfiction is easier for new authors to break into than fiction.

3. New fiction authors should write at least two novels in the same genre to build a readership base.

4. You don't always need an agent.

5. A good agent is your guide through the publishing process as well as your business partner.

6. Rejections are business decisions, not an indictment of you or your work.

7. Agents and editors don't have time to deal with amateurs. Therefore, be professional in all your dealings.

8. Six-figure advances are the exception, not the rule, especially for first-time authors.

9. From the author's perspective, nothing in publishing ever happens quickly.

10. No matter how many setbacks you encounter, the only person who can tell you you're not a good writer is you.

Introduction

▶ According to the International Publishers Association, U.S. book publishers put more than 65,000 new titles in print in an average year. No one keeps track of how many manuscripts are rejected in an average year, but you can be sure the number is phenomenal; even assuming that one in ten manuscripts gets published (and that's probably quite a generous assumption), that means every year well over half a million book ideas never go anywhere.

Why do so few book proposals make it to print? Contrary to the popular belief among many would-be writers, still writhing with righteous indignation over their latest rejection slips, it is not because authors are at the mercy of the capricious whims of editors or agents who are incapable of recognizing the rare and beautiful even when it is served up on a platter. In virtually every instance, a book idea is rejected because it fails to meet a publisher's standards of salability.

Those standards are high, and justifiably so. Publishers will spend a minimum of $50,000 to acquire, print, and promote a given book; in order to stay in business, the publishing house has to choose those titles that it expects will be profitable. Authors, especially first-time authors, often get so wrapped up in their own projects that they fail to recognize the very real business needs of the publishers to whom they hope to sell their work.

Talk to any editor or agent who has been in the publishing business for a few years, and he or she likely will give you the same list of common mistakes first-time writers make in trying to sell their ideas. Sometimes their ideas aren't original, or they haven't found that unique slant that will catch an editor's attention. Sometimes authors pitch ideas that don't fit in with a publisher's line, or they don't take the trouble to find the right publisher for their project. Sometimes there just isn't a demonstrable market of readers for the project.

Unfortunately, many authors are vague about how the publishing industry works and unfamiliar with the tools editors and agents use to decide which proposals land in the dead file and which earn the elusive acceptance letter. It's like going fishing, except that you don't know what kind of fish you want to land, where to find them, or what kind of bait they like. You wouldn't expect to be very successful at fishing if you didn't have this basic knowledge, as well as the tools to do the job, would you? Yet, all too often, writers send their works off like an amateur angler, hoping to hook a contract without knowing exactly what a particular publisher is looking for or even where that publisher's readers are.

No one, and especially no book, can guarantee that your next book proposal will set your telephone ringing with flattering contract offers. But you can make your proposals more complete, more energetic, and more professional. That alone will make your ideas seem like tiny islands of peace in a sea of pandemonium, naturally drawing the eye of any editor or agent and giving your work its best opportunity for thorough consideration. Eventually, you might just hit that magical combination of the right idea at the right time with the right publisher for the right readership—and, just like that, you'll be a published author.

Chapter 1

What Do You Want to Write?

The writing life has been glamorized in fiction and film, leading many aspiring writers to believe it consists of lounging for hours in quirky diners with a cup of coffee, a legal pad, and a pen, dreaming up your next great opus. There's nothing wrong with this vision; for lots of writers, it may even be fairly close to reality. But if you're serious about building a writing career, you'll have to take much more specific and much less glamorous action.

Setting a Goal

Successful people in virtually any field usually have at least this one skill in common: They visualize where they want to be five, ten, or more years in the future, then they work their way back to figure out what steps they need to take to get there. For aspiring writers, the long-term goal may be one published book, several books, or even the celebrity that comes with publishing a bestseller. Whatever your dream is, the trick to making it come true is planning the best way to get there, and then sticking to your plan.

Goals and Projects

There's an important difference between goals and projects. Goals are broad in nature, and there may be several ways to achieve a given goal. Projects are smaller in scope and usually have an ordered method, a series of steps, that will lead to completion. If you want to own a house someday, that's a goal. If you want to add a sunroom onto your house, that's a project.

ESSENTIAL

Most writers prefer projects to goals, because they like knowing the steps to follow to finish a project. That's why books about writing give you advice on developing your plot, creating characters with depth, and so forth; each of these is a step that, taken in the correct order, moves you toward completion of your project, and each in turn moves you closer to achieving your goal.

Your goal is to be a published book author. Your project is the book you're working on. You might reach your goal in a number of ways. Even if you're a fiction writer, you might land a contract for a nonfiction book before you can sell your science fiction novel. In this way, you'll have achieved your goal of becoming a published book author, though not the way you envisioned it. Meanwhile, your science fiction novel is a project for you to work on, and your chances of selling that project increase dramatically if you already have a book credit in your portfolio.

Time-Based Goals

People who work creatively, whether they are writers, actors, musicians, or painters, sometimes set time limits for themselves to achieve their dreams. You might think in terms of publishing your first book by the time you're twenty-five, for example, or you might give yourself three years to get your book published. These kinds of internal deadlines help keep many people motivated to pursue their goals. And it is certainly a valid way to avoid the "someday" trap and stay focused.

Unfortunately, time-based goals also have a down side, especially when they're too broad or used as stand-alone goals. The down side is failure. If you don't have other ways to track your progress, the ability to meet a self-imposed deadline becomes your only measure of success. This can be devastating when your twenty-fifth birthday passes or three years go by and you don't have that first book contract. If your overall plan doesn't include other ways to gauge your progress, you are likely to feel like a failure—even if you have racked up other publishing credits in the meantime.

ALERT!

If you've said, more than once, "One of these days I'm going to write a book," but haven't taken any steps toward realizing that ambition, you're caught in the "someday" trap. Giving yourself time-based goals—like a deadline for finishing your outline or your first chapter—can help you break the "someday" cycle.

If you stop to think about it, the time-based goals you give yourself are completely arbitrary, no matter what they're based on. Any number of factors might prevent you from getting your first book published before your twenty-fifth birthday or within three years of finishing your manuscript, none of which may be within your control. Self-imposed deadlines work best when matched with smaller, realistic goals—ideally ones that are within your power to control.

Accomplishment-Based Goals

Goals based on completing specific tasks—especially specific tasks within a larger project—are usually more realistic and more satisfying, especially for the beginning writer. Even published pros can be daunted by the idea of sitting down and writing a whole book; it's too large a job to get your mind around all at once. That's why so many writing books advise you to break big projects down into smaller, more manageable elements.

Any writing project, whether it's a magazine article or book-length work, can be broken down into smaller parts. A novel, for instance, needs a plot, settings, and characters; instead of just starting at page one and forging ahead, you can write a short narrative of your plot that will serve as a sort of roadmap to help you stay on course when you write. You can write a descriptive piece about the settings in your story to help you visualize them more clearly. And you can write mini-biographies for each of your main characters, which gives you a chance to focus properly on each of them before you toss them all together into your story.

Nonfiction projects can be broken down in similar ways. A mission statement for your book tells you what you want to accomplish with your writing. A chapter-by-chapter outline helps you define the material to be covered and how it is to be organized. A list of resources or questions that need to be answered helps focus your research efforts.

FACT

Publishing in general is highly competitive, and fiction markets are especially difficult for new authors to break into. You can improve your chances of getting published if you stay open to other opportunities, even if they're out of your favored genre. A nonfiction book credit is still a book credit, and it will probably help you as you market your fiction.

Smaller goals like these serve two purposes: They help you progress toward your overall goal of writing a book, and they help keep you motivated and on track. When you finish your plot narrative or your nonfiction outline, you get to revel in a sense of accomplishment that otherwise would be postponed until you completed the entire book. And when you feel like you're making progress toward your overall goal, you are more likely to stick with it instead of feeling stuck.

Accomplishments and Deadlines

Time-based goals work best when they are combined with accomplishment-based goals. Tie your self-imposed deadlines to the smaller elements in your book project. Instead of pressuring yourself to get a book published before the next Leap Year, resolve to have your nonfiction outline done in the next thirty days. Give yourself a week to write the mini-bio for your protagonist, then devote the following week to the mini-bio of your protagonist's love interest, and so on.

Combining these elements gives you a tangible measurement of your progress; you can look at what you've done and know that you've used your time wisely to move a step or two closer to your goal of getting published. You're less likely to get discouraged in the long run, because you direct your energy at taking charge of the things you can control rather than at the things that are beyond your control.

Working against your own deadlines is good practice for when you do get a publishing contract with legally binding deadlines. By setting your own deadlines to complete various writing tasks, you learn more about how you write—the kind of pace you're comfortable with, for example—and will be better able to judge whether you can meet deadlines requested by publishers.

Plotting Your Career

Many writers focus their energy on their current projects or on their overall goals without giving much thought to career planning. You might get where you want to go by waiting for inspiration and opportunity to strike; lots of writing careers have been made that way. But most beginning writers benefit from defining their goals, identifying the things that will help them achieve their goals, and then laying out a career plan to follow.

Choosing a Genre

Like actors, writers are often "typecast" into specific categories. A non-fiction author may make a name for himself writing business books, or a fiction author may become known as a mystery writer. This is not to say that you can't make the jump from one genre to another, but when you're at the beginning of your career, you should plan to write at least two books in the same genre before switching.

Following up your first book with another in the same genre serves two purposes. First, readers tend to expect certain things from certain authors. A reader who read your first gothic novel will expect your second offering to be a gothic novel, too, and she likely will be disappointed if you switch to fantasy; therefore, sticking with the same genre helps you build a base readership. Second, but just as important for beginning authors, selling a second book in the same genre helps build your self-confidence because it proves that getting your first book published was not a fluke.

FACT

Some writers pour all their energy into one book project at a time, preferring to write the query, proposal, and partial or full manuscript before even thinking about whether they want to do a second project. Pacing your projects so that you have one in each stage at all times helps remind you that there are other ideas waiting to be written, so lack of progress on one project isn't quite so discouraging.

Projects and Stages

Professional authors often have three or even four projects going at the same time, albeit in different stages: one project that has been published and that the author is now helping to promote, one that is in the writing stage, one that is in the marketing stage, and even one that's in the dreaming-up stage. These authors always have something to work on and something to look forward to.

Of course, juggling projects this way requires a great deal of organization and discipline. Deadlines for the project you're writing might interfere with promotional efforts for the published book, and the project being marketed might sell sooner than expected. Some authors arrange their days with blocks of time devoted to each of their various projects. Some even have separate desks and filing cabinets—one set for works in progress, and one for works that have sold and need to be promoted.

If you're a beginning writer, you don't have too many projects to worry about, but you do have some juggling to do. While you're waiting for responses to your query letter, you can polish your proposal so it's ready to send when an agent or editor asks to see it. At the same time, you can collect material and make notes for your next book idea, so you'll have the preliminary work done when you're ready to write your next query letter.

Building Your Portfolio

Another critical element in plotting your career is developing your credentials and publishing credits to boost your attractiveness as a new book author. (Chapter 15 offers detailed information on ways to collect useful credentials.) Ideally, your portfolio should relate directly to your book project. If you're marketing your science fiction novel, it will help if you've published short stories in a respected science fiction magazine or if you've published technical articles in science journals. For nonfiction projects, newspaper and magazine credits on a similar topic will make a good impression with a prospective agent or editor.

These small projects may seem inconsequential when compared to your goal of landing a book contract, but they are an integral part of most successful writing careers. Indeed, many published book authors supplement their income and keep their names before the reading public with magazine articles and short stories. Some even find ideas for their next book while they're researching or writing these shorter pieces.

The Personal Project

Most writers focus on what they want to write—the genre and topics for which they feel a particular affinity. The aspiring romance novelist writes about romance, and the aspiring domestic diva writes about the home. These are passionate projects, the ones that motivate us to sit down at the computer or typewriter and pour our souls onto the page.

Beginning writers often get discouraged when they find that agents and editors don't share their passion for their projects. Rejection slips and even constructive criticism make many would-be writers feel at best pessimistic about their prospects of realizing their dreams. One aspiring writer, wounded by a critique that accompanied a rejection of his first novel, lamented, "If I can't write this (genre), what am I supposed to do?"

The answer, echoed by virtually every professional author, is "Keep trying." The subject or genre you feel passionate about may not sell today or even this year, but its time may come next year or the year after. While you're waiting for the market to catch up to your vision, you can study your craft, hone your skills, and look for other opportunities to help you realize your writing ambitions.

ESSENTIAL

Look for ideas that can cross over between books and magazines. Is there a chapter in your nonfiction book that could be adapted for a magazine article? Can you condense a subplot from your romance novel to write a new short story? Finding different ways to use the same material saves you time and energy, and cross-marketing your work like this can help boost your career.

The Business Project

Business projects have three main advantages for writers: They promote your career, they generate income, and they provide opportunities to hone your writing skills. These projects usually aren't personally compelling and would not have been your first choice. In fact, business projects will often come to you (as opposed to your seeking them out) through an agent or editor who thinks you might be a good fit—even if they've rejected a proposal from you before. For example, your agent or an editor may have rejected your mainstream novel, but may peg you for a book about small business planning because your author's bio indicated you've taught seminars on that topic for several years.

The best example of a business project is a nonfiction title for the writer who dreams of making a name for himself as a novelist. His heart is in fiction; that's where he finds the passion to write. But the path to getting published may well include a detour down the nonfiction lane, if he's open to the opportunity.

Many writers have a hard time accepting this premise; they believe they should only write in the genre or on the topic they feel passionate about. It's often especially difficult for would-be fiction authors to open themselves to the idea of writing nonfiction. But there are two factors that make the concept of the business project important to you as a writer. First, the hardest part about becoming a published book author is getting that first book credit. Second, it's often much easier for new writers to get that first book credit with a nonfiction project than with a fiction book.

QUESTION?

How often do agents and editors solicit writers for projects?
It doesn't happen all the time, but it's frequent enough that you should keep an open mind about these kinds of opportunities. A publishing house may decide it needs a book on a specific topic to fill a niche in its list, and its editors will ask agents if they can recommend a writer for that project. Agents often keep reminders of prospective authors' areas of expertise for just such situations.

Write What You Know

Sometimes the biggest challenge for writers is coming up with a good story or a good topic. Most writing instructors advise students to write what they know about and avoid the things they don't know about. If you live in a small Midwestern town and have never traveled overseas, the instructors say, set your novel in Paris, Iowa, not Paris, France. This is good advice, as far as it goes. But for our purposes here, it doesn't go far enough.

All of us know more than we think we do. We have work experiences, hobbies, and life experiences that, with a little practice and a slight change in the way we view our knowledge, can be transformed into compelling premises for a book. The challenge is to take a step back and look at your experiences from an outsider's point of view.

Work Experience

Most of us spend most of our days working at something other than writing books, so the workplace is a good spot to begin the search for potential book ideas. We all know that we can adapt our workplace as a setting for a novel, or capture traits and mannerisms of our coworkers for our characters. But there are other possibilities, too.

Have you been working in a particular field for several years? Is there an issue in that field that needs to be addressed, and do you have ideas on how it should be done? Your years of experience would be a great asset when you're pitching this book idea to agents and editors.

Even the most mundane job can present book possibilities. Suppose you're a waitress in a sports bar. You could identify seven main customer types and write a book about them. Maybe you could write an hour-by-hour account of a typical Friday night in your establishment. Or you could write a book about major sporting contests and how the clientele and mood of the place differs between a regular-season baseball game and the World Series.

Personal Hobbies

Many writers abandon their other hobbies, preferring to concentrate attention on their book manuscripts. But a hobby can be the basis of a winning book proposal, especially in today's society, when leisure activities like collecting and crafts are so popular. Perhaps your own hobby is unusual enough that there aren't any books about it, or perhaps the books that are available don't reflect your own experience. If you have engaged in your hobby for years, that gives you credibility in writing about it.

Life Experience

Each of us experiences life in his own way, and each of us has experiences that touch us differently. You may take your life experiences for granted and don't see them as a resource. To give yourself a different perspective on the things you've done and the things that have happened to you, try making lists of them. Then find a friend or relative who knows firsthand about these happenings, and ask him or her to describe the event to you. Looking at your own life from someone else's point of view can be eye opening; your relative or friend may have a different memory of the event from yours, and may even ascribe different motives and emotions than you do.

FACT

Most writers are familiar with the advice, "Write for the market." Author Fay Weldon cautions that "the market" doesn't mean agents or editors; "the market" is your reader. Always write with your reader in mind, and have faith that eventually an agent or editor will catch on to "the market."

What Fascinates You?

You don't have to be an expert on a topic to write about it, and you aren't required to experience firsthand the things you write about. Ann Rule writes true crime stories, usually murder stories, but that doesn't make her a murderer. *The Boston Globe* staff wrote a book about the child sex abuse scandal in the Catholic Church, but that doesn't mean any of those writers were personally abused by a priest.

One of the great things about writing books is that it can be your excuse to add to your store of knowledge. You can choose a subject that interests you—space travel, marine biology, history, mathematics, global economics, basketry, basketball, or any of a million and one other themes. Your personal interest in the topic, combined with good research, can get you started. Add to your topic an angle that hasn't been used yet, and you may have the makings of a great book idea.

You can further leverage your interests by combining a plot point or setting for your novel with a potential nonfiction book; do the research once and get two book ideas out of it. If your novel involves modern whaling, for example, you might be able to turn your research for your novel into a layman's guide to whale watching. And if you get your whale-watching guide published, you'll have an impressive selling point when you begin to market your whaling novel.

Grist for the Idea Mill

Beginning writers sometimes feel that they were born too late; all the good ideas are already taken, and some of them are overused. One particularly cynical critic once said that there are only six plots for fiction, and three of them are used regularly. It's enough to make the novice despair of ever coming up with something fresh.

Fortunately, it doesn't matter whether that critic was right or not. We keep writing, and our readers keep reading, and no amount of cynicism will change that. The trick, especially for beginning writers, is to get the idea mill churning reliably, and that is simply a matter of knowing where to look and what to look for. Here are three simple steps to start the wheels turning:

1. **Read, read, read.** Newspapers, magazines, books, and Internet sites are home to ideas just waiting to be mined. A short item on a ten-car pile-up on the interstate might give you a starting point for your next short story; a single quote from a government official may trigger an entire plot line for a spy thriller.
2. **Think, "What if?"** Whenever you read, ask "what if" questions. What if the second car in that ten-car pile-up had not tried to change lanes? What if the government official had made his comment two years ago? "What if" questions let you unleash your own imagination and make you an active thinker rather than a passive receiver of information.
3. **Look for holes.** There are always at least two sides to every situation. As you read, look for aspects that haven't been given their due. The story on the ten-car pile-up probably covered the aspects of weather, speed, emergency response, injuries, and effects on other motorists. But there might be other aspects that didn't get much attention, such as whether all the drivers involved were insured, or how one's religious faith comes into play after a traumatic event.

FACT

Try putting yourself in another person's place to see a new angle to an old subject. There are lots of books about how to provide the best customer service, for example; are there any written from the customer's point of view? Has the topic of leadership been tackled from the point of view of the follower? Searching for different perspectives and unanswered questions can lead to terrific book ideas.

Once you get into the practice of searching for ideas, your problem will be reversed: Practically overnight, you'll find that you have too many ideas and not enough time to devote to them all. To make sure you don't lose any of those ideas, devise a system for keeping track of them. It doesn't have to be fancy or extensive. Many writers use 3" x 5" index cards to write short notes about possible book ideas and then store the cards in a recipe box. This system is simple to use and doesn't require a lot of space.

It's Time to Write

Some writers advise you to write every day, whether you feel like it or not. The argument for this is twofold. First, like any other artist, you must practice your craft, and, second, making yourself write every day instills the discipline you'll need to finish your projects. Committing to some writing time every day also helps you make writing a priority; this is important for those who dream about writing but never seem to find the time to sit down and do it.

Do you really need to write every single day? It may seem excessive; after all, few other disciplines require you to work seven days a week, 365 days a year. Besides, when it comes to any creative endeavor, the mind and the muse both need time to rest. You won't ruin your writing career if you take an occasional day off, or even an occasional week's vacation. As with most aspects of writing, the time you need to devote to it depends on your lifestyle, your other commitments, and what you want to accomplish.

Just as important as time to write is a place to write. Whether you can convert the spare bedroom into an office or have to block off a corner of the living room with a folding screen, set up a place in your home devoted to writing. Having your own space where you can leave the tools of your trade about without worrying about other people messing around with them will make things a lot easier.

Depending on What You Write

When you're working on fiction, it's a good idea to write every day, or nearly every day. You can lose tone, minor plot points, and the genuine feel for your characters if you wait too long between writing sessions. Most writers who advise you to write every day are thinking in terms of book-length fiction, where these factors are more important and you could more easily lose track of them.

Nonfiction is different, because each chapter is more like a long magazine article—a piece that can stand on its own. (The exceptions to this are biographies, true crime stories, and other works that follow a preset chronology, where continuity in tone, plot, and character development are important.) When it comes to writing nonfiction, you probably won't lose the feel of the whole if you allow several days to elapse between chapters.

A Window of Opportunity

Some people are at their most creative in the early morning. Others can't get going until late at night, when the rest of the world has gone to bed and they are alone and free to imagine whatever they like. Still others can write productively at almost any hour of the day, as long as the inspiration is there.

How you write is as personal as what you write. If you aren't sure when your muse is most active, experiment with writing at different times of the day under different conditions and examine the results. You may find that you do your best work in the hour or two before breakfast, or that you need Bach or the Beatles playing softly in the background to stimulate the flow of ideas and words. Or you may find that you need a couple of hours in the neighborhood diner with a pad of paper, a pen, and a bottomless cup of coffee.

Setting a Schedule

Once you figure out the time and place that's best for you and your writing, work it into your routine. Some writers recommend setting aside the same time every day to be devoted to writing, because this makes writing a regular habit rather than an occasional hobby. This sort of schedule is particularly useful if you have trouble working writing time into your daily life. It also can be useful if you have a family; you can schedule your writing time from 8 P.M. to 10 P.M., for example, and let family members know that this time is off-limits for other activities.

Most writers prefer to have blocks of time, rather than a spare few minutes here and there. For most of us, it takes a little while to settle down, organize our ideas, and begin writing. Having an hour (or two or three or four) blocked out will give you more time for this kind of settling in.

ALERT!

Too much time sometimes can be a problem too, because work usually expands to fulfill the time allotted for it. If you find yourself spending a good share of your writing time staring into space or otherwise avoiding the actual writing, try cutting back on your writing hours. If you only have an hour to write, you might find yourself getting down to work sooner than if you give yourself two hours to do it.

Life as a writer is tough, uplifting, hectic, exciting, frustrating, liberating, and disheartening. As often as not, it's all those things at the same time. Many, many would-be writers never get the hang of the ups and downs of the business and give up on their dreams of getting published. The rest of us are convinced that the ultimate reward, seeing one's name on the cover of a book, is just over the horizon, and that's what keeps us going.

Chapter 2

The Business of Publishing

Many authors, even published pros, have only the sketchiest of notions about how the publishing industry operates. Everybody knows the basic steps: You submit your proposal, get a contract, finish the manuscript, and then, months later, you get a bound copy of your book in the mail. But there are dozens of intricate maneuvers behind each of these steps. Understanding these intricacies can help reduce your impatience and frustration as you seek to get your work into the public's hands.

How Publishing Works

There's a romantic notion prevalent among writers that the key to success is getting your manuscript into the hands of an editor who recognizes its wondrous quality, and then it's nothing but celebrating. It's true that an editor who is enthusiastic about your work can help convince the decision-makers in the publishing house to take a chance on you. However, there are lots of other ingredients that go into the making of a contract offer, and few of them are within the editor's control.

Acquisitions Process

An editor rarely has the final say on whether a publishing contract is offered. Those decisions typically are made in "editorial meetings" by the publication board (informally called the "pub board"), a collection of editors, marketing and publicity staff, and the publisher or editor-in-chief. The pub board may meet once a week or less often; editors have a few minutes to pitch the projects of interest that have come across their desks. They may ask their colleagues to look over the proposal or manuscript, or they may recommend offering a contract.

There are many ways for a project to get torpedoed in a pub board meeting. A marketing rep may balk, saying he'll have a hard time building buzz about such a book. Someone may point out that a similar book the house put out five years ago sold poorly. There may be other publishers coming out with similar titles, or the project may be too much of a stretch to fit into the publisher's usual line. No matter how well written a proposal or manuscript may be, these kinds of objections in the editorial meeting can kill the project.

If the editor receives a positive response to her pitch at the pub board meeting, often she'll get approval to "run numbers"—that is, research the expenses and sales records of similar titles. She'll go back to the pub board with those figures; if any of her colleagues have read the proposal or manuscript, they'll offer their opinions. Then, depending on whether the colleagues liked it and whether the numbers show the publisher can make money, a "go" or "no go" decision is made. If it's a "go," the editor-in-chief will authorize the editor to make an offer for the book. If it's a "no go," the editor will send out a rejection.

As difficult as it is to get that first book contract, getting good marketing support for your book can be even harder. Publishers set promotion budgets for their entire list, and the amount of money dedicated to promoting a specific title can vary dramatically. This budget—and it may be quite small—has to cover advertising, special bookstore displays, and all other promotional costs. That's why it's so important for you to determine what you can do yourself to promote your book.

This lengthy back-and-forth process is the main reason publishers take so long to respond to your submissions. It's also why the slogan, "No news is good news," is so widely adopted among experienced authors. Once in a great while, you might find a publisher straining at the leash to get your signature on a contract. But most of the time, and for most authors, it's a case of waiting, waiting, and waiting some more.

The Editorial Process

You can expect to work with at least two and often three different editors as your manuscript is developed. The acquiring editor—the one who pitched your idea to the pub board and made the contract offer—is your first point of contact. He's the one you work with while you're writing your book. You'll deliver your manuscript to him, according to the schedule in the contract, and you'll work with him to resolve any problems or issues that come up during the course of the work.

When you turn in your final manuscript, the acquiring editor will read through it and may have questions or suggestions for you. At some houses, the acquiring editor will then turn the manuscript over to a development or project editor. The development editor focuses on the structure and content of the work and may have a whole new set of questions and suggestions for you.

Finally, your manuscript will go to a copyeditor, who may be working in-house or as a freelancer. The copyeditor checks style, spelling, grammar, punctuation, and syntax; she also does fact-checking. Again, the copyeditor will usually have another set of questions and suggestions for the author.

When this process is completed, your manuscript will go to a typesetter, who will create page proofs of what the final pages will look like. Generally, you'll have a chance to look at the proofs and make minor changes, if necessary. (At this stage, any major changes to your manuscript jeopardize the production schedule and cost the publishing house lots of money, so the editors will work closely with you to make sure the big stuff gets taken care of early on.)

Distribution

Once the manuscript is finalized and the design team has created the cover, page layout, illustrations, and other elements, the book is printed and bound, then shipped to the publisher's warehouse for distribution. Sales reps already have taken orders for your book from booksellers, and the publisher has sales contracts in place. These contracts usually allow the bookseller to return any unsold copies for a full refund; they also may cover such items as in-store displays and cooperative advertising, like a Borders newspaper ad that features your book.

FACT

About 8 percent of all books sold in the United States are purchased through Internet retailers like Amazon.com. Independent and small chain booksellers account for about 15 percent of sales, and mass merchandisers and warehouse outlets like Wal-Mart and Costco together claim about 13 percent of sales. Large bookseller chains like Borders and Barnes & Noble make the lion's share of sales.

Because these special arrangements are so expensive, publishers typically reserve this treatment for books on which they expect to make a considerable profit. Most new titles are considered "midlist" books—that is, books that are expected to make some money, but not expected to achieve blockbuster sales. These books get shelf space in the stores, but aren't singled out to attract the buyer's eye.

Publishing Expenses

Publishers spend a minimum of $50,000 producing a new title, from acquisition to production to delivery to marketing. Many books never earn back the initial investment, which makes publishing a risky venture. That's why publishers look for at least a few highly commercial books; the revenues from the bestsellers help support the publication of midlist books.

Every publisher has unavoidable costs. Hardcover printing costs about 8 percent of the retail price; distribution costs between 1.5 percent and 8 percent, depending on whether the publisher has to pay an outside company for this service. Wholesale and retail booksellers typically buy the books from the publisher at around 50 percent of the retail price. The author's royalties range from about 10 percent to 15 percent, depending on the volume of sales.

The following chart shows what a typical publisher pays out and gets back for a hypothetical hardcover book, priced at $25, that sells 10,000 copies:

	Per Copy	Total (multiplied by 10,000 copies)
Retail price	$25.00	$250,000
Printing cost	$2.00	$20,000
Distribution cost	$2.00	$20,000
Bookseller discount	$12.50	$125,000
Author's royalties	$2.50	$25,000
Net revenues for publisher	–	$60,000

The chart shows a tidy net revenue for the publisher. But keep in mind that the $60,000 generated by this one title has to help pay for all the other costs the publisher incurs—wages and benefits, insurance, legal costs, office expenses, marketing, and so on. Most publishers, even the big conglomerates, operate on a modest profit margin of between 5 and 10 percent.

FACT

There's a widespread perception that publishers have cut back on the number of new titles they produce each year. In fact, new title lists have been growing for the past few decades, even faster than book sales. New midlist titles in particular have seen steady growth over the past ten years.

A Day in the Life of an Editor

An editor's workday is a cacophony of meetings and messages, contracts and crises. Virtually every editor is juggling several projects at a time. She's in the process of negotiating contracts for new titles; she's riding herd on books that are being written by her authors; she's working with the development editor and design team on manuscripts that are going through the editorial and production process; and she's working with the publicity and marketing departments on promoting books that are about to hit the stores.

The official business day at most New York publishing houses runs from 9 A.M. to 5 P.M. But editors typically work ten, twelve, even fifteen or more hours a day, plus weekends, and most of them do so for relatively small salaries. It isn't unusual for an editor to get into the office at 8 A.M. or earlier, to catch up on voice mail and e-mail messages before the telephone starts ringing and the day's round of meetings begins. If he has time, he may go through dozens of queries, requested proposals and manuscripts, and unsolicited proposals and manuscripts that each day's mail deposits on his desk. He may even find time to write a rejection letter or e-mail.

By 9 A.M., most editors are entering the daily routine of meetings. Nearly every day, your editor will have a meeting with the production department to talk about any issues for manuscripts that are being prepared for the printer. She may meet with the art director to discuss cover art for her books, or with the editor-in-chief to discuss negotiations for new titles.

In between these meetings, the editor will periodically check voice mail and e-mail messages and squeeze in time to reply to the most urgent ones. His lunch hour may be spent at his desk returning those calls and e-mails, or he may have a lunch meeting scheduled with an agent or an author. After lunch, he has more meetings to attend and more messages waiting for him. By 5 P.M. his desk is full of packages from FedEx, UPS, and the post office; his inbox has memos and catalog copy and page proofs that need his attention; and there's a fresh batch of voice mail and e-mail messages waiting.

It isn't until after the office closes for the day that the editor has time to read through the stacks of queries, proposals, and manuscripts that have accumulated in his office. He may spend an hour or two at his desk sorting through them, selecting the ones he wants to read on the couch that night and packing them up for the trip home. If he's lucky, he'll get through today's stack by 10 or 11 P.M. And tomorrow, he'll run the same marathon all over again.

Submitting Your Idea

Now that you know what a typical editor's day is like, you can understand why editors get so peeved when hopeful writers don't pay attention to the guidelines for submitting their material. It isn't that editors are particularly rigid or controlling. They simply don't have the time to read material that isn't right for them or respond to writers' unnecessary e-mails and phone calls.

ESSENTIAL

You stand the best chance of catching an editor's attention by following the writer's guidelines for submitting material; it shows that you respect the editor's time and that you've done your research. Market directories like *Writer's Market* offer specific instructions, and some publishers have their submission guidelines posted on their Web sites. With such readily available resources, there is no excuse for not giving an editor what she wants.

It's critical that you do your homework when submitting your material. Match your book to appropriate publishing houses and to editors who handle similar kinds of projects. Find out what the editor prefers to receive from writers—will she read unsolicited proposals or manuscripts, or do you have to send a query first? What is the editor's format preference (electronic, snail mail, etc.) for submissions?

Finding a Good Fit

Editors are all too familiar with writers who take the scattershot approach to submitting their material, aiming at anything with "publishing" or "press" in the company name and praying for a hit. Just as your book has to have a specific audience, your marketing efforts need to be targeted to publishing houses that fit your type of writing. You do yourself no favors—and might even do yourself untold damage—by sending your how-to book to a publisher that specializes in women's fiction.

Also consider the right person to contact within the company. At many publishing companies, different editors are responsible for specific lines or imprints. Make sure you address your submission to the appropriate editor; don't assume that your material will be passed along to the right person. It annoys the recipient, and it makes you look unprofessional. If you can't target the right editor, how can an editor assume that you know how to target your readership?

Following Submission Guidelines

In writer's groups and on writers' Internet discussion boards, you'll sometimes find people who advise you to ignore a publisher's or editor's submission guidelines. You may be advised to send an e-mail query even though the guidelines call for "snail mail" (the U.S. Postal Service) or send your entire manuscript when the guidelines ask for proposals only. The theory behind this advice is that you set yourself apart from the crowd by deviating from the guidelines. This theory may be true, but it's not good for your image. Editors and publishers establish guidelines so they can handle the sheer volume of submissions smoothly and effectively. When you ignore these guidelines, you throw a wrench into the machinery, causing delays and frustration.

The guidelines will tell you what to submit to the editor and how to send it. Many editors won't consider unsolicited proposals or manuscripts, just because they don't have time to read them all. Instead, they require a query first; if the query interests them, they'll ask for more. This can be frustrating for the writer, who feels that her work has been rejected sight unseen, and this is why it's so important for aspiring authors to master the art of the query letter. Very often, the query is your only opportunity for impressing an editor.

Some editors ask for electronic submissions, but most still prefer hard copies, largely because so much of their reading is done away from the office. Even when an editor accepts proposals or manuscripts electronically, chances are he prints out a hard copy to review. Writers tend to like the speed of electronic submissions, but don't let your expectations run away with you. Even if an editor accepts e-mail queries or proposals, he probably won't respond any faster than he will to a snail mail submission. You may save two or three days getting your material to him, but he's still going to take six to eight weeks (or longer, depending on his workload and what you send) to get back to you.

ALERT!

Don't give an editor (or an agent, for that matter) a deadline to respond to your material. Directories list the response times for each publishing house, and that's how long you should expect to wait for an answer. Telling an editor that she only has a week or two weeks to consider your material won't endear you to her; in fact, it's more likely to make her send back a form rejection without even reading through the rest of your submission.

What to Expect from a Publisher

Your dealings with publishers almost always will follow the same pattern. You submit your query to the appropriate editor. The editor likes what she sees in your query and asks you to send more material. For fiction, she may ask for the first three chapters or the first fifty pages, plus a synopsis (see Chapter 11 for more information about fiction proposals). For nonfiction, she may ask for a proposal and one, two, or three sample chapters (see Chapter 12 for details on nonfiction proposals). It's important that you send exactly what the editor asks for. Don't forget, the editor is incredibly busy. You can help her do her job and make a good impression by following her instructions.

After you send the requested material, you're in for a period of waiting. This can range from a few weeks to several months; market directories will give you an idea of the average reporting time. Patience is essential here. Editors don't like to field calls or e-mails from anxious writers wanting to know if their material has been read yet. If you haven't heard anything, assume that the editor has not gotten to it. When she does get to it, you'll know. You'll either receive a rejection letter or, if the outcome is favorable, an e-mail or phone call with the good news.

If the publisher wants to offer you a contract, the editor will be authorized to negotiate with you (or with your agent, if you have one). Usually, the publisher or editor-in-chief will give the editor a cap on the amount of the advance she can offer, but that won't necessarily be the first figure she mentions. If her cap is $25,000, for example, she might start out at $20,000; that way, if you insist on a higher advance, she can offer the $25,000, which makes her look like a hero to you but doesn't force her to go back to her superiors to get more money.

Other terms in the contract will be discussed—royalty rates, delivery dates, and so on. When you reach a verbal agreement on the contract terms (discussed in more detail in Chapter 19), the editor will ship the contract out for your signature.

The steps for this dance between editors and new authors are virtually always the same. Once you get established, you may be able to skip some of the preliminaries, but until then, you'll be expected to play by the same rules everybody else has to follow.

What a Publisher Expects from You

Publishers are always looking for new talent, and they know that beginning writers aren't always familiar with the often-confusing maze of the publishing business. They don't expect you to have the same level of knowledge as an editor with years of experience. But they do expect you to be professional and honest in your dealings with them.

Professional Courtesy

Editors are plagued with wannabe writers who have no respect for the editor's time or expertise. They flood editors' inboxes with vapid e-mails; they call incessantly, demanding to speak with the editor about their work or just to chat; they challenge every suggestion, even the most constructive ones. These writers are the ones that make editors question their choice of profession and fantasize about a "normal" career in a field that doesn't involve dealing with authors.

Your professional attitude will set you apart from the crowd. Give the editor time to do her job. Accept rejections and suggestions for changes with grace. Limit your e-mails and phone calls to topics that really matter; don't call or write just because you're bored or need somebody to hold your hand. These small gestures, coupled with your terrific writing, will endear you to an editor and make you one of her favorite authors to work with.

Timeliness

From the author's perspective, publishing moves at a glacial pace. It takes weeks to get a response to your query, several more weeks to hear back on your proposal, and several more weeks to see the contract. Then you have a number of months before the manuscript has to be turned in, and months after that before you see the final product. When you're looking at a year or even two before your book is in the stores, it's easy to develop a casual attitude toward deadlines.

But deadlines are the sacred cow of publishing. A publishing house's entire year is planned according to a multitude of deadlines, many of which you won't even be aware of. Delays mean extra costs, holes in the catalog, and disgruntled salespeople. If you're two months late turning in your manuscript, that puts the development editor two months behind schedule, which in turn puts the production department two months behind. And if every author is two months late, the carefully crafted plan for the whole publishing house is in a shambles. That's why it is so important for you to deliver your material on time.

Honesty and Integrity

Publishers expect their authors to be honest. That means creating original work—no plagiarizing or unauthorized "borrowing" of another author's material. It means telling the truth in your author's bio—you cannot claim bestseller status when you haven't achieved it or paint yourself as an expert when you don't have the credentials to back it up. It means living up to the promises you make, making sure your manuscript matches what you promised in your proposal, delivering your work on time, and being willing to work with your editor to improve your copy. Dishonesty in any of these areas will, at the very least, tarnish your reputation; you could even put your entire writing career at risk.

Many of the larger publishing houses won't deal with unagented authors. There are several reasons for this. One is that agents act as pre-screeners for editors and publishers; they won't submit material that is inappropriate or not up to standards. Another is that agents know the business and the vocabulary of contract negotiations, and they can distinguish between reasonable and unreasonable demands.

Get to Know Potential Publishers

Like authors, publishers come in all sizes, shapes, and specialties. The major houses are the best known, in large part because they are the ones that generate huge publicity for books that win seven-figure advances. Many authors set their sights solely on the big players, but there are plenty of opportunities with the plethora of smaller, lesser-known publishers.

Major Publishers

The major houses, like Random House, are part of multinational corporations and usually have several imprints, each with its own distinct identity. As a rule, they tend to focus on books that are likely to have significant commercial success; literary fiction and nonfiction are likely to be overlooked by the big houses. The sheer size of these publishing houses gives them clout in attracting authors and marketing their titles through booksellers and the media. But this very influence can make it difficult for new authors to break in, unless they have an exceptional book.

Midsized and Small Presses

It used to be that midsized and small presses struggled to get their books into bookstores. Often, their books could only make it into independent bookshops. Interestingly enough, the increasing popularity of superstore bookstore chains like Borders and Barnes & Noble has helped smaller publishers get their titles into the mainstream retail markets. This has happened in part because of consumer demand and in part because the superstores need a larger inventory to fill their shelf space.

Smaller presses don't have the economic resources of the publishing giants. They can't offer the massive advances or huge marketing budgets, and this fact sometimes makes both authors and agents shy away. However, the midsized and small presses will take beginning authors that larger houses turned away.

FACT

Even if your book doesn't make the bestseller list, it can generate respectable revenues for quite a long time. According to a study conducted for the Authors Guild, backlist books—those that have been on bookstore shelves for a year or more—can constitute as much as 50 percent or more of a bookseller's sales.

Small and medium publishers have served as the launching point for many new authors. In fact, many of the large publishers routinely review the titles published by their smaller competitors, looking for promising books that they can pick up to publish in paperback, for example. Starting your career at one of the smaller publishers can lead to lucrative offers from the big players.

University Presses

University presses have begun expanding their lines from traditional scholarly books to more mainstream nonfiction. Reductions in financial commitments from their universities and declining purchases from academic libraries have helped fuel an increase in the number of general-interest titles acquired by these presses. Some even publish fiction titles.

Like their small-press counterparts, university presses can't offer large advances or a big marketing budget. However, they can provide a starting point for your career. Remember, the hardest part about breaking into the book-writing business is getting that first book published. And having a book published by a prestigious university press can add a good deal of heft to your credibility.

Chapter 3

That's the Agent's Job

Published authors have widely differing opinions on the need for literary agents. Some are adamantly opposed to bringing a third party into the relationship between editors and writers, while others are just as adamant in declaring that, without their agent's help, their career never would have gotten so far. While it's true that you don't always need an agent to succeed in publishing, the fact remains that almost four out of five manuscripts purchased by major publishers today come from writers with agents.

What an Agent Does

A literary agent is a writer's guide throughout the publishing process, from submitting materials to signing the contract and collecting royalties. But a good literary agent does far more than just send out manuscripts and negotiate royalty rates. A good agent also is a writing coach, cheerleader, traffic cop, and business partner.

FACT

Beginning writers might wince at having to share their hard-won book earnings with a middleman, but partnering with the right agent is a worthwhile investment for those who envision a long and lucrative career as an author.

Coach and Critic

Agents tend to have a broader perspective on the publishing business than writers or even editors. Writers are focused on what they produce or want to produce; editors are focused on the needs of the publisher they work for. Agents deal with a variety of authors and genres and with a spectrum of publishers, large and small. They keep track of which new imprints—lines of books or publishing divisions—are starting up (and what kind of material they're looking for) and which are not doing well. They know which editors are moving on to bigger houses, and they stay in contact with editors they've worked with before, no matter which publisher that editor is currently working for.

One of the benefits of this wide-ranging experience is that agents know what particular publishers are looking for and can be more effective in targeting proposals and manuscripts to specific publishing markets. When a writer has a good idea for a book, an agent will assess the idea based on what he or she knows of the current publishing market and then offer suggestions to strengthen the proposal or manuscript. The agent's goal always is the same—to create a salable product.

Altering your manuscript or proposal to fit the market is a lot like altering clothes. If you buy a suit, and the trousers are four inches too long, you won't wear the suit until the trousers are hemmed to fit you. Likewise, if your book project doesn't quite fit the publishing market, you probably won't be able to sell it until you've made the appropriate alterations. An effective agent suggests tailoring for your project, making recommendations that will help your project better fit the market.

Constructive criticism from an agent is not meant to be hurtful; it is intended to help you craft the kind of manuscript a publisher will want to buy. You don't have to accept an agent's suggestions, but understanding the motivation behind those suggestions can take much of the sting out of the criticism.

Cheerleader

A good agent should be honest about her client's prospects of getting published but also enthusiastic about the project's potential. Because so much of the twenty-first-century publishing world seems to move at a nineteenth-century pace, it's easy for writers (especially first-time writers) to lose their energetic optimism as the publishing process drags on. Your agent, on the other hand, is intimately familiar with the vagaries of publishing and can offer both insight and encouragement, even when things don't seem to be going well.

Besides cheering you on, your agent gets other people excited about you and your work. Many people have a hard time boosting themselves, whether in a job interview or in their authors' bios; most of us have been taught from toddler-hood that it's not nice to brag. The agent has no such compunction about boasting. Part of his job is to promote his clients' talent, as well as their actual work. A good agent will revel in convincing editors that you're the next Toni Morrison or David McCullough.

Traffic Cop

A good agent will resolve issues with publishers that you won't even be aware of. When he's selling your project, he handles all the contract negotiations, then presents you with a complete offer to consider. You don't have to worry about things like the number of free copies you'll receive when your book is published, or how the royalty rate changes based on the number of copies sold, or even whether the royalty rate is based on the list price or the wholesale price of your book. Your agent knows the industry standards for all these details, and he will negotiate the best deal possible for you.

Most agents will keep you posted on developments as they market your project to publishers. Some agents prefer to wait until the marketing is completed, then give you a summary of the responses. Others will send off a quick e-mail whenever they get a response from a publisher, positive or not.

Your agent's duties don't end with the signing of the contract. Even as you write your manuscript for the publisher, your agent will be in contact with your editor, resolving any issues that might arise, answering the editor's questions, and continually keeping the editor excited about you and your book. Nine times out of ten, you won't even know that these conversations are taking place. Your agent wants you to concentrate on writing and won't bother you with minor details.

Likewise, if you have an issue that needs to be brought to your publisher's attention, your agent acts as a go-between. Any number of things can change the complexion of your book even as you're in the middle of writing it. New developments in medical research might warrant a change in your book's outline. The technical adviser you're working with on your architecture book may fall ill and be unable to assist you. Your agent, when aware of such developments, can work with your editor to accommodate him.

Business Partner

The only way a reputable agent makes money is by selling clients' manuscripts to publishers. The typical agent's commission for domestic sales is

15 percent of the author's revenues, including all advances and royalties. Because the agent is paid from the writer's revenues, many writers think of themselves as the employer and the agent as the employee. But this is a poor model for the agent-author relationship, and, indeed, can cause innumerable problems on both sides.

A better way to think of the relationship is as a joint business venture. As the writer, you supply the goods to be sold; the agent supplies her expertise in the publishing industry to find a market for your goods and negotiate the best sale terms. This partnership allows each of you to do what you do best and ultimately results in profitable and fulfilling careers for both of you.

The "joint business venture" model also implies longevity, which makes sense both for agents and authors. The longer you stick with your agent, the better the two of you will work together, and the more successful your partnership will be. In the early stages of your career, your agent will be akin to an athlete's trainer, teaching you the business and helping you turn your raw talent into salable projects. Because of the time and energy involved in training new writers, effective agents usually prefer authors who are interested in building careers, and writers who are serious about their careers look for agents who have that long-term philosophy.

FACT

An agent's commission is usually higher for foreign sales because such sales often mean hiring a co-agent in the overseas market, with whom the commission must be split. Foreign-sales commissions typically range from 20 to 25 percent of an author's revenues.

This is not to say that once you find an agent, you should stick with him no matter what. There's no point in staying with an agent who isn't enthusiastic about representing you, for example, whether it's because the agent himself is ineffective or because he doesn't usually handle the kind of books you want to write. Sometimes, too, your personality and the agent's just won't complement each other. If your relationship with your agent isn't working, for whatever reason, consider finding another.

A Day in the Life of an Agent

An agent's business day is hour after hour of continually changing, and sometimes competing, priorities. The nature of the business ensures that no two days will be exactly alike. The most carefully planned schedule in the world will disintegrate in the face of the unexpected, and the unexpected pops up almost daily—sometimes several times a day.

Contracts

For most agents, the first priority each day is handling unsigned contracts. These are contracts that have been negotiated between the agent and publisher but not executed yet; the agent reviews each contract to make sure it reflects what was agreed to in the negotiations, then forwards them to the author for her signature. Publishing contracts can be time-sensitive, meaning they have to be signed and returned to the publisher within a certain number of days. Besides, the sooner the contract is signed and returned to the publisher, the sooner the agent and the author receive their advance payments.

Author Payments

The next priority for most agents is processing payments to authors. Publishers cut checks payable to the agent, who then deposits the check (usually in a separate agency bank account) and writes a new check, minus the agent's commission, payable to the author. Typically, a publisher sends the first half of the advance payment with the executed contract (a contract that has been signed by all parties), and the agent forwards a copy of the executed contract with the author's payment.

Pending Offers

Next on the agent's to-do list is negotiating pending offers from publishers. This can be a lengthy and painstakingly detailed process, and the agent has to make sure that conditions agreed upon in previous negotiating sessions make it into the final contract. Usually, the publisher makes an offer, which the agent then discusses with the author. After the author agrees, the agent proceeds with the negotiations. There can be several back-and-forth sessions before a deal is finally reached.

ALERT!

Publishers prefer that agents make all contract change requests at once, so the author should discuss any special needs before negotiation begins. It requires organization and forethought on your part, but it saves much time and frustration when the agent can proceed in an orderly fashion.

Marketing

An agent is in business to sell manuscripts, so a big part of her job involves soliciting publishers by telephone, e-mail, or snail mail. Often, an agent who is negotiating a pending contract on one project or talking with an editor about a manuscript in the writing stage will take advantage of that meeting or phone call to pitch another project the publisher might be interested in. Effective agents will do this habitually, mainly because it saves time for everyone.

Firefighting

Any of the previously mentioned priorities can be relegated to the bottom of the to-do list by unexpected crises. Agents who have been in business for any length of time have known days when all they can do is put out fires. Questions from editors or writers arise that need immediate answers. Authors who are under deadline pressure encounter problems with finishing their manuscripts. Sometimes it takes all the agent's time and energy to take care of these urgent issues, and the items on his to-do list for that day get pushed to the next day.

Finding an Agent

Because of the sheer volume of queries, proposals, and manuscripts agents receive every day, some literary agencies shy away from new writers. These agencies will rarely accept new clients unless the new writers have been referred by existing clients. That's the bad news.

The good news is that there are lots of agents who are willing or even eager to work with new authors. The chance to "discover" new talent motivates these agents to open the mail every day and spend their evenings and weekends wading through stacks of proposals. When they find a writer with potential, it's like finding a sapphire in a salt mine.

There are several ways to find an agent who might be interested in representing you. Print directories of agents and publishers, such as *Writer's Digest Guide to Literary Agents*, have listings that include names, addresses, genres, and submission guidelines for agents. *The Literary Marketplace*, commonly known as the *LMP*, also carries these listings; your public library should have the latest edition in its reference section.

QUESTION?

Do I need an agent who lives in New York City?
No. Your agent should have good contacts and a good reputation with editors at major publishing houses, but overnight delivery services and technology like the fax machine and e-mail have made it easy for agents to do their jobs from virtually anywhere.

Another good way to find agents who can sell the kind of book you're writing is to visit your local bookstore. Look in the section that has books similar to yours; if you're writing a travel book, for example, check out books in the travel section. Read the acknowledgments in these books to see if an agent is mentioned and make a note of the agent's name; then check that agent out in the print directories or one of the Internet sites listed in Appendix A of this book. Pay special attention to those agents who are praised by their clients in the acknowledgments.

Submitting Your Idea

To catch an agent's attention, you'll need to send in a submission. The process is similar to submitting your material to a prospective publisher. First, you have to match your material to an agent who handles books similar to the one you plan to write. Next, you have to find out how the agent prefers to receive submissions. Does she ask for queries only, or can you send your proposal without a query? Finally, you have to find out how the agent prefers to receive your materials (via snail mail or e-mail only, for example). Agent directories are the best places to find this information, as well as the correct name and address of the agent you want to solicit.

Matching Your Material

Sending your illustrated children's book to an agent who handles adult nonfiction is like walking into a car dealership and trying to buy an ice cream cone. In both cases you'll be told, politely but firmly, to go elsewhere. This can't be stressed often enough: Send your queries and proposals to agents who handle the type of book you're writing.

Like publishers, agents tend to carve niches for themselves. The publishing industry is so competitive and can change so rapidly that most agents must concentrate on a few select genres in order to keep up with the latest developments. Generally, only literary agencies with large staffs will take on all genres, and even then these mega-agencies will have agents who specialize in different types of books.

Most agent directories include information on the types of books a given agent is interested in. Some directories even list titles that were recently sold by an agency. Read the listings carefully and make your own list of the agencies that look like a good match with your book. Then do additional research on these agencies to make sure they are reputable and honest in their dealings with authors. When you've got your list narrowed down to those whose specialty most closely matches your book and who have good reputations in the industry, you're ready to prepare your submission.

Sometimes agents do represent works outside their usual lines, but this happens most often with established clients. When you're just starting out, stick with the agents who deal with your type of book and take advantage of their expertise and contacts in that area.

What to Submit

An agent's listing in a directory will tell you what she wants to see from you. For most agents, the first step in approaching them is the query letter (see Chapter 10), a one-page business letter outlining your book and your qualifications to write it. The agent will decide from your query letter whether she wants to see more.

Some agents will read unsolicited proposals, and a few even accept unsolicited manuscripts; "unsolicited" means you can send your proposal or manuscript without first sending a query letter. If the agent accepts only solicited proposals or manuscripts, you must send a query first; if the agent likes your query, she will invite you to send more material.

How to Submit

Agent directories also will tell you how an agent prefers to receive material. Most still prefer to receive hard-copy submissions via the U.S. Postal Service. There are a couple of good reasons for this. One is that it's easier for many people—writers, editors, and agents included—to read a printed page. Another is that most agents spend much of their working days at the computer and don't want to be tied to their desk during their evenings and weekends when they have the time to look through the submissions. If the listing says something like, "E-mail queries not encouraged," stick with regular mail.

FACT

Your courtesy and professional attitude will pay off. Agents want talented, professional clients, and the impression you make in the courting stage can determine whether an agent thinks it's worth taking a chance on you.

Sometimes you'll run across writers who advise you to e-mail your queries or proposals to all agents, even those who expressly ask for snail-mail submissions. You might get lucky, occasionally, but you are more likely to get a rejection by taking this kind of shortcut. The message you're sending is that you either don't pay attention to or don't care about following instructions, and that message won't help you make a good impression. These rules usually ease once you're an established author or client. While you're trying to break in, however, you present a more professional image if you follow the guidelines set by the agent.

As with most publishers, your dealings with a reputable agent will follow a standard path. You begin by sending a query; the agent likes your query and asks to see your proposal or manuscript; after the agent reviews your proposal or manuscript, she will either send a rejection letter or give you a call to talk about representing your work. It's extremely rare for a reputable agent to offer to represent you based on your query alone.

The Phone Call

During that phone call, the agent has an agenda to discuss with you. He may want to know more about you and more about your book; he may have suggestions for strengthening your proposal to make it more attractive to publishers. This conversation also is an opportunity for each of you to size up the other and decide whether you want to work together.

During that first phone call from an agent, it's appropriate to ask all those pertinent questions that have been simmering in the back of your mind since you first sent off your query. The Association of Authors' Representatives (AAR), which establishes codes of conduct for literary agents, has a dozen recommended questions each author should ask of potential agents. Here are some of them:

- How long have you been in business as an agent?
- Who in your agency will actually be handling my work?
- How do you keep your clients informed of your activities on their behalf?
- Do you consult with your clients on any and all offers?
- What are your commission rates?
- Do you issue an agent-author agreement?

If the agent is not an AAR member, ask if she follows the AAR Canon of Ethics. AAR prohibits its members from charging any up-front fees, no matter how those fees are labeled, and bars agents from receiving "secret profits"—kickbacks from editors or so-called "book doctors," or proceeds from a self-publishing house. The AAR also requires members to have business bank accounts, separate from their personal accounts, so that the agent's personal funds are not commingled with clients' revenues.

ALERT!

AAR membership is not the be-all-end-all to prove an agent's legitimacy. Some reputable agents choose not to join, and some haven't yet met the experience requirements to join. Adherence to the AAR Canon of Ethics, however, is a good gauge of an agent's honesty and dedication to fair business practices.

The Right Agent for You

When you sign on with an agent, you're agreeing to pay for the agent's expertise and contacts in the publishing industry, so it's reasonable to ask about an agent's performance. Keep in mind, however, that you're not entitled to know everything about an agent's business—only those things that are pertinent to your decision to sign up with him.

Disclosing Information

A legitimate agent should be willing to tell you about her sales in general and about notable aspects of her sales, but she won't necessarily be willing to share details with you. Don't take this reluctance as evidence of anything sinister: Many agents tend to be protective of their clients because they want their writers to concentrate on writing, not provide references for prospective clients. Instead, an agent is more likely to want to talk about your project—how suitable it is for the current publishing market, and how receptive editors at different publishing houses might be.

Most agents will not discuss books that have been sold but haven't yet been published, and they won't talk about books they're marketing right now. No reputable agent will tell you what kind of advance a given title received or what the royalty earnings on a given title were. This is confidential information; it's inappropriate for you to ask for it and highly unethical for an agent to give it to you. Remember, too, that once you're a client, you won't want your agent revealing your financial information to would-be writers.

Likewise, most agents will not reveal client lists. If he has permission from the author to identify that author as a client, the agent may choose to do so, but rarely will you find an agent willing to reveal his full client list to you or give you contact information for his clients. Again, look at this situation from the other clients' point of view. Once you've signed with an agent, you'll want him to get your permission before offering your name and contact information as a reference for prospective clients.

FACT

The very best indication of an agent's performance is the number of titles sold to royalty-paying publishers. The AAR requirement for new members is ten sales within the past eighteen months. An agent who is new to the business should start making sales within six to twelve months.

Good Attitude

A good agent will paint a reasonably optimistic picture of the chances of selling your book. Naturally, she expects to be able to find a publisher; otherwise she wouldn't be interested in representing you. But she won't fill you up with promises of six-figure advances, bestseller status, movie rights, and the like. Good agents know how volatile the publishing market can be, and they know better than to make such outlandish promises.

On the other hand, you don't want an agent who sounds pessimistic about your prospects. If an agent isn't enthusiastic about your book idea when she's talking with you, she probably won't be enthusiastic about it when she's talking to an editor.

Author-Agent Contracts

You may come across well-meaning people who'll tell you that only scam artists posing as literary agents require contracts with authors before a book is sold. In fact, many (if not most) reputable agencies have standard contracts with their clients that spell out such terms as the scope of representation, the agent's commission, additional expenses, and the responsibilities of each party. An author-agent contract is more the rule than the exception these days.

Agent-author agreements cover virtually all aspects of your business relationship. Here are four of the most critical areas:

1. **Scope:** Often, the agent is granted exclusive rights to represent all your book-length work, in all formats and media, worldwide. Once in a while, an agent will contract to represent just your current book project, but this is unusual. It's also quite rare for an agent to represent shorter work, such as short stories, magazine articles, and individual poems; payments for these works are much lower than for book sales, and the agent's time isn't worth the 15 percent commission.

2. **Duration:** Most contracts have a term limit, often ranging from one to two years. Many initial contracts cannot be terminated for a set period—six or twelve months, for example—but have a termination clause that kicks in after that initial period. A typical termination clause allows either party to pull out of the agreement with thirty to ninety days' notice. The agreement should also specify what happens if you want to take your book project to another agent.

3. **Commission:** The agreement will spell out what the agent is entitled to receive as a commission on sales—usually 15 percent for domestic sales and a higher percentage for foreign sales.

4. **Handling of payments:** In a typical agent-author agreement, the agent is empowered to receive all the author's advances and royalties from the publisher, take her commission from those proceeds, and send the remainder to the author.

It's important to take this seriously. You should always have a reasonable time to review and sign the contract.

ALERT!

Be wary of any contract with an agency that requires you to pay up-front fees. Even reputable agents who pass mailing, telephone, and other business costs on to their clients won't charge those fees until after a book is sold. An agent who wants money up front is likely making his living from those fees, not from selling authors' manuscripts to publishers.

Your End of the Bargain

An agent doesn't expect you to be an expert in the business of publishing; after all, one of the main reasons you seek an agent is so you can put his expertise to work on your behalf. But agents do expect you to be courteous and use common sense. A pleasant attitude from you helps motivate an agent to work for you; a negative attitude can do just the opposite.

Agents expect you to give them what they ask for. If an agent wants to see a synopsis and sample chapters, don't inform him that you had already sent the synopsis with your query. Include another copy of it with your sample chapters. If he asks for the first twenty-five pages of your manuscript, send the first twenty-five pages; don't send pages 110 through 135, even if you think those are your strongest.

Agents expect you to respect their time. Don't pressure an agent to respond to your proposal by a certain deadline. If you do, chances are he'll give your material nothing more than a cursory read-through, if that. Instead, give the agent a reasonable period to review your work and don't pester him with e-mails or phone calls asking if he's read your proposal. If you haven't heard anything, it means he hasn't reviewed it yet; when he does, you'll either get a phone call or a rejection letter.

Loyalty is also important. If an agent is interested enough in your book to give you tips on making your proposal more marketable, don't take his advice and then shop the new, improved proposal to other agents. Give that agent—the one who gave you his free, expert advice—first shot at representing you.

Finally, agents expect you to keep your word. If you tell an agent that he's the only one who has your proposal, don't send it to other agents. Also let the agent know if your proposal has already been turned down by an editor, so the agent will know not to solicit that editor again. If you promise to deliver requested materials by a certain date, make sure you meet that deadline. It's all too easy to get a bad reputation in the publishing world; if you don't do what you say you'll do when you're looking for an agent, how can that agent expect you to live up to a publishing contract?

FACT

The expectation to be honest also applies to the originality of your work. Plagiarizing from any source, including the Internet, is the cardinal sin in publishing; it will get you blacklisted, if not sued.

Chapter 4

Working with Others

Book publishing offers plenty of opportunities to pair your talents with another's. Movie stars, politicians, and other prominent persons often hire ghostwriters to pen their autobiographies or other books. Sometimes an expert in a particular field has a great idea for a book but needs a professional writer to polish the proposal or manuscript. Collaboration is one way for a beginning author to land that elusive first book contract, and a good collaboration can result not only in a publishing credit but also in a successful book.

A Professional Relationship

No matter whom you're collaborating with, working with others on a book project demands a professional relationship. Whether it's your spouse, your mother, your best friend, or a complete stranger, for the purposes of the book project you are business partners. That means you should share a vision for the book and respect each other's contributions and viewpoints. The extent to which you can develop a professional relationship with your collaborator may be the determining factor in whether your experience is a dream come true or a nightmare.

These days, it's easy for writers to collaborate with just about anyone just about anywhere. E-mail, fax machines, and low-cost long-distance telephone service make communication almost instantaneous and extremely simple; you don't even have to meet your coauthor in person in order to work together on a project. The opportunities for collaboration are no longer limited by location, so you should have no trouble finding someone to work with if this option interests you.

FACT

Collaboration can help improve your writing skills. A University of Michigan study in the mid-1990s found that students who collaborated on assignments became better, more flexible writers than students who worked on assignments alone. Computer-based collaboration via e-mail and message boards improved students' writing skills even more dramatically, the study found.

A Shared Vision

Collaborations work best when both parties agree on what they hope to accomplish with the project, beyond simply getting the book published. You should be able to find common ground on how to approach the subject of your book, what information to include, and what you want readers to take away from your book. Ideally, you and your coauthor should act as a team, working together toward the same end.

Fiction often presents stubborn challenges for collaborators. Often, no two people will view characters, plot, settings, or other novel elements in exactly the same light, and this can cause friction and frustration as the work progresses. Sometimes egos are harder to manage in fiction projects, as well; writers invest so much of themselves in creating a unique universe peopled by unique characters, it can be difficult for them to separate themselves from their creation. Fiction writers who can step back from their work and discuss it objectively with their coauthors tend to have an easier time than those who cannot detach themselves from what they have imagined.

Nonfiction carries different challenges for collaborators. Even when two authors agree on the overall message or theme of the project, discord can arise over questions of tone, subtopics, research citations, and hundreds of other details. You and your collaborator might disagree on how certain facts or events should be interpreted and explained, or even whether to discuss certain facts or events in your book. Again, the ability to step back from the work and discuss such disagreements as objectively as possible is an essential ingredient in successful collaboration.

Sometimes it's helpful to write a mission statement for your book that describes its scope and what you want readers to get out of it. If you and your collaborator agree on a mission statement, it can help both of you stay focused on your ultimate goals when disagreements arise.

Respect for Each Other

You don't have to agree on everything to have a successful experience with your collaborator. In fact, disagreement can lead to a better book proposal and manuscript—as long as it is done with mutual respect. You might be able to point out perspectives that your partner has overlooked; your partner might have information that you aren't aware of. Honest and friendly discussions often breed good ideas that otherwise might never come to the fore.

Having a thick skin is an asset in the publishing business, and it's especially important in collaborative endeavors. One of the advantages of working with a collaborator is that you get immediate feedback on your writing, but this can turn into a disadvantage if you're overly sensitive to criticism. You don't have to concede every point when your coauthor has a different idea, nor do you have to fight every suggestion from your coauthor. Give-and-take is an essential ingredient in successful collaboration; an open mind and a respectful attitude will ensure that your project benefits from it.

Dividing up the Work

Anyone who ever worked on a group science project in elementary school knows that the division of labor on a given task seldom works out evenly. During a joint writing project, it can feel at times like you're doing the heavy lifting while your collaborator kicks back in a hammock with a glass of iced tea. Interestingly, if you asked your collaborator, you likely would find that she has the same perception of you. And at the end of the project, both of you may feel that you carried more than your share of the load.

The truth is that there will be times, even in the most closely divided projects, when one of you is pulling more than their share of weight. In the best circumstances, those times will more or less even out over the course of crafting your proposal or manuscript. To keep this to a minimum and avoid feelings of resentment, it's best to decide in advance which portion of the work each of you will do.

Assess Your Strengths

How you divide the labor depends largely on the type of project you're working on and the talents and skills each of you brings to the collaboration. Ideally, you and your collaborator should be able to play on each other's strengths and compensate for each other's weaknesses. If you're a technical expert, for instance, your collaborator may bring a layman's perspective to your topic that will allow you to connect with a broader readership. If you're better at thinking up interesting plot twists, your collaborator should excel at creating interesting characters. One advantage to working with a collaborator is that, when you're properly matched, neither of you has to overreach in order to achieve your goal.

Spell Out Assignments

If you and your coauthor both know from the beginning which areas of the project you're responsible for, you'll be less likely to step on each other's toes during the process. You can divvy up assignments in whatever way makes sense to you. You might agree to write all the odd-numbered chapters, with your collaborator in charge of the even-numbered chapters. You might be responsible for all the writing, subject to input, review, and approval by your collaborator. Or you might decide that you should write the portion of the manuscript that deals with technology and your collaborator should write the portion that deals with people who use the technology.

FACT

Collaborative works can be more time-consuming than solo efforts because you and your coauthor will go back and forth, reading and commenting on each other's drafts. When you construct the framework for working together on a project, be sure to take this need for extra time into account so you can set reasonable deadlines for various stages of the work.

However you decide to split up the tasks, make sure you and your collaborator discuss all the details before you begin work. Knowing ahead of time what each of you expects from the other helps avoid anger, confusion, and resentment down the road.

Assigning the Responsibility

When two people work on one project, they both are theoretically responsible for the project's shape and success. But, like the workload, the degree of responsibility isn't always equal. One of you may be responsible for doing the actual writing, while the other is responsible for fact-checking and making sure the proposal or manuscript achieves the goals the two of you established at the beginning of your work. Within those broad areas of responsibility are smaller but equally important obligations.

If you are to take your coauthor's research and turn it into readable chapters, for example, your coauthor is responsible for supplying you with the information you need. Furthermore, he may need to make himself available to you to answer questions or clarify material. Depending on the type of project, your coauthor may also be responsible for arranging access to additional documents or sources to supplement his information. His responsibility in the project comprises all these obligations; if he can't meet them, the project itself is directly affected.

As the writer in this scenario, you have a different set of responsibilities. You have to make sure you have the material you need to write the proposal, chapter, or manuscript; if pieces are missing, you are responsible for letting your coauthor know what you need. When it comes to the actual writing, you are obligated to give your coauthor sufficient time to review and, if necessary, edit or correct your work. Failure to live up to these obligations will ultimately affect both your working relationship and the project's chances of success.

Before you begin a collaboration, make sure you and your partner both understand and agree to your respective responsibilities. Define each of your duties up front, and discuss any concerns or potential problems. Open communication at the beginning of the process can avert serious problems once you're buried in your work.

ESSENTIAL

In any collaborative effort, one person must have final authority over the work. In nonfiction works, that final authority generally resides with the expert in the field the book covers (or the subject in the case of autobiographical works). In fiction, deciding who takes the lead in approving copy depends on how you've structured your working arrangement. In any case, this is an important decision that should be made before work begins.

Sharing the Credit

One of the main incentives for collaborating on a book, especially for beginning writers, is to get that all-important first book credit. Coauthor status looks just as good in your author's bio and can do just as much to help you market your next book idea as sole authorship.

QUESTION?

Whose name goes first in the "A and B" sequence?
If one of you is an expert on the topic your book covers, that person's name usually should go first; in fact, a publisher may insist on it. If both of you are experts, or if that criterion doesn't apply to your book, the easiest solution is to list your names alphabetically.

"And," "With," or "As Told To"

When you think about teaming up with someone else for a book, then, it's important to discuss how you'll share the credit. There are three common ways coauthors share billing on a book cover:

Jane Jones and John Smith
John Smith with Jane Jones
John Smith as told to Jane Jones

Deciding which billing to use depends largely on the circumstances surrounding the collaboration. "And" is most often used when the two authors have more or less equal responsibility for creating the work. That doesn't necessarily mean that each of you writes 50,000 words of a 100,000-word manuscript. One of you may do the bulk of the writing, while the other supplies her expertise, research, and other materials.

"With" is often used when one of you is an expert and the other is a writer. Doctors and other professionals, for instance, often team up with professional writers for book projects because writers tend to be better at putting complex and technical ideas into everyday language. The "with" designation in the credit subtly alerts the reader that the first person listed is the authority on the book's topic and the second person listed is the one who makes the information readable for a general audience.

"As told to" is most often used in autobiographical books, although there may be other types of books in which this kind of billing is appropriate. Less subtly than "with," the "as told to" designation tells the reader that the first person is the one the book is about, and the second person is the one who put the story into words.

The difference among these designations is fundamentally insignificant as far as your writing career is concerned. Having "with" or "as told to" in your billing doesn't diminish the accomplishment of getting published. You're still a credited coauthor, and that's what will matter most to publishers when you market your next book idea.

Ghostwriting

Actors, politicians, and other famous people routinely employ ghostwriters for their autobiographies and other books. While the collaboration process is much the same as for any other joint book project, the main difference—and the main disadvantage for beginning writers—is that you don't get credit for the writing. Under a ghostwriting arrangement, the copyright and all other rights belong to the person whose name appears on the work.

That said, ghostwriting could be a lucrative business if you aren't concerned about putting your own name on a book. The most common ghostwriting arrangements give the writer a flat fee to create the work, but you can negotiate for a percentage of royalties instead. Sometimes it's more advantageous for you to accept a lower flat fee—or none at all—in exchange for, say, 50 percent of the royalties, particularly if the book is expected to become a bestseller.

Splitting the Money

Collaborations are often arranged on a fifty-fifty basis, but an even split certainly is not required and may not be appropriate in some situations, depending on how the work and responsibility are divided. Your best strategy is to determine money-sharing arrangements on a case-by-case basis.

Valuing Each Other's Contribution

There may be instances in which it makes sense for you to ask for more or less than a straight split. If your coauthor is going to supply all the research and information, and your responsibility is to organize and write the proposal or manuscript, that's a fairly even distribution of labor; and a fifty-fifty split is appropriate. However, if you have to supplement your coauthor's contribution with your own research, that might be worth another 10 percent (or more) of the proceeds from the book, depending on how much extra work is involved.

Alternatively, you might agree to a smaller cut if your workload is significantly lighter than your coauthor's. For instance, your collaborator already might have done the bulk of the research and writing, and your contribution is a matter of rewriting here and there, perhaps with a little reorganizing to make the material flow better. In this situation, your share of the work will take less time and effort, so taking a smaller share of the revenue is fitting.

Assigning a monetary value to the work, expertise, and time each of you brings to a project can be tricky; you don't want to undervalue either your contribution or your coauthor's. The most important thing is that you and your collaborator feel that the money-sharing arrangement you make is fair to both of you.

Upfront Fees

The issue of writers charging upfront fees to work on book proposals is a controversial one. Although legitimate writers sometimes charge these fees, unscrupulous practitioners have been known to demand unreasonable upfront payments from would-be collaborators and then fail to deliver a salable proposal or manuscript. As a result, many people tend to look askance at writers who require payment before a publishing contract is offered.

ALERT!

Don't expect a publisher to pay for any specific expenses you incur while researching or writing your book. You (or your agent) might be able to negotiate a larger advance if there are extraordinary expenses attached to your work, but that is only a "maybe." For the most part, publishers will view your expenses as part of your own investment in the work.

Certainly, there are legitimate arguments to support reasonable upfront fees. Creating a marketable book proposal or manuscript takes time and creative energy, and a writer who spends his time and energy on your proposal can't spend that same time and energy on another project. Asking for modest compensation for the use of those assets is both licit and appropriate.

On the other hand, exorbitant upfront fees should make you wary. If a writer wants, say, $10,000 to prepare your proposal or manuscript before you have a publishing contract, ask if the fee will be deducted from her share of the advance if you sell the book. If not, consider looking for another collaborator.

Working Expenses

Usually, collaborators are responsible for their own expenses. If you have to mail something to your coauthor, you foot the bill for it; if he has to ship something to you overnight, he pays for it. The same applies to all the normal costs of doing business—long-distance phone calls, copying, and so on. In a normal collaborative work, these costs will be minimal, and the easiest way to address them is for each collaborator to assume responsibility for his own expenses.

However, there may be instances when extraordinary expenses can be expected, and this can be a factor when it comes to deciding how to split proceeds from a book sale. For example, if you have to travel to South America for a month to do research for your project, you might want to take that expense into account when negotiating the split. You may decide to absorb those costs, or you might be able to arrange for reimbursement out of the publisher's advance if you sell the book.

Dealing with the Agent

It is impractical for two people working on a single project to have two agents representing that project. Virtually all reputable agents want the exclusive right to market the works of the authors they represent, and that exclusivity extends to joint works. If you and your collaborator have different agents, you'll have to come to some arrangement for representing your joint proposal. Many agents decline to work with other agents unless the other agent specializes in a different field, such as foreign rights or film rights.

If your agents are willing to work together, one agent will be designated the "agent of record" and will be responsible for marketing your project, but the two agents should split the normal commission (as opposed to each receiving the full commission). As always, anything you work out in these circumstances should be put in writing, and copies of the arrangement should be kept by you, your collaborator, and each of your agents. A written agreement is the only insurance you have in the event of a dispute over representation of the work.

Obviously, it's much easier to proceed with marketing if you and your collaborator begin with the same agent. Indeed, most collaborative works—especially those between strangers—are arranged through the agent. Typically, an agent will have a client or potential client who has a good idea for a book but who needs the services of a writer to create a salable proposal. She'll then match the client with a writer who is interested in the topic and available to do the work; the client and writer will discuss how to structure their working relationship and the agent will provide a collaboration agreement.

Before you leap into a collaboration with someone you don't know, try to set up a face-to-face meeting or at least a telephone conversation, to get a feel for each other and how you might work together. Collaboration is going to be much easier for both of you if there is some professional chemistry; if you think the two of you wouldn't work well together, it's best to wait for another opportunity.

Putting It in Writing

A formal collaboration agreement is essential to maintaining a professional relationship. Aside from establishing the rights and responsibilities you and your collaborator have for your project, a strong written agreement spells out how disputes are to be resolved and what happens if either of you decides to withdraw from the project. If you don't have such an agreement, copyright ownership and other issues may have to be decided in court. A collaboration agreement in publishing works much the same way a prenuptial agreement works in marriage: It doesn't come into play unless there's a problem.

If you have an agent, he should be able to provide a collaboration agreement for you. If you don't have an agent, the publisher may have a standard agreement for you and your collaborator to sign. A good collaboration agreement should spell out the following points:

- Responsibilities of each party
- Deadlines for completing the proposal or manuscript
- How to split advances and royalties
- Wording of authorship credit
- Who has approval authority
- How disputes will be handled

FACT

Another option for dealing with the rights to use materials is a buy-out clause. If you and your collaborator create a book proposal but decide not to work together after the proposal is finished, a buy-out clause would allow one of you to market the proposal independently in exchange for a fee. Such a fee can be specified in the agreement or defined as a percentage of the advance in the event of a publishing contract.

A collaboration agreement should also specify what happens to the work already done if you and your collaborator decide, for whatever reason, to stop working together. If you've divided the project so that each of you can easily identify which parts belong to which collaborator—you plan to write the chapters dealing with business and legal issues, and your collaborator will complete the chapters dealing with personalities, for example—the easiest solution is for each of you to retain your own materials (and the rights to those materials). But most collaborative projects are not so clear-cut, and it can be difficult to separate your contribution from that of your collaborator. A typical collaboration agreement will prevent either party from using materials covered by the agreement without the written consent of the other.

Warranties and Representations

A typical collaboration agreement includes clauses that assure each party is legally free to enter into the agreement and that each party's contribution to the project is his or her own work and doesn't violate copyright, libel, privacy, or other laws. These clauses apply to both you and your collaborator. Properly worded, they also afford protection to you should your collaborator violate her warranties, and vice versa. Without these clauses, you could be held liable for your collaborator's mistakes in the event of a lawsuit.

In plain English, if your partner contributes material that is judged to be libelous or an invasion of privacy, the typical indemnification clause in your collaboration agreement would require your partner to take financial responsibility for that judgment. If you were the one who contributed libelous or privacy-invading material, you would bear the costs of any judgment. Warranties, representations, and indemnification clauses work to your advantage and to your collaborator's advantage because they keep both of you honest in preparing the work.

For almost all collaborations, you should offer your services on a nonexclusive basis. This keeps you free to work on other projects—even other collaborative projects. Of course, it's important to make sure that other projects don't interfere with your obligations to your current work.

Agreements with Friends and Relatives

Many inexperienced writers think they don't need a formal collaboration agreement when they're working with friends or family members. While it can feel awkward to introduce a business note into a personal relationship, it is just as vital to put your collaborating relationship in writing under these circumstances. You can significantly reduce the risk of misunderstandings and hard feelings that may be fatal to your personal relationship by establishing the ground rules for your collaboration in advance. Think of your collaboration agreement as an insurance policy to protect the health of your personal relationship.

The Publisher's Interest

Virtually every publishing house will want an assurance that you and your collaborator have a written agreement in place that spells out each of your responsibilities and how proceeds from the project are to be split. In most cases, you don't have to provide the publisher with a copy of your collaboration agreement, but your contract with the publisher usually will refer to that agreement. Even if your collaborator is a relative, chances are you'll need a formal agreement.

Chapter 5

Researching the Market

Market research should be an integral part of preparing a book proposal, whether you want to write fiction or non-fiction. Chapters 2 and 3 show you how to research the market for potential agents and publishers. But before you try to sell your book to them, you have to know who your potential readers are. And you have to be able to demonstrate to potential agents and publishers that there is, indeed, a readership out there just waiting for your book.

Establishing Your Audience

Whenever you have a great idea for a book, the first question to be answered is, "Who will read this?" The more specific information you have about your potential readers, the better. For fiction, your research will be mainly for your own use as you craft your tale. You need to know who your reader will be, what elements readers (and therefore agents and editors) look for in a particular story, and where your book will appear on the shelves.

You don't need market statistics for your fiction proposal, but you do have to identify the genre and exact word count of your manuscript in your query and cover letters. New fiction authors are usually compared to published authors in the same genre, so let an agent or editor know that your work is "similar to Toni Morrison" or "in the style of Douglas Adams." This helps an agent or editor visualize where your book might fit in the market.

For nonfiction, you need to convince an agent or editor that the world needs your book. You want her to look at your proposal and think, "How have we gotten along without this book before now?" To evoke that reaction, you have to do your homework and back up your claims of a wide potential readership with hard numbers whenever possible. You also need to come up with ideas for reaching your targeted readers.

Who Buys Books?

Before you begin looking for those details that are relevant to your project, it's helpful to have a general understanding of the overall reading public. The statistics cited here are from the *2002 Consumer Research Study on Book Purchasing*, a survey conducted by Ipsos Book Trends and published in late 2003 by the Book Industry Study Group (BISG). While these figures can fluctuate—and readers of specific genres are not discussed—they do provide a good "big picture" snapshot of who buys books, where they buy them, and why they buy them.

In general, people who buy books in the United States tend to be older, wealthier, and more highly educated, according to the BISG study. Women buy more than half of all books sold. About 40 percent of all books are purchased by people fifty-five and older, and more than half are purchased by people fifty and older. More than half of all books are bought by people with household incomes of $50,000 or more, and fully one-third are bought by people with household incomes of more than $75,000. Nearly 40 percent of the people who purchase books have at least some college education.

FACT

According to the Authors Guild, a successful fiction book sells 5,000 copies and a successful nonfiction book sells 7,500 copies. You can reasonably expect about 1 percent of your potential readership to actually buy your book. That means, ideally, you should be able to identify a potential readership of at least 500,000 for your fiction and at least 750,000 for your nonfiction.

Obviously, this doesn't mean that all your work should be aimed at a 55-year-old, college-educated woman who has money to burn; remember that half or more of all book buyers don't fit that profile. Besides, people have different interests, concerns, and tastes. That fifty-five-year-old woman might be more interested in a book about protecting her retirement nest egg than in buying a new house, while a thirty-something woman's immediate concern is how to save enough to get out of her apartment and into a house. Likewise, the fifty-five-year-old may have a ravenous appetite for historical romances, while the thirty-something would rather curl up with a good thriller.

What Books Do People Buy?

Books for adults account for seven of every ten book sales, the study reported. Popular adult fiction is the lead category, claiming more than 50 percent of the American book market. About 30 percent of books sold are hardcover, and about 33 percent are trade paperbacks (softcover books with a larger trim size and, often, more formal look, than mass-market paperbacks).

Mass-market paperbacks—the smaller paperbacks you often find on supermarket racks—represent more than 35 percent of all book sales.

Here's how book sales rank by category, with 1 being the most popular:

1. Popular fiction (mainstream, thriller, fantasy, historical, adventure, mystery, romance, science fiction, etc.)
2. Nonfiction religious (inspirational, New Age, philosophy, theology, family, history, prayer books, etc.)
3. Crafts/cooking (collecting, photography, hobbies, home improvement, etc.)
4. General nonfiction (biography, true crime, true adventure, humor, military, history, etc.)
5. Psychology/recovery (popular psychology, family/children/relationships, health and exercise, etc.)
6. Technical/science/education (computers, business and economics, medical, science and math, social sciences, etc.)
7. Art/literature/poetry (literary fiction, art and architecture, performing arts, etc.)
8. Reference (study guides, dictionaries, etc.)
9. Travel/regional (domestic and foreign travel guides, etc.)

Keep in mind that changes in current events and popular culture can alter these rankings. For example, before the September 11, 2001, terrorist attacks, the nonfiction religious category ranked third, behind cooking and crafts. After September 11, there was a significant surge in demand for books offering words of wisdom and ways of coping with the shock, grief, and anger felt after the attacks. Conversely, the demand for travel books dropped precipitously after the attacks.

How Do Readers Buy Books?

According to the BISG study, half of all book purchases are impulse buys. That means that 50 percent of people who buy books don't set out to purchase a specific title; instead, they tend to browse the bookstores or book sections of other retailers—or they browse online—and make their decisions based on how the book strikes them at the moment. Other research has shown that the average person spends about eight seconds looking at the front cover of a book and fifteen seconds reading the back cover.

FACT

Only a tiny percentage of new books ever get reviewed by the big players like the *Sunday New York Times Book Review* and *Publishers Weekly*. On average, the *Times* reviews approximately 3 percent of all newly published titles in a given year. *Publishers Weekly* covers more titles, about 11 percent of new titles annually.

Many surveyed readers report that word-of-mouth is one of the top three factors in their decision to buy a book. Word-of-mouth can come from book reviews in newspapers and magazines, or recommendations from friends, relatives, and colleagues.

Assessing the Competition

Just because someone else has already written a book similar to yours doesn't mean you don't have a salable idea. But agents and editors will want to know how your book differs from those already on the market. What you need to know, and what you need to tell agents and editors, varies according to the kind of book you're writing.

Fiction Research

For fiction, it's most helpful to point out books that are similar to yours; if your story is reminiscent of Tony Hillerman, for example, an agent or editor will start thinking of ways to tap into that vein of readers. Go to your local bookstore and see which books are being aggressively marketed with front-table displays, posters, and so on. Make a note of the authors, titles, publishers, and genres of these books, and check out the acknowledgments for agents' and editors' names; this will help you target potential agents and editors for your book.

Do I need to find out how many copies of a competing book were sold?

No. Publishers have access to much more accurate copies-sold data than you can find, and that information is an integral part of their decision to purchase a manuscript. However, if a similar title has made the bestseller list, point that out in your cover letter or proposal.

Nonfiction Research

Nonfiction books need to stand out from the crowd in order to catch an agent's or editor's eye. No matter what your topic is, chances are there's a similar book out there somewhere. You need to find out what those titles are, what their focus is, and who is likely to be most interested in them. You may have a great idea for a book on herb gardens or the history of the potato chip, but until you know what other books have to say on those topics, you can't fine-tune your idea.

It's important to note here that your idea of a competing book may not be the same as an agent's or editor's idea of a competing book. Let's say you want to write a complete guide for babysitters about how to keep children safe and what to do in various emergencies. Maybe there isn't another book quite like this on the market. But perhaps there is a babysitting book that covers this material in one of the chapters. An editor may consider that a competing book, especially if that book is published by his own house. If the existing book is selling well, the editor may be interested in yours to be marketed as a companion guide; on the other hand, the publisher may not want any new titles that could siphon sales from the existing book. If the existing book is not selling well, chances are the house will be leery of taking on a similar title, unless you can convince the editor that yours will do better.

Online booksellers like Amazon.com are excellent sources of information about books in print. Even upcoming books—those to be published within the next four to six months—are often listed on these sites. You can find out the publisher, the format, and often even the table of contents, or maybe read excerpts of competing books.

ALERT!

Amazon.com and other online booksellers usually list sales rankings for titles. For your purposes, these rankings are irrelevant because they only reflect sales on that particular site. Many authors assume the rankings show how many copies a particular title has sold, but that's not true: The No. 1 seller on Amazon.com may have sold 1,000 copies, while No. 3,642 sold 910 copies. Your best bet is to ignore the sales ranks altogether.

Finding Your Angle

Once you know what other books are on the market, you can begin to narrow the focus of your own book idea. Ideally, your book should present a fresh angle that hasn't been explored by others. This is where the techniques for generating book ideas discussed in Chapter 1 come in. Think critically about the material covered, how it's presented, and whom it's for.

Underserved Markets

There may be a dozen or more available titles on your topic, but that doesn't mean they're appropriate for every reader. Let's say you want to write a book about professionalism in the workplace. There may be lots of books about this, but most of them may be aimed at supervisors, managers, and executives, who are most responsible for setting the tone and upholding standards of behavior. Perhaps your book could focus on what entry- and midlevel employees can do to promote a professional atmosphere, addressing such issues as attire, language, makeup and jewelry, and even workspace decoration.

As discussed in Chapter 1, there are many potential audience segments for virtually any topic. Customer service books can be targeted to employees and managers, or to customers who want to know how to resolve problems or get the level of service they're looking for. Personal finance books can be targeted to middle-aged couples who are worried about retirement planning or to new college graduates who have concerns about handling and saving money. When you look at the competition, think about which readers those books have ignored.

A Different Perspective

Lots of books offer advice from experts in various fields, from finance and self-help to legal issues and even cooking. But sometimes there's an opening for a "real-life" perspective on a topic. "Expert" advice sometimes doesn't translate well into ordinary lives. Few people have the patience to decipher legal documents, for example, so putting legal language into plain English provides a service to the layperson who may need information on divorce, living wills, partnership contracts, and the like.

In fiction, a different perspective may mean telling a tale from an unusual point of view. Granted, you won't get far if you try to sell a Gothic novel told from the hero's point of view instead of the heroine's. But perhaps you could tell your Western story from the point of view of the stable hand instead of the gunslinger. *Black Beauty* and *Call of the Wild* were told from the point of view of, respectively, the horse and the dog, and were much more effective than if the authors had used human narrators.

Filling a Void

Chapter 9 discusses potential holes in the title list according to the reader's age group; there may be books on a given subject for beginning and middle-school readers, but nothing geared toward young adults. This is one kind of void to look for when doing your research. Other voids may be found in general categories (although it's fairly rare to come up with a completely new topic) and in individual publishers' lists.

Take this book as an example. Adams Media, the publisher, has a book called *The Everything® Get Published Book*. But there was no title on Adams's list that focused specifically on writing book proposals. This book filled a void in Adams's *Everything®* series. The slant is different enough to distinguish it from the other, related book, and adding this title gives Adams more comprehensive coverage on subjects likely to appeal to aspiring writers.

That really is the key to filling a void, whatever that void may be. Combine a clear idea of your reader with a topic carefully structured to match that reader's needs, then look for publishers who have already demonstrated, through their title lists, that they are interested in the same reader you want to reach. If you can do that, you're already miles ahead of many writers.

Reaching Your Readership

For fiction, you don't have to worry much about how to market your book to the reading public. Once you've identified the genre and length of your work, marketing is the publisher's responsibility. Your job in fiction is to write your best possible story and target agents and editors who are likely to be interested in your manuscript. After your book is published, you'll focus on what you can do to help promote the book, such as readings and book signings, and maybe even appearances on the public speaking circuit.

For nonfiction, though, you can improve your chances of getting a "yes" from an agent or editor if you show that you know where your readers are. Take that book on herb gardens, for example: If it's aimed at people who don't have space for a traditional garden, your readers most likely live in apartments, and the highest concentration of apartment-dwellers is in major cities. In this case, then, it may make more sense to send a review copy of your book to the gardening or food editor at the *San Francisco Chronicle* than to rural newspapers. That's the kind of thing you would point out in the promotion section of your proposal.

It's also helpful to know where readers buy their books. This varies from genre to genre. For example, online booksellers like Amazon.com and Barnes & Noble's Web site account for about 8 percent of all book purchases. But only 1 percent of all children's books are sold online; more than 25 percent of children's books are sold through book fairs, clubs, and mail-order catalogs. On the other hand, most adult trade paperbacks are sold through traditional bricks-and-mortar booksellers, whether large chains or independents.

Agents and editors want to know that you've given some thought to creative and innovative ways to reach the potential readers you've identified. For nearly every new title, the publisher will send a review copy and press release to major newspapers and possibly magazines, but very few of those books ever will be the subject of a review. Particularly for nonfiction, agents and editors will want to know about other possible marketing venues for your book.

Thinking beyond the bookstore can help you zero in on your audience. If you're the manager of a popular day spa, for example, and your book is about relaxation and stress-reduction, you could tap into the spa's customer base for potential book sales. An agent or editor will take notice if 200,000 people visit your spa every year, and 10,000 of those have signed up for your spa's mailing list.

Book Clubs

There are dozens of book clubs that promote titles to their members, usually via direct-mail catalogs. Some of these are general-interest, with an eclectic mix of fiction and nonfiction titles. Some are highly specialized, targeting readers of romance, mystery and suspense, science fiction and fantasy, even military and history categories. If your book would fit well into a book club's title list, mention that in your cover letter or proposal.

Associations and Organizations

Social and professional organizations are fertile ground for finding readers who already have an interest in your book's topic. Your high fantasy novel, for instance, probably would appeal to Renaissance re-enactors, and there are several such organizations around the country; you might even be able to sell your book at some of the countless Renaissance fairs. Veterans groups would make a sensible target for your memoir of Pacific Theater military operations during World War II. Your herb gardening book might hold special appeal for members of gourmet cooking clubs.

Many of these groups have newsletters for their members, and these newsletters might accept advertising or reviews of your book. Some even have mailing lists, which you or the publisher might be able to use for a direct-mail or e-mail promotion.

Specialty Publications

Don't overlook magazines in your market research. While it can be incredibly difficult to get your book noticed by national magazines, the possibility still is there, and you should take this into consideration. At the very least, circulation figures can help bolster your argument that there's a market for your book. *Bon Appetit* has a circulation of well over 1 million—an impressive market to reach with word about your herb gardening book, and a tempting target for a publisher.

Market directories like *Writer's Market* include vital statistics on a broad range of magazines, often including a profile of the magazine's readership. This should be a core part of your research. You can use this information to further refine your book idea and zero in on your target audience.

Keep in mind that your research is mainly designed to show a potential agent or editor that there is a strong available market for your book. Most of your ideas for promoting your book will never be implemented, for a variety of reasons, but that shouldn't concern you. As long as you can demonstrate that you have studied the market and thought seriously about whom and where your readers are, you'll have an edge over the innumerable wannabe writers who don't do their homework.

Chapter 6

Mass-Appeal Fiction

More than half of all books sold in the United States every year are novels aimed at adults. There are a dozen broad fiction genres, or categories, and dozens more subgenres, each with its own distinguishing elements. Mass-appeal fiction tends to cross gender, education, and income lines, attracting a broad range of readers. These genres also tend to have the most "break-out books," titles that, often unexpectedly, reach bestseller status.

Action/Adventure

Action/adventure stories are always popular, and the more realistic, the better. Readers of these stories often have experience in the military or law enforcement, and they're interested in weapons, martial arts, and paramilitary tactics as much as they are in the characters of their favorite stories. Settings for these stories can be exotic, but they must be authentic, and the foes are villains from real life—mobsters, terrorists, drug dealers, psychopaths. War and its aftermath are popular backdrops for the action/adventure story, but nearly any setting will work, as long as the danger is real and palpable.

Common Themes

The action/adventure novel almost always involves a heroic quest of some kind. It may be a quest to find a missing artifact or missing people, or to expose wrongdoing, or to bring the bad guy(s) to justice, or even to win a sporting contest. The protagonist is compelled to go on the quest, either willingly or unwillingly, and both people and nature contrive to place obstacles and dangers in his (or her) path. The odds are always stacked against the protagonist, and they mount steadily through the course of the story.

FACT

Although traditional action/adventure heroes and stories tend to have military, war, martial arts, or postapocalypse backdrops, these kinds of stories can take place anywhere, with almost any type of lead character. The Indiana Jones movies are an excellent example. Although war heightens the stakes, archeology is the main background for endless intrigue, danger, travel, and adventure, and a college professor becomes a reluctant hero in the quest to save the free world.

Woven through the quest theme are other, underlying themes that motivate the protagonist into following his course of action. Revenge, torn families, internal demons, and the search for redemption are common motivators in this genre; they can spur the hero to action, but, just as often, they can hinder his progress and even create more problems for him. The quest is the "what" of the action/adventure story. The underlying theme is the "why" that propels the hero into the quest.

Typical Characters

Action/adventure protagonists usually are male, although there are a growing number of books that feature female protagonists or two protagonists, one male and one female. Generally, action heroes and heroines must be quick thinking, self-sufficient, and brave, even recklessly so. They trust their gut instincts, and when they don't, they pay for it. They usually don't trust other people, certainly not strangers, and sometimes not even their nearest and dearest. Again, when they trust the wrong people, they pay for it.

The antagonist can be human, an animal, or even a force of nature. The protagonist may or may not know who or what his enemy is; sometimes the hero battles many of the villain's minions throughout the story but doesn't know until the climax just who is responsible for his travails. More often, however, both the reader and the protagonist know whom the bad guy is, and the emphasis is on how the protagonist will defeat the bad guy.

Characters, good and bad, have to be established through action, not through exposition. They must act logically according to how you've drawn them. A timid person won't react violently at the first provocation, for example, but a steady build-up of danger, frustration, and anxiety can realistically cause the most timorous of characters to lash out.

Plot and Pacing

Chases, rescues, showdowns, and cliffhanger scenes are staples of the action/adventure novel. Action sequences involve physical conflicts and usually physical danger to the hero or to the people around him. The hero must outwit, and sometimes outfight, the villain at nearly every turn.

The reader looks for risk, danger, and excitement; he wants to feel his pulse racing as he follows the hero through the story. But even these factors can become bland if they have the same flavor in each scene. The writer's responsibility is to vary the action scenes enough to surprise the reader, and to use language that puts the reader in the hero's place during each sequence. Excessive description of the setting, the problem, even the violence, can put fatal brakes on your story; if it slows down too much, the reader will give up on you and your hero.

Professional action/adventure authors often talk about "watching" the scenes in their stories before writing them down. They mentally choreograph the sequence over and over, watching it play out like a movie in their mind's eye. Only after they have a clear vision of how the scene should look do they sit down to translate it onto the page.

Pacing is an important part of keeping your action sequences effective. Because of the genre's emphasis on realism, remember that both your characters and your readers need time to catch their breath now and then. Your protagonists have needs. They get tired. They need to eat. They need to discuss strategy with their partners or talk out points that have confused them during their adventures. You can give them temporary safe harbor to do these things without sacrificing excitement or suspense. The key thing to remember is that digressions from the main plot should always help develop characters, explain a point, or build suspense.

Horror Fiction

Stephen King says horror fits into one of four thematic categories—ghosts, vampires, werewolves, and "things without a name." Whatever the mechanism for wreaking havoc among mere mortals may be, horror invariably explores the dark side of human nature. Fear and anxiety are this genre's stock in trade, and the form continually evolves to keep pace with modern society and all the new fears and anxieties progress brings.

History of the Genre

Although it wasn't dubbed "horror" then, the genre was born in the mid-eighteenth century with Horace Walpole's *The Castle of Otranto.* Bram Stoker's *Dracula* and Henry James's *The Turn of the Screw* came more than 130 years later. All were considered mainstream literature in their day. It wasn't until the late 1960s and 1970s that a few popular novels-turned-even-more-popular-films—namely *Rosemary's Baby* and *The Exorcist*—convinced publishers to actively market "horror" as its own genre.

The 1980s saw an explosion in horror fiction, some of it good, some of it not. The genre became so pervasive that publishers, authors, and readers alike began to see horror as formulaic and predictable. By the 1990s, the air had gone out of the horror market to such an extent that many publishers stopped identifying their stories as "horror," and booksellers began eliminating the horror sections from their shelves.

Today, horror is reclaiming its audience by reintroducing high-quality plots and characters, and through a good deal of cross-breeding with other genres, such as mystery, science fiction, and even historical fiction. Some horror fiction is still not marketed as horror per se, but as "supernatural" fiction or something similar. The protagonists in horror fiction have changed, too: Instead of mortals plagued by demons and the undead, today's heroes and heroines often have supernatural powers themselves.

Horror Subgenres

Horror fiction may be crossbred with mystery, action/adventure, romance, fantasy, and even literary fiction. Fantasy elements are common in horror, especially when the theme involves traditional quasi-human monsters like vampires and witches. Characters often have special powers or attributes, such as telekinesis or immortality. Sometimes the protagonist has these qualities, too, but is unaware of them until confronted with the villain. In other cases, the protagonist is a reformed villain, perhaps seeking redemption by fighting his former brethren or protecting innocents. The quest is also a common element in fantasy horror.

Horror may contain erotic elements, as in Anne Rice's *Interview with a Vampire*. "Erotic" can be as innocuous as romantic suspense, or it may be subtly sensual. Sex scenes are seldom graphically explicit; rather, sensuality is used as a weapon to seduce victims—and thereby the reader.

The common element in all horror fiction is its ability to evoke pure fear. The reader wants to be frightened, startled, anxious about what will happen next; she wants to feel her pulse quicken and her breath come in shallow pants as she follows the story. As long as you can produce that kind of visceral reaction, you can mix and match nearly as many elements as you want into your horror novel.

ALERT!

Most publishers shy away from so-called "extreme" horror—that is, overly graphic descriptions of physical violence. Horror readers want to be horrified, but they don't really want to be nauseated by gruesome blood-and-guts details. You can build suspense and fear more effectively by describing only what needs to be described and leaving the rest to the reader's imagination.

Mainstream Novels

Mainstream stories are those that don't fit conveniently into one of the other genres, although they may borrow several elements from other categories. Because they don't belong to a specific genre, these stories don't have to conform to a specific set of rules. Generally, mainstream fiction is set in a contemporary setting, but some mainstream authors have used historical settings in their novels.

Whatever the time period, mainstream fiction uses story, setting, characters, and language to explore some aspect of the human experience in a realistic way. Plots are important in mainstream fiction, but there is room for more complex character development than in some of the other genres. Mainstream novels tend to appeal to a broad range of male and female readers.

Unfortunately, mainstream fiction can be harder to market, especially for beginning authors. Unlike science fiction or westerns or technothrillers, whose readers know what to look for in the stories they like, mainstream readers never get quite the same feel from one author to the next. That's not a bad thing, but it does mean that there is no built-in readership to target. Big-name authors like Amy Tan and John Irving can rely on their fan base and name recognition to help promote their works. New authors are often compared to a big-name author in marketing efforts to give readers a hint of what they can expect between the book's covers.

FACT

Fiction genres in their simplest sense are marketing categories, designed to help readers find the kinds of stories they like and so boost sales. Bookstores arrange similar stories together under these broad categories and subcategories; you won't find a fantasy novel in the western section, for example. Though most genres have been around for decades, even centuries, they are fluid enough to keep up with the demands of contemporary readers.

Mainstream fiction is sometimes categorized as commercial fiction, but that's a misnomer. Commercial fiction covers books that are expected to sell particularly well; they may be mainstream, or they may be genre works. Not all mainstream fiction will have terrific commercial success.

Finally, some people confuse mainstream fiction with literary fiction. Definitions of "literary" are necessarily subjective, and some mainstream work may also be literary work. In general, though, literary fiction may sacrifice plot to characterization, may contain more dialogue and less action than mainstream or genre fiction, and may offer several layers of meaning within the primary story. Mainstream fiction tends to be more straightforward and more plot-driven than literary fiction.

Mystery/Suspense

Mystery and suspense novels both present puzzles to be solved, but they approach them in different ways. In mystery stories, the crime—murder, theft, kidnapping—happens early in the story, and the protagonist spends the rest of the story figuring out what happened; the villain is never revealed until the climax. In suspense stories, the plot is built around what's going to happen; we know who the villain is early on, and the emphasis is on foiling the villain's scheme rather than unmasking him.

Mystery and Its Subgenres

Mysteries are always popular with readers, and readers who find a mystery author they like will try to read all that author's novels. There are several ways to craft the mystery, and each has its own appeal. For example, many readers like amateur detective stories, especially if the lead character is a series detective, like Agatha Christie's Jane Marple. The private detective is another popular character and one that it is easy to build a series around. Sue Grafton has made a living with her Kinsey Millhone Alphabet Murder Series, featuring a gritty female private detective whom readers have followed from *A Is for Alibi* right through the mid-2004 installment, *R Is for Ricochet*. Publishers also tend to like series detectives—of any variety—because of this reader loyalty.

From the author's perspective, there are advantages and disadvantages to creating a series detective. On the plus side, a series character gives you much more leeway to develop that character's life and personality. On the minus side, you can get bored writing about the same character over and over again; it can become harder to keep the character fresh and invigorating, and later books can suffer from this lack of enthusiasm.

Other subcategories in mystery fiction include the police procedural, where the focus is on the technology and process of sifting clues and snaring the criminal. The "caper" mystery tells of a major jewel heist, bank robbery, kidnapping, or other crime (usually not murder) from the criminal's point of view, with an emphasis on the planning, equipment, and gang involved in the caper.

Finally, there is the "cozy" mystery, which wraps violence in a cocoon of wealth, elegance, and refinement; characters in "cozies" are well bred and well heeled, and the hard-core violence takes place offstage. Agatha Christie is the grand dame of the "cozy," but this subcategory remains popular today, with such authors as Sarah Graves (*A Home Repair Is Homicide* books) creating their own series of comfortable whodunits.

Suspense Novels

As noted, the suspense novel differs from the mystery in that the major violent scene comes at the end, rather than the beginning, of the story. The protagonist and antagonist are clearly defined at the outset, and the plot builds around the main characters' efforts to outdo or escape each other. Generally, the stakes keep building for the protagonist until he or she has to change his or her own behavior or come to some sort of self-discovery in order to survive. The interesting twist in suspense is that your protagonist can be the bad guy, as long as you make him or her sympathetic and someone the reader wants to root for.

Characters, settings, and plots in suspense novels are almost limitless. Think of such movies as *Enemy of the State* or *The Fugitive*, where ordinary people are put in extraordinary situations, where they must use all their wit and strength to win out against equally smart and strong adversaries. No matter what the background, the essential element of suspense remains the same: The reader's anticipation builds steadily, and he can't put the book down until he finds out what's going to happen.

Romance Novels

According to Ipsos Book Trends, romance is the most popular fiction category, accounting for nearly one in every five fiction book sales. Romance Writers of America reports that 93 percent of romance readers are women. Half of them are married, and almost two-thirds have attended college. About 2,000 romance titles are issued every year.

At its most basic, the romance has three components: A man and a woman meet early in the story; they face conflicts and obstacles in their relationships; they finally make it to the happy, emotionally satisfying ending. Once those components are in place, the details of plot, setting, and character are up to you, and there are several established subgenres at your disposal.

Up-and-coming subgenres include the Christian romance, which introduces a spiritual element to the traditional romance and often focuses on a single woman struggling to stay true to her faith in today's world. Romances featuring Latina and African-American heroines also seem to be gaining popularity among editors, in response to reader demand.

A good share of romances are written by men, but they almost always use feminine pseudonyms. The people who read romances expect a decidedly female point of view in their stories. A man's name on the cover tends to turn readers away.

ALERT!

Most romance editors warn writers not to get too hung up on subgenres, because the popularity of a specific subgenre (such as time travel or paranormal romances) is hard to predict. No matter how you mix categories, the single most important ingredient in a romance is a fresh, sophisticated love story.

Historical Romance

Generally, historical romances take place any time during or before World War II. Often, they are set during the Civil War, or in the American Old West, and the fictional characters travel in and out of historical events. Any historical period can provide the background for your story. Some epic historical romances traverse continents and oceans and cover a year or more in the characters' lives.

Although the characters and stories are fictional, readers of historical romances expect the historical details to be accurate. You'll need to research the culture and customs, modes of transportation, clothing, food, and even entertainment of the period carefully to give your story the authentic flavor readers crave.

Regency romances are historical romances that are set in England in the early 1800s; the immense popularity of this subcategory warranted its separation from the general historical romance genre. Regency stories have a strong focus on the society, culture, and customs of the day and how these factors influence the interactions among characters.

Contemporary Romance

Contemporary romances are usually set in the present day, but they also can be set in any post–World War II era. Settings for contemporary tales may range from a small Midwestern town to a metropolis, or even exotic overseas locales. As with historical romances, the details about setting, clothes, and so on must be accurate. Although romance readers pick up their favorite novels for an escape from real life, they still want a believable story.

Other Subgenres

Romances can incorporate any number of other genres in their stories. Fantasy romances, for instance, transport the reader to another world, populated with mystical creatures, magicians, sorcerers, and the like, but the focus remains on the love story between a man and a woman. Likewise, contemporary romances may use suspense, humor, or mystery to weave their tales. In every genre and subgenre, though, the main story is the relationship between a man and a woman.

FACT

There is a difference between romance and what is known as women's fiction. Where the romance spotlights the relationship between the heroine and the hero, women's fiction allows friendships, family ties, and other issues to play just as important a role. Generally, women's fiction relies more on complex characters and subplots, while romance deals almost exclusively with how the couple gets together in the end.

Sci-Fi/Fantasy

Science fiction and fantasy have different characteristics, but they are often marketed together in bookstores and libraries. Science fiction builds on current scientific knowledge and theory or starts from the premise that current scientific theories will be proven wrong in the future. Fantasy, on the other hand, often creates other worlds that may bear little if any resemblance to our own; these worlds are populated with odd creatures and strange people who use magic, sorcery, talismans, and an assortment of other-worldly skills and talents. In both genres, the writer doesn't have to worry much about the reader's willing suspension of disbelief; the reader is out for escapism, and her disbelief is suspended as soon as she picks up the book.

Sci-Fi Elements

Science fiction can take a number of forms, from the futuristic vision of *Star Trek* to the alternate humanity of *Animal Farm*. Aliens, parallel universes, accidents or incidents that change history, new frontiers, postapocalyptic life, the dangers of technology—any one of these elements or a dozen others (and in virtually any combination) is a commonly occurring factor in science fiction. In most cases, the writer is expected to explain the technology, basing it either on known science or on a repudiation of known science. The main exception to this rule is the "space opera," a futuristic version of the western, in which the battle between good and evil—with virtue emerging triumphant—takes precedence over the hardware.

So-called "hard" science fiction is based on real, present-day science and usually features one or more of the "hard" sciences like physics, chemistry, astronomy, and mathematics. A plot that can't survive the excision of the science element is called "hard" science fiction. Conversely, "soft" science fiction is based more on the social sciences, like sociology and psychology. "Soft" science fiction tales can often be transferred to any other setting without losing their basic integrity.

Fantasy Elements

Fantasy novels generally take place in mystical worlds with creatures like dragons and unicorns. A fantasy world may be earthlike, but it is usually far removed from the earth we know today; the exception is "modern" fantasy, where magic, sorcery, and other elements are fused in a contemporary setting. So-called "high" fantasy usually has a medieval setting and features strong class distinctions, often pitting staunch and true peasants against sly and greedy noblemen. Mythology and the Arthurian legends often provide the seed of the fantasy plot.

Like the action/adventure genre, fantasy usually involves a quest of some sort. The protagonist may set out to rescue a damsel in distress, to find a lost treasure, or to recover a magic amulet from an evildoer. Usually, the hero or heroine is young and naive, but possesses extraordinary courage and is helped in his or her quest by a wise and powerful mentor. Fantasy often takes on the flavor of an epic, spanning vast territories and introducing large casts of characters to the reader.

In fantasy fiction, morality is usually unambiguous. The characters are involved in a battle between good and evil, and evil nearly always appears to be stronger, smarter, faster, and more likely to win than good. To be able to resist the force of evil, the protagonist gets help from his allies, but in the end he must draw upon his own undiscovered resources to claim victory.

Chapter 7
Targeted Fiction

Targeted fiction includes genres featuring special characteristics that readers—and therefore editors—look for. Most such fiction has unwritten rules about plot lines, characters, settings, and so forth, rules created in nearly equal parts by what readers expect and what publishers know readers look for. Still, there's plenty of room for your own creativity within the broad parameters of these targeted categories.

Espionage/Thriller

Many observers predicted the demise of the spy/thriller story when the Cold War ended and the Berlin Wall came down. But modern-day dangers have proven to offer compelling stories for the novelist, and readers are increasingly seeking out this very specialized category. According to Ipsos Book Trends, the espionage/thriller genre is growing fast, increasing its market share by more than one-third in recent years.

The focus in this genre is on linear plot action. The story almost always involves a race against time and features lots of chases, showdowns, and rescues. Vigilante justice is a recurring theme, and treachery, subterfuge, and conspiracy are the norm. Heroes and heroines trust themselves, occasionally a partner, and their weaponry; everything else is suspect. Villains are drawn from real-life bad guys: terrorists, drug traffickers, unethical scientists, and corrupt politicians. Sometimes the antagonist is known from the beginning of the story; often, the villain's operatives are known, but the identity of the mastermind remains shrouded until the climax.

ALERT!

Current events can make for compelling, "ripped from the headlines" plots, but this technique can count against you when it's time to sell your novel because editors will be wary of a dated story line. You can tie your plot to a real-life event, but your themes should transcend that event to capture readers' attention after the event is over.

Spy Stories

Although they have lost some of their clout since the breakup of the Soviet Union, spy stories still have a loyal and devoted readership. The Vietnam War and the first Persian Gulf War are popular backdrops for espionage tales, as are the Middle East and China. The proliferation of nuclear capabilities in such countries as Iran, North Korea, India, and Pakistan provides a "clear and present danger" to national and international security, and therefore offers the seed of a good espionage plot.

There are half a dozen common plots in the espionage line:

- Rescuing someone from a hostile country
- Preventing someone from entering a hostile country
- Preventing a hostile power from obtaining technology or information
- Capturing technology or information from a hostile power
- Preventing a hostile power's invasion or takeover of another country
- Preventing an overthrow of our government

The espionage world can be as glamorous and exciting as the one in which James Bond operates, or it can be a grim, taxing, and seamy world, where good and evil are stirred into shades of gray and the happy ending is merely one in which the worst fate is averted for now. Whichever portrait you paint, readers will expect detailed descriptions of weapons, surveillance equipment, and other gadgets, as well as realistic representations of tactics.

Technothrillers

The technothriller has grown out of the gadgetry of the traditional spy story and is highly popular, especially among readers with a military or law enforcement background. Authors like Tom Clancy have helped foster this interest by focusing on state-of-the-art technology in weaponry, information-gathering, communications, and military air, sea, and land craft. The technology is nearly as important as the plot and characters, and often even provides the *raison d'être* of the plot. While the technology represented in these novels always is cutting-edge and may even be experimental, it never crosses into the bounds of science fiction.

Scientific Thrillers

Although they sometimes deal with plots of stolen germ-warfare agents or mishandled microbes, today's scientific thrillers usually focus on stories where science is both the cause of and ultimate solution to the problem. Michael Crichton's *The Andromeda Strain* dealt with an invading plague from outer space, while his more recent *Prey* explored a technology that was created by humans but threatened to exterminate them. Man's propensity for creating new technology or meddling in the forces of nature, and then being unable to control it, is a common theme in scientific thrillers.

Courtroom Drama/Legal Thriller

John Grisham has almost single-handedly elevated the staple courtroom drama to the status of legal thriller. Where Erle Stanley Gardner used the courtroom as a setting for unraveling a mystery and ensuring justice was served, today's legal story often incorporates all the traditional elements of an action/adventure or spy plot, with harrowing chases, narrow escapes from death, and lots of conspiracy and sleight-of-hand. The protagonist usually is a lawyer or law student with an unambiguously righteous cause; suspense comes from both the action and from wondering whether good will prevail.

Gothic Fiction

Gothic fiction is really a specialized form of romantic mystery. It is perhaps the most formulaic of all category fiction, with fairly rigid rules for characters, settings, and plot lines. It incorporates elements of the suspense novel, in that the reader anticipates some disaster happening to the heroine, and elements of mystery, since the heroine usually doesn't know who the villain is until the end. Romance and at least the promise of a happy future with the right man also are integral parts of the plot.

In the past, almost all Gothic stories by unknown or relatively unknown authors were published only in mass-market paperback, which necessarily limited marketing efforts; paperbacks are seldom reviewed by major media, and they usually don't get front-of-the-house placement in bookstores. However, in recent years, more publishers have issued hardcover Gothic fiction, and a writer with the skill and talent to inject fresh ideas into this genre—without breaking the taboos, of course—has a good chance of finding a hardcover publisher. Hardcover Gothic novels even have been known to appear on the bestseller lists occasionally.

The Gothic Formula

The Gothic heroine is young, attractive but not necessarily beautiful (and never a sexual being), often orphaned and always alone in the world. Needing to make a living, she takes a job as a secretary or governess with a moneyed family living in an old and isolated house. Everyone in the house, family members and servants, is a stranger to her, and they all are suspicious in some way. Shortly after her arrival, the heroine is plunged into some mystery, usually involving the death of someone in the house, and she becomes endangered herself, either through her efforts to solve the mystery or through some kink in the villain's mental makeup. Some Gothic stories invoke the supernatural, which may be genuine or a machination of the villain.

Modern romantic suspense stories have adapted the Gothic formula to suit today's society. Its heroines are more independent, but still vulnerable and imperiled; there is still a strong romance element; and the heroine often rescues herself from the danger, then falls into the hero's arms. While not traditional Gothic, these romantic suspense stories have found large and loyal audiences.

Throughout the mystery, romance develops between the heroine and a man, who may be a member of the household or a neighbor. Sometimes, the heroine is torn between two eligible men, and the one she favors invariably turns out to be the villain. If there is only one possible love interest in the story, he must be the good guy, because one of the rules of Gothic fiction is that the heroine finds true love by the end of the story.

Settings for Gothic fiction always are isolated and lonely, and the weather plays a large role in foreshadowing danger, evil, and madness. Think *Wuthering Heights*, with the wind and rain lashing the barren moors. The setting is as much a character as the people in the Gothic, and does as much to endanger the heroine. She must be trapped both by circumstance and by geography; peril and suspense cannot be sustained if she can just run out the front door and hail a cab.

Gothic Taboos

Gothic heroines are always delicate, slightly timid, emotional, and given to stereotypically female fears, anxieties, and reactions. There is no room in this genre for a self-sufficient, overly courageous woman. While she may be intelligent and resourceful to a certain degree, the Gothic heroine always ultimately relies on a man to rescue her. Gothic tales are always told from the point of view of the heroine, never from the hero's point of view.

The heroine must grow through the course of the story, working to change a major character flaw in steps as the plot progresses until she finally triumphs over both the villain and her own shortcomings. Her reward for her travails is the happy ending. Any Gothic that doesn't culminate in marriage or the promise of true love likely will be rejected by publishers.

Finally, the Gothic requires a more moderate pace than the categories it borrows from. Scene-setting and foreshadowing are important; high-energy action scenes are rarely used. Unlike mysteries, which can have two or more murders, most Gothic stories have no more than one death. Unlike suspense novels, there usually is no race against time and seldom any direct chase sequence. Instead, the tension mounts for the heroine (and the reader) from the anticipation of impending doom.

Graphic Novels

To fans and creators of the form—and even to publishers and booksellers—the term "graphic novel" is woefully inadequate to describe the scope of this body of literature. It's misleading even to think of it as a genre, because graphic novels cover everything from traditional superhero comics to autobiographies, memoirs, and literary fiction. At its most basic, a graphic novel is any square-bound book, hardcover or paperback, that tells its story in a comics format.

The graphic novel has been around for at least twenty-five years. Will Eisner is generally credited with clarifying the form in his 1978 release, *A Contract with God*, which was published outside the traditional comic book system and aspired to be a serious work of fiction, as opposed to the usual comic fare of superheroes and supervillains. Since then, publishers have issued graphic novels covering all manner of stories, from collections of comics that originally were serialized in comic book form to *Maus*, a memoir of the Holocaust by Art Spiegelman.

Today, large publishers issue graphic novels under separate imprints; at Random House, for example, graphic novels are handled by Del Rey, the publisher's sci-fi/fantasy imprint, and Pantheon. Four Walls Eight Windows, Sasquatch Books, and even Little, Brown have published graphic novels. The market seems to be growing; a Time.com article on this literary form in November 2003 quoted a Borders official as saying that graphic novel sales have had the largest percentage growth of any book category in the last four years. One graphic novel, Neil Gaiman's *Sandman: Endless Nights*, even made it onto the *New York Times* bestseller list.

The storytelling guidelines of other genres apply just as forcefully to the graphic novel. The main difference is that the illustrations cover most, if not all, of the description and exposition you would find in a text-only novel. Action is essential in a graphic novel plot; you have to have action to propel the illustrations. Dialogue must be crisp and clean, and characters almost never launch into long soliloquies. Readers must be able to identify with the characters, and they must care what happens to them.

Historical Novels

This genre combines all the elements of good fiction with meticulously accurate details of life in another age. Real-life people often appear as secondary characters in historical fiction. Sometimes historical figures even are primary characters in a subcategory known as "faction," in which the writer conceives some scenes and dialogue that are fictional but consistent with what these real-life characters might have said and done.

Authors of historical novels recommend reading only material related to the time frame of your story while you're writing. This technique helps you stay in your history, so to speak, and keeps you attuned to the tone, voice, and attitudes of the period you're writing about.

Readers of historical novels typically are interested in being transported to another time and place. They want to know what life was really like in pre–World War I England, for example, or colonial America. They want to experience the sights, sounds, smells, and flavors of the era, and they demand authenticity in these areas. Of course, readers also want a good tale to go along with their history, and in this regard the historical novel can blend with elements of virtually any other genre.

Cross-Categories

Most historical novels contain some bits of the action/adventure novel, using both people and nature as adversaries. Natural and manmade disasters are common ways to add action and adventure to the historical plot. A tornado or flood can change a family's fortunes in a heartbeat; a fire, accidentally or intentionally set, can lay waste to a town or even vast stretches of forest or prairie.

Mystery and suspense often play significant roles in the historical novel. Romance may be a part of any historical novel, although it is usually incidental to the main plot unless the writer is aiming to write a historical romance. There are even inspirational historical novels, in which faith and spirituality form the basis for characters' decisions and actions.

FACT

Saga novels sometimes are called *roman-fleuve* works, a term that means "novel stream." Because they cover so much time and so many characters, the pacing of a saga novel tends to run fast, then slow, the way a river does. The challenge for the writer is to balance the action, drama, and suspense over the course of the novel.

The Historical Saga

The saga or generational novel is a massive work that centers on one family and follows their story through three or more generations. The problems, conflicts, and dangers of the times are complemented by the internal forces that shape the family dynamics—greed, love, jealousy, competition, misunderstandings, and betrayal. Usually, the head of the family is a powerful man or woman, strong, determined, often domineering, whose personality shapes and often overshadows those of the rest of the family. Occasionally, a saga will be covered in a series of books, but more often they are confined to one lengthy book of 150,000 words or more.

Inspirational/New Age

Inspirational and New Age novels have been gaining popularity, along with their nonfiction counterparts, especially since the September 11, 2001, terrorist attacks. Readers look for stories of hope and fulfillment, with characters whose faith helps them cope. The category can range from nondenominational tales, which stress spirituality but don't endorse any particular religion, to evangelical Christian stories that apply traditional Christian teachings and morals to their stories. Some of these books sell millions of copies, and top-tier authors regularly earn six figures.

Inspirational and religious fiction encompasses every other genre of fiction. Mysteries set in religious communities or with church leaders as protagonists have been around for years. Science fiction infused with spirituality is becoming more popular. Even romances that explore issues of faith and religiosity are finding a readership eager for such ingredients in their novels. Violence has become more acceptable in inspirational fiction, although it's still muted compared to other genres. However, references to alcohol and sex (even marital sex) are still considered taboo.

ESSENTIAL

Inspirational fiction isn't limited to religious presses. Harlequin launched a new line in late 2004, with planned releases of a new title every other month in 2005. These titles cover everything from the tribulations of dating to juggling family, social, and work obligations, but the underlying theme in all the stories is how women stay true to their Christian beliefs and values in today's world.

Although Christian fiction dominates the market, there are opportunities for writers to explore other faiths. Finding the spiritual enlightenment of Buddhism in a materialistic American society, determining the relevance of ancient Jewish traditions in the twenty-first century, or seeking the true teachings of Islam in a world where extremism grabs the headlines—these themes and others have made several appearances in recent fiction titles. The biggest mistake most writers make is sounding too preachy; editors look for well-told stories with realistically flawed but spiritual characters and an expertly gentle touch when it comes to moralizing.

Westerns

There was a time, not too long ago, that the Western novel seemed to have suffered the same fate as the Old West itself. The dawn of the space age turned readers' attention and imagination to new frontiers, and publishers quickly shut down most of the Western novel mill, instead focusing on other, more profitable genres. Then, in the mid-1980s, several authors managed to publish not traditional Westerns, but "novels of the West," which recast the traditional Western in more realistic terms and recaptured readers' interest in that period of American history. Sagas like Larry McMurtry's *Lonesome Dove* and Max Crawford's *Lords of the Plain,* even with their strong Western flavor, were marketed as mainstream fiction and proved to publishers that the market for Westerns was still vibrant.

That market still seems strong today, and publishers once again are turning out both single titles and series in paperback and hardcover. Once in a while, a Western—or, more commonly, a "novel of the West," with its more literary flavor—will score major book awards (*Lonesome Dove* won the Pulitzer Prize) and bestseller status.

FACT

Westerns typically are set between 1865 and the turn of the century, when the country was still recovering from the Civil War, and there were vast stretches of wilderness to be explored and settled. The lack of organized law enforcement, the dangers of new territories, and the possibility of fortunes to be made are common themes in every type of Western novel.

The Traditional Western

The Western may be the only truly American form of literature. Western author Matt Braun points out that the young United States, at least as seen by its immigrants, had no grand mythology or legends of its own, no deep past from which to draw superheroes and arch villains. The westward expansion after the Civil War provided the grist for genuinely American fables, and the dime novels and pulp magazines of the late 1800s and early 1900s brought to a mass audience the exciting feats and exploits of larger-than-life characters like Wyatt Earp, Buffalo Bill Cody, and Jesse James.

Today's traditional Western builds on that mythology. These are relatively short tales, around 70,000 words, and focus on a single story line; the length doesn't allow for more complex subplots or a cast of thousands. Traditional Westerns draw on the stereotypes familiar to us all from John Wayne movies and television shows like *Gunsmoke*. The heroes are immediately identifiable as good guys, the bad guys are clearly bad guys, and justice wins in the end.

The Historical Western

The historical Western acknowledges the mythology of the genre but paints a more realistic picture of life in the Old West. The good guys have human weaknesses and failings; the bad guys may be motivated by greed or revenge, but they are rarely 100 percent evil. Historical figures, realistically portrayed, often make appearances in these stories, sometimes even as primary characters, and the plot may be tied to historical events. Accuracy is critical in the historical Western. You may make up dialogue between historical characters and your fictional ones, but you can't wrinkle history by shifting events to different locations or times, or by having a historical figure appear in Tombstone when he was really in Denver.

Western Story Lines

There are seven main themes in Western story lines. Your protagonist can be a lawman caught in a conflict with an outlaw of some type. The hero usually has to overcome some obstacle to deal with the outlaw; mere conscientiousness isn't enough to sustain the reader's interest in the main character. Conversely, your protagonist may be an outlaw, though he can't be one who is unsympathetic. An outlaw who kills without provocation, for example, is a lousy hero. But he can be a train robber, for instance, who has been forced into a life of crime by circumstances beyond his control. If you choose to make your protagonist an outlaw, you have two choices for the ending: Either you can reform him (as long as the reformation is consistent with his character), or you can let him escape. Readers and therefore editors will reject a moralistic, "crime doesn't pay" ending.

Other themes include the cattle story, which may take the form of cattle drives, conflicts between cattle and sheep ranchers, disputes over water or land rights, or a number of other problems associated with cattle ranching. Closely tied to this is the "battle between titans" theme, pitting two prosperous antagonists against each other; one big rancher may fight another big rancher or the railroad baron, for instance. The economics of the time, and the impact of those economics on the town, valley, or territory, provide the motif.

Finally, there are the themes of revenge, opening the West, and conflicts or wars between the cavalry and Native Americans. When revenge is the theme, the protagonist's actions have to be justified and understandable to the reader. The opening-the-West theme can provide endless conflicts among characters with competing personal interests in development and progress, but the ecological/environmental argument is taboo here; in the late 1800s, there were no concerns about irreplaceable natural resources, and you won't impress readers or editors by imposing a twenty-first-century sensibility on nineteenth-century issues. This is part of the historical accuracy demanded by today's readers.

ESSENTIAL

Just as most romance publishers will insist that male authors use female pen names, most publishers of Westerns will insist that women authors use male pen names or gender-neutral bylines, such as initials. The reasoning is the same in both genres: Readers expect a certain viewpoint and will turn away from authors who don't fit their perception of the proper viewpoint.

Likewise, today's cavalry-versus-Indians theme cannot devolve into racial stereotypes of Indians as wild savages and Army men as pure souls. You can explore bigotry and intolerance in the context of the period you're writing about, but readers expect a more accurate picture of the true relationship between American Indians and the U.S. cavalry, which, as often as not, involved the cavalry victimizing and persecuting the Indians. Make sure you paint an unbiased and accurate portrait of all your characters.

Chapter 8

Nonfiction Categories

Nonfiction presents a wealth of opportunity for the aspiring writer. You can turn a hobby or an area of interest into a salable proposal; you can even team up with an expert in a particular field who needs your skill with words to get his ideas out to the public. Nonfiction also can give you an entrée into publishing. In general, it's easier for an unpublished author to get that first book contract with a nonfiction title, and once you have a nonfiction book to your credit, it's easier to break into the fiction market.

Self-Help Books

The market for self-help books is enormous. People are always looking for ways to improve themselves and their relationships, to get their lives going in the direction they want. As one editor described it, there are three kinds of readers in the self-help market: those who are in trouble and need help, those who have had troubles in the past, and those who like to read about others' troubles.

FACT

Virtually every self-help author has impressive credentials that give him or her a strong aura of authority—a clinical psychologist, for example, or psychotherapist. If you don't have those kinds of credentials, chances are your proposal in this field will be rejected. To improve your chances, try to find a partner who does have the required background. (For more information on working with a coauthor, see Chapter 4.)

Self-Help Subcategories

Books about human relationships—and how to make them better—form the foundation of many of today's self-help books. Topics run the gamut, from dating to marriage, from being a parent to dealing with your aging parents, from coping in a single-parent family to smoothing the transition to a blended family. Sometimes the focus is on knowing and understanding your own personality; sometimes it's on understanding the people around you and the dynamics of your relationships with them. These books typically offer practical advice, often in the form of exercises, for dealing with common problems that crop up in any close, extended relationship. *Men Are from Mars, Women Are from Venus* by John Gray and *Self Matters* by Phillip McGraw (a.k.a. "Dr. Phil") are two bestselling examples in this category.

Addiction and recovery books used to focus solely on alcohol and substance abuse, but today the category is much broader. There are books about sex addictions, addictions to work, even addictions to miserable relationships. Again, authors of these types of self-help books nearly always have some kind of professional expertise and extensive educational backgrounds in their fields.

Success is a major theme in many self-help books, and it is defined in many different ways. *Who Moved My Cheese?* by Spencer Johnson helps the reader adjust to changing roles and goals in the workplace, for example. *The One-Minute Manager* by Kenneth Blanchard and *7 Habits of Highly Effective People* by Stephen Covey address ways to be more efficient and more effective at work; some of the techniques also can apply to other areas of your life. Other books focus on figuring out what you want to accomplish, changing careers, living your dream, and so on.

Self-Help Credentials

Relationship and addiction/recovery books lean heavily toward psychology and sociology, and the authors of these books usually have extensive professional experience as therapists or counselors, as well as advanced degrees in psychology or social work. It's virtually impossible for the layman to sell this type of book unless you're collaborating with such an expert; readers tend to gravitate toward those authors who have a proven track record in helping people work out their problems, so that's what editors look for in considering proposals.

Your own life experience can qualify you as an expert for other types of self-help books, though. If you've had a successful career in sales, for example, you have the expertise most agents and editors will look for when considering a book on proven sales techniques. Your background in running and growing a small business can provide the authoritative feel for a guide on small business strategies.

The self-help shelf is crowded, with lots of self-help authors having other platforms to promote themselves and their books. To break into this category, you'll need exceptional credentials, a solid promotion plan, and a topic or angle that will help your book stand out. Agents and editors will reject any proposal that looks like an imitation of existing books.

How-To Guides

Instructional books can cover virtually any topic imaginable. Getting organized at home and at the office, building model airplanes and trains, gardening and landscaping, creating a business plan, collecting dolls or coins or stuffed animals, managing your finances or your time, raising and caring for pets—think of an activity, and you have a potential how-to book idea.

How-To Elements

A salable how-to book provides essential information and step-by-step instructions for the reader and often includes lots of photos and illustrations. Your book can be targeted to readers who already have a basic understanding of your topic, or it can be aimed at newbies; the level of information you provide will be dictated by your audience. The volume in your hands, for instance, is intended primarily for new authors who need information on how publishing works and how they can polish their ideas to improve their chances of getting published. Some of the information presented here may seem elementary to experienced authors, but it's essential for the beginner.

How-To Credentials

Many how-to books are written by well-known experts in the field, but being an expert is not necessarily a requirement. In fact, it's possible to build a reputation as an expert by writing a book or a series of books on a given topic; once you've done the research and gotten your book published, the general public usually will assume that you are an expert. After all, the word "author" is an etymological cousin of "authority."

Publishers' requirements for how-to credentials vary. Some will insist on existing expertise or at least a strong professional background on your topic. Others will accept books written by laymen, as long as they include generally accepted principles or advice from other experts. Much also depends on whom your targeted readership is. If your book about coin collecting is aimed at novices, a publisher probably won't insist that you be certified as an appraiser. If you're trying to reach an audience that already is highly knowledgeable, however, your credentials probably will have to be stronger.

Biographies and Autobiographies

Biographies usually cover well-known figures, either historical or contemporary, though sometimes an "unknown" with a compelling life story can make a good subject (consider Helen Keller, for example). Whether the subject of your biography is living or dead, this category entails a great deal of research. Public and private documents, as well as interviews with the subject, friends and relatives of the subject, or descendants, are the essential building blocks for crafting a thorough and well-written biography. The best writers of this genre use the storytelling elements of fiction to paint word pictures of people and places, building tension and suspense where warranted, and connecting the dots for the reader throughout the tale.

Biographies vary in terms of what they cover. Books on historical figures like George Washington, Thomas Edison, or Catherine the Great may include details about the person's entire life, or they may break down the subject's life into segments. One book may focus on Edison's many failed inventions before the light bulb and the telephone made him famous, for instance. This technique serves two purposes: It allows the biographer to pour his energies into the part of the subject's life that interests him most, and it also leaves open the possibility of a series of books about the same subject, which can be attractive both to the author and to the publisher.

FACT

Celebrity biographies can be authorized or unauthorized. "Authorized" usually means you have the full cooperation and support of the subject, while unauthorized may mean that you've never even met the subject, or that the subject objects to some of the material in your book. Autobiographies by famous actors, political personages, or other celebrities often carry that person's byline but are written by ghostwriters, who usually don't get credit for their work.

Subjects for biographies come from virtually every area of life. Movie stars and Broadway actors are common subjects, as are political figures. The business world has its own set of stars and celebrities: Bill Gates,

Warren Buffet, Martha Stewart, Katherine Graham. Those who have achieved wealth, fame, and all the trappings of material success are popular subjects; equally popular are those who have fallen from grace, such as Richard Nixon or the CEOs from the many corporate scandals of recent years.

Reference Category

The reference category is more than just dictionaries and encyclopedias. These days, readers of all ages have almost insatiable appetites for information, and there is a market for reference books that have a unique slant. There are several books about how things work, from basic machines to today's omnipresent digital gadgets. The *Uncle John's Bathroom Reader* series, with more than a dozen volumes, provides interesting anecdotes and trivia, while *Vivaldi, Of Course!* is a series of tough quizzes on fifty core subjects, aimed at highly educated readers. Unlike the hardbound, all-inclusive encyclopedias of yore, today's reference books often are trade paperbacks aimed at a general readership, with very specific content. Examples include guides to over-the-counter medications, civilian airplanes, military hardware, even vegetarian-friendly restaurants in the major cities of the United States.

These kinds of reference books also include technical guides, such as manuals on how to use computer software, or guides to state labor and tax laws for employers and business owners. Study aids for various exams, such as the Civil Service exam or entrance tests for college, graduate school, medical school, and law school, also are a popular subcategory.

In many cases, you don't have to be an expert to author a targeted reference book. You do, however, have to know how to research your topic to provide useful information for the reader. That may mean getting access to experts in the field, and your ability to do that can influence an agent's or editor's opinion that you're the best person to write the book. Because your book will be marketed as a reference book, the quality of your research and accuracy of your information must be impeccable. Your reputation, and that of your publisher, will be riding on it.

True Tales

Truman Capote is generally considered to have invented the modern version of what he called "the factual novel," a true story based on traditional journalistic reporting techniques but told in the best fashion of dramatic fiction. Since Capote's *In Cold Blood* in 1965 and Joseph Wambaugh's The *Onion Field* in 1973, readers' appetites for well-told true tales of crime, adventure, and all the attendant human emotions has grown immensely. In recent years, Ann Rule, a former police officer, has made a second career with her factual novels of true crime, including at least three No. 1 bestsellers, covering such real-life events as the disappearance and murder of a high-ranking staffer in the Delaware governor's office *(And Never Let Her Go)*.

Effective true-tale writing involves extensive research. Official documents like court transcripts, incident reports, and arrest records, as well as some financial information, usually are public record, though it may take some persistence to get hold of them. Private documents like letters and diaries can help fill in the blanks in the public record, if you can get access to them. Finally, you can expect to conduct lots and lots of interviews with the people involved—not just with the principal actors, but also with their friends, neighbors, and relatives.

True Crime

Tales of kidnapping, murder, theft, espionage, and conspiracy find a ready audience when they are real-life cases. Readers look for the real story behind the headlines. They want to know what the players in the drama thought and felt, and what motivated their actions. Though the outcome is already known, the artful writer builds suspense by delving deep into the characters' psyches, revealing the reasons for what might seem inexplicable on the surface. There is a sense of inevitability in these works, a feeling that all the players in the drama are moving inexorably toward their fate, both before the crime is committed and afterwards, when law enforcement begins piecing its case together and the miscreant is caught and tried.

In some cases, the crime is never solved: D. B. Cooper, who parachuted from a jet over the rugged mountainous wilderness between Seattle and Reno with $200,000 in ransom money; the escape and eventual fate of a handful of inmates of the infamous Alcatraz prison; the truth behind the brutal slayings of Lizzie Borden's parents. All these are true-life mysteries, and they are all the more compelling because the questions as to what really happened remain unanswered.

ALERT!

Writers have to be particularly careful about libel when writing this kind of story. Especially when the accused has been acquitted, the way you paint your real-life characters can have serious repercussions when your book is published. You may wish to consult with an expert in libel law before submitting your manuscript to a publisher.

True Adventure

The true adventure story has in many ways supplanted the fictional one, because so many true-life adventures are more exciting and satisfying than anything the most imaginative writer could dream up. Real-life exploits, from the search for a shorter passage to the Orient to the exploration of space, provide all the ingredients of a rip-roaring adventure tale: human beings on a quest for riches, fame, or knowledge; nature, in all its untamable fury; danger and discovery, hardship and hope.

Think of the doctor who made headlines a few years ago; at a scientific outpost in Antartica, she first diagnosed herself with breast cancer, then had to treat herself using only the supplies on hand, because the weather prohibited any attempt to transport her to a better-equipped facility. Think of the *Apollo* 13 mission, when the world waited anxiously for days to find out if the three astronauts would make it safely back to earth. Think of the Lewis and Clark expedition through the uncharted interior of North America, or the scaling of Mount Everest, or the final voyage of the *Andrea Gail*.

As with true crime stories, readers expect to get inside the heads of the characters in an adventure. They want to know what the people thought, felt, and said, as well as what they did. The same rigors of research and interviewing that are required for writing the true crime story apply to writing the true adventure story.

Inspirational/Religious Writing

Interest in the inspirational/religious category has burgeoned since the terrorist attacks on the World Trade Center and the Pentagon. Even readers who don't consider themselves religious are looking for ways to promote spirituality in their lives. The *Cup of Comfort* and *Chicken Soup for the Soul* series tap into this need by providing inspirational anecdotes, sayings, and philosophies without promoting or identifying with a specific religion. Likewise, interest in and demand for books about the various organized religions have increased as people look for a deeper understanding of their own or others' faiths and religious principles.

FACT

Sometimes controversial fiction books can spark a whole new subcategory of nonfiction books. Dan Brown's *The Da Vinci Code,* for example, gave rise to at least ten nonfiction books that countered or supported Brown's theories on the early years of the Catholic Church and what Jesus' life may really have been like.

Who Are the Readers?

Successful books in this category can be aimed at a general readership or at narrow segments of the populace. The key is identifying the issues and concerns facing a particular demographic, whether it's broken down by family role, occupation, or hobby. Mothers and fathers have different worries than teenagers; nurses might find inspiration in different areas than accountants; NASCAR fans may look to different sources of hope and direction than quilters. The better you know your reader, the more effectively you can focus your book.

Religious Studies

Religious books are usually written by scholars or practitioners of the faith. They can be intended as study guides for members of that religion, or as educational materials for people wanting to learn more about the religion. Religious books of the study-guide type usually take the form of prayer books, devotional materials, interpretations of holy texts, or modern translations of scripture. Books designed to educate nonmembers of the faith usually provide more of an overview, including information on the history and evolution of the faith, ancient and modern practices, and so on.

Health Category

The health category covers more than just diet, exercise, and fitness, though these topics are perennial mainstays. Heightened awareness of such issues as obesity, heart disease, diabetes, cancer, dementia, and a broad assortment of other diseases has created a need for easy-to-understand manuals on monitoring and improving your health. Usually, readers of these books require more than just advice on how to protect their health; they also want information on how the body works and the science behind the methods that are advocated. This can provide quite a challenge to the aspiring writer, especially since research is continually challenging long-held ideas and perceptions of such things as hormone replacement therapy for menopausal women and the ideal combination of food groups for maximum health.

Lifestyle Topics

Lifestyle health books examine such areas as diet, fitness, and mental and emotional well-being. They are usually meant for a general readership with an interest in all-around health, and topics often are dictated by current trends. The low-carbohydrate diet trend has given rise to numerous protein-rich cookbooks. The demands of modern life have fueled interest in books on stress management and reduction, and related topics like meditation also have seen a surge in interest. Exercise books that are strictly instructional have been sidelined by more holistic fitness books that look not just at exercise but also at the physical and psychological benefits of regular activity. As life expectancy has increased, books that deal with maintaining an active and healthy lifestyle into old age also have found a strong readership.

ALERT!

The health category is exceptionally crowded these days, and it can be very difficult for a new author to break in. Agents and editors typically look for exceptional credentials, coupled with sound science and a slant or angle that readily differentiates your book from the rest. Even with these attributes, though, few of the myriad proposals on health issues ever get published.

Issue-Specific Topics

As awareness of various chronic and acute diseases has increased, so has demand for reader-friendly books on such topics as heart disease, diabetes, breathing disorders, and the like. Relatively newly diagnosed syndromes or those that are bubbling up into the national consciousness, such as chronic fatigue syndrome, attention deficit-hyperactivity disorder, and seasonal affective disorder, lead to new niche markets for books on these topics.

The readers of these types of books are usually directly affected by the issue covered. Either they have the disease or health problem themselves, or a close relative or friend suffers from it. That fact naturally limits your potential market, but it also can provide specific entrees to reach your readers through associations, support groups, and Web sites.

In general, the more specific your health topic, the heftier your credentials have to be. Most of these books are written by doctors or researchers. There may be opportunities for you to collaborate with an expert, especially if the expert has trouble relating technical information in everyday language, but rarely—if ever—will an agent or editor take on a project like this from someone without the precise technical background.

Travel Writing

Travel books can be a particularly hard sell these days. Never a huge share of the nonfiction market, the demand for travel books has dropped dramatically since September 11, 2001, as Americans eschewed overseas travel and continued the trend of staying closer to home for leisure trips. That said, there may be opportunities in the travel category if you find the right angle to tie into current trends and forecasts.

Travel books are usually purchased by people who are actively planning or considering a trip to a specific location. Rarely do people buy travel books out of general curiosity. When organizing your travel book, remember to provide the essential information travelers need, such as contact and price information for lodging and dining options, train schedules, directions to attractions, and so on.

Regional Travel

Many travel books focus on a specific region of the country like New England, the Southwest, or the Rocky Mountains. These books usually spotlight lesser known attractions and activities, and include at least a little of the area's history and culture. Readers of these guides want to know where to stay, where to dine, and where to shop, as well as what there is to do. Often, they look for suggested itineraries and how much various activities and amenities will cost.

Interest in regional travel has increased over the past several years, as Americans have abandoned lengthy vacations in favor of shorter trips, usually staying closer to home. Activities and sites that provide insight into American history and culture also are enjoying greater popularity, as travelers—especially those with children—show a heightened desire for so-called "heritage tourism." Book proposals that tap into this growing travel segment may have a better chance of piquing an agent's or editor's interest.

Other Travel Topics

After the slump following the September 11 attacks and the economic slowdown, traveling seems to be picking up again, but today's travelers have different concerns. There is less interest in overseas travel, and even leisure travel to big cities seems to have tapered off in recent years. Safety and security issues, and the delays caused by extra security measures, are of more concern to today's travelers. Both business travelers and leisure travelers are placing more emphasis on value; they don't necessarily want the cheapest fare or lodging or meal, but they do want high-quality service and amenities for their money. Travel books that take these new factors into account have a better chance of tapping into an otherwise overfilled niche.

Et Cetera and So On

The great thing about the nonfiction market is that there is virtually no end to possible book topics. Humor, history, sports, military subjects, art, music, architecture, interior decorating, economics, even research itself—all are vibrant subjects with nearly limitless slants and focal points. The trick is to find that overlooked angle and match it up with potential readers.

Although agents and editors tend to be wary of any book that seems dated, trends in popular culture can provide the seed of a broader, more timeless book topic. As always, the best nonfiction book proposals will combine extensive research on the topic with a thorough understanding of the marketplace. Without that powerful combination, it can be difficult for the new writer—and even for established pros—to break into these categories. But agents and editors are always looking for great ideas from talented writers who know how to make their ideas scream for attention.

Chapter 9
Children's Books

The children's book market presents an interesting dichotomy. The phenomenal success of J. K. Rowling's *Harry Potter* and Lemony Snicket's *A Series of Unfortunate Events* books shows that writing for children can be a rewarding endeavor in every sense. However, most people in the publishing industry still view children's books as a difficult market to break into—in part because few children's books capture the widespread audience of a *Harry Potter,* but also because few writers understand the specialty of writing for children.

What Children Read

Publishers of children's literature generally break down their books by age group. By their second birthday, children are just learning what a book is, while middle-school children are reading so-called chapter books. For the writer, this broad spectrum of book types and age groups presents many opportunities, both in fiction and nonfiction.

FACT

Children of all ages are eager to learn, and younger children especially tend to like books that help them understand the world around them. A well-written story targeted at a specific age group is likely to catch an agent's or editor's eye, no matter what the genre.

Picture Books

The picture book category has a number of subcategories, again determined by the child's age group. "Baby books" are picture books for infants and young toddlers, and most are designed to assist some aspect of the child's development, such as the motor skills involved in holding a book and the cognitive skills to turn pages in order. Baby books may be wordless or may include very short stories like nursery rhymes.

So-called "toddler books" are for children ages one to three. These books also are short on text—usually 300 words maximum—and often involve learning concepts like simple counting, identifying familiar animals, and so on. The average toddler book is twelve pages long and may be produced in a variety of formats; the most common is the "board" book, in which the pages are constructed of sturdy cardboard.

The age range for other types of picture books varies by publisher, but usually they are meant for three- to six-year-olds. Stories for these books are lengthier, typically between 1,000 and 1,500 words. The story should be told through one main character, and that character should be one that very young children can identify with. Illustrations still carry much of the story in these books, and the plot, though simple, requires lots of action.

In picture books, descriptions are often eliminated because the illustrations show what otherwise would be described in the text. Dialogue should be kept to a minimum—it can be boring to read aloud and it's boring to draw; illustrations in picture books should always show action.

Easy-Read Books

Easy-read books are aimed at children who are just beginning to read by themselves, usually between ages six and eight. These books still have lots of illustrations (often one on every page), but they are formatted more like books for older children. The reason for this is simple: six- to eight-year-olds are beginning to feel like "big kids," and they aren't interested in books that look like they're meant for babies.

Easy-read books can vary greatly in length, often depending on the publisher. Some of them are as short as 200 words; others are as long as 2,000 words. These books aren't as simplistic as the old "See Spot Run" primers many of us grew up with, but they should be written in short sentences that address one idea at a time. There may be two to five sentences per page. As with picture books, easy-read books require a single main character and lots of action.

Chapter Books

Designed for the six- to nine-year-old and sometimes called "transition" books, early chapter books form a bridge for young readers between illustration-heavy picture books or easy-read books and more text-heavy chapter books. The style for these books is similar to the easy-read style: one main character in an action-packed plot, told in short, simple sentences. These books still have illustrations, but they are usually black-and-white drawings, and they are more scattered. Chapters are typically two to three pages long, and an entire book will run around thirty pages in manuscript format.

Chapter books for readers ages seven to ten are a little longer—between forty-five and sixty manuscript pages—and have slightly longer chapters, usually three to five pages. The stories for this age group are a little more complex, and the sentence style also can be more complex, but paragraphs usually are no more than four sentences long. "Cliffhanger" chapter endings, or endings in the middle of a scene, are common, designed to keep the reader turning pages.

Middle-Grade Books

Middle-grade readers are eight to twelve years old, and they tend to read lots of different types of books. Favorite fiction genres fill the genre spectrum, from mystery to science fiction, contemporary, and historical. Also popular with middle-grade readers are series books, which feature the same characters, either in different stories or in a continuing saga like the Lemony Snicket books.

FACT

Good books intended for children often capture a strong adult readership as well. According to Ipsos-NPD Book Trends, only 41 percent of the "Harry Potter" books sold in 2003 were for readers younger than fourteen. The majority were purchased for readers fourteen and older.

Middle-grade books make a great leap from early chapter books, both in length and in complexity. Manuscripts burgeon to between 100 and 150 pages. Sentence structure is more complex. Subplots and secondary characters weave in and out of the main story, and themes become more sophisticated.

Young Adult Books

The "young adult" or YA category is one of the most fluid in children's books. Some publishers consider their YA lists suitable for any reader between the ages of twelve and nineteen. Others have broken this category down into two sets: young teenagers (ages ten to fourteen) and young adults (ages twelve to sixteen).

This category is the last demarcation between children's literature and adult literature. Themes, plots, and subject matter all are more complex in these books than in earlier categories, though some child-appropriate sensibilities still apply. YA publishers often have specific guidelines, especially for fiction. For example, a young teen romance may culminate in a kiss, but rarely will a publisher accept more explicit physical scenes for this age group.

Hi/Lo Books

Hi/lo books are those aimed at children whose interest in a topic is high, but whose reading skills are below average for their grade level. Generally, these stories are simpler than the typical YA book, but they are fast-paced with lots of dialogue. Fiction books in this category usually have contemporary settings and realistic dilemmas. Nonfiction hi/lo books deal with hot topics that sixth- through twelfth-graders are interested in.

Children's Fiction

Children's fiction has the same elements as adult fiction: strong characters and a good story line, well executed. The genres are similar to those for adult fiction. Although the style and structure of the stories are less complex, you can't take your readership for granted. Children require your best writing and storytelling skills.

Problem or Character Stories

The difference between a "problem" story and a "character" story is mainly one of emphasis. "Problem" stories may highlight a particular issue such as divorce, moving to a new town, bullies on the playground, and so on; when the emphasis is on the problem, character development often gets shortchanged. "Character" stories focus on the protagonist and his or her thoughts and feelings in dealing with problems. Both types involve contemporary, realistic settings and characters that reflect people the reader might encounter in real life. Both the protagonist and the reader should grow in some way by the end of the story.

Mysteries

Children of all ages like mysteries. These stories require fast action and suspense; characterization, though still important, often takes a back seat to plot. For younger children, the mystery usually is more of a puzzle to be solved, and the "crime" usually falls short of murder. Theft, missing persons, pranks and other puzzles are more common plot lines for younger readers. Murder mysteries can be appropriate for young teenagers or young adults, but the violence is emphasized much less than in adult murder mysteries.

For readers of all ages, the focus in a mystery is on clues, red herrings, and a logical conclusion that wraps up all loose ends. Mysteries can incorporate other genres, as well. You might place your mystery in a historical setting or mythical place, for example, or you can put a humorous spin on your mystery.

Adventures

The adventure story pits the protagonist against incredible odds and usually involves both people and nature as adversaries. In this genre, the central character has some goal to achieve, either through her own desire or to meet some critical need. Surprises and obstacles are integral to an adventure story, and often the various twists will raise the stakes for the protagonist.

Believability is key in this type of story. The reader must believe that the adventures he's reading about really could happen, even if the location is exotic or the story is set in a different time. The protagonist has to reveal her character through her own words and actions, and she has to achieve her goal through her own efforts.

Sports and Careers

Old-fashioned sports stories almost always featured a superhuman hero—a two-dimensional character, typically male, who always wins in the end. Today, the trend is toward more realistic characterizations of both boys and girls, who have flaws and weaknesses and who may not always end up on the winner's dais. As with the problem or character story, the central character learns and grows from what he experiences on and off the field.

Likewise, today's career stories shy away from idealistic notions of various professions and instead offer more balanced views of occupations. The concepts of choosing and pursuing a career are more often dealt with in nonfiction, but good career fiction can find a home. Again, the approach should be realistic, with characters learning both the good things and not-so-good things about their career options.

Myth and Fantasy

Myth and fantasy stories provide the ultimate escape for children, taking place in different times and different worlds among creatures of endless diversity. The central plot in a myth or fantasy story usually involves a quest of some sort. The central character typically is young and innocent and has to prove herself by completing the tasks set for her. Magic and the struggle between good and evil are stock elements of these stories.

Science Fiction

Science fiction has long enjoyed popularity with children, but today's sci-fi themes go well beyond the traditional lines of space travel, aliens, and beyond-the-pale technology. Contemporary authors use the genre to examine social issues and human characteristics through a different prism. Like myth and fantasy stories, science fiction requires a well-developed alternate universe. Even when the characters are of different species, the reader must be able to identify with them.

Historical Fiction

Historical fiction is a blend of fact and fantasy. You can make your story anything you like, set in any era you like, but your research must be impeccable. Children, like adults, expect that the historical details you present in your story will be accurate; they have little patience for basic errors in things like clothing, technology, popular culture, foods, and social mores. That said, a compelling story and well-drawn, interesting characters still are essential to this genre.

YA Romance

Romances seem to be just as popular with young girls as they are with adult women. There are several imprints of romance books aimed at twelve- to seventeen-year-old girls, and the "rules" of YA romance are similar to those for adult romances—the main difference is that, in traditional YA romances, the relationship is rarely consummated. Plot lines focus on the trials facing teenage girls; issues such as popularity and self-image are prevalent. The cast of characters usually is small, and the reader knows the story will end happily, with the girl getting the right boy.

Children's Nonfiction

Children have an almost insatiable appetite for knowledge of any kind, which makes nonfiction for children particularly attractive to the aspiring children's author. If you can make a subject fun, lively, and easy to understand, chances are you can fill a much-felt want in the children's nonfiction market.

FACT

Nonfiction can provide interesting topics for picture books, and can appeal in the picture-book format to readers as old as ten years. Nonfiction picture books for these older children typically run about 2000 words and can be up to forty-eight pages long.

Like adults, children have a wide range of interests and hobbies. Here are just a few categories you could select for your nonfiction projects:

- Sports
- History
- Biography
- Animals
- Fossils
- Space exploration

- Music
- Dance
- Engineering
- Cultural diversity

These are broad topics, of course, but there are countless possibilities for a children's book in each of these categories—plus dozens of others. If you want to write about sports, for example, you could write a book about basketball, football, soccer, baseball, or hockey; you could cover a lesser-known sport, such as lacrosse or dirt-bike racing, or you could write a book about skateboarding, snowboarding, or other extreme sports popular with today's youth. If your interests lie more along engineering lines, you could write a book about kites, their history, how they're constructed and why they work. If you're interested in history, you could write about popular toys of the eighteenth century.

As with any other type of book writing, you must study the market and find a niche or angle that has been overlooked. If you want to write about horses, for example, you might find that there are several books for very young readers and several more for young adult readers, but nothing for middle readers. If you craft your book to target this overlooked age group, you improve your chances of selling your proposal.

Of course, children's nonfiction, like children's fiction, must be written at an appropriate level for your reader. An eight-year-old will want to know different things about horses than a five-year-old, but the eight-year-old's vocabulary will be different from a fifteen-year-old's. It's important to write for your specific reader: Make it too simplistic or too difficult, and you've lost your audience.

Think about Your Readers

When you're writing for children, the age group you're targeting will be determined by the age of your main character. Generally, children want their heroes and heroines to be a year or two older than they are, never younger. Unlike adults, who often yearn to be children again, kids are eager to grow up and carry no nostalgia for the phases they've already lived through. A seven-year-old isn't interested in a five-year-old main character, and a ten-year-old isn't interested in a seven-year-old main character. If the hero of your story is seven, you're writing for the five- to six-year-old reader.

ALERT!

Diminutive terms such as "Little Sally" or "Little Jake" can turn children off your book. Kids look forward to being big enough to do the things they read about; they don't want their main characters to be "little."

Although they like to read about children their age or a little older, most kids aren't terribly interested in reading about adults, especially in fiction. The best children's fiction keeps adult characters to a minimum. The focus is always on the child in the story and how he copes with the problems he encounters.

Older children might part ways according to gender when it comes to interest levels in various subjects; boys may be more interested in sports stories, and girls may be more interested in romances, for instance. However, the trend in children's books, especially for younger readers, is to try to appeal to both boys and girls. Many of today's children's books feature both boy and girl lead characters, and many of them weave diverse, multicultural traits into their plots.

Many beginning writers make two common errors in their children's stories. Either they write from an adult's point of view, or they talk down to their readers. Children are pretty astute when it comes to judging tone, even in the written word, and they'll cast aside any book at the first hint of preachiness or condescension. Once you've determined the age group your story is aimed at, spend some time with children that age to get a feel for what they know, what they think about, and what they like, and keep those characteristics in mind when you're writing.

Illustrating Your Manuscript

Unless you're a professional artist, you should leave the illustration details to the publisher. You can make brief suggestions about drawings or pictures that might be included, but for the most part this is the purview of the editor. If she has been in the field for a while, she has a lot of experience in matching written material with artists, and she has a vivid imagination that enables her to see possibilities that you probably won't even think of.

In most cases, you won't meet the person who illustrates your text. In fact, many publishers discourage direct contact between the author and the illustrator because they don't want to deal with messy disputes over "creative vision." Typically, the publishing house will send your text to an illustrator, and you'll get a chance to see and comment on the illustrator's work when it's done. The editor acts as an intermediary between you and the artist.

FACT

When you're thinking out your picture book idea, you might make a dummy book, with the text laid out as you envision it in the final product. But when you submit your picture book story, use the standard manuscript formatting. Type your story straight through, double-spaced, with your name or story title and the page number at the top of each sheet.

Overview of the Market

There is good news and bad news when it comes to marketing your children's book. The bad news is that the field, both for fiction and nonfiction, is highly competitive. Publishers may receive 1,000 or more unsolicited submissions every week; of those, more than 90 percent will be rejected out of hand. Less than 1 percent might eventually be offered a contract.

The good news is that many of those rejected submissions simply miss the mark. A proposal or manuscript that combines a good story, good writing, and an understanding of the audience for which it is intended shines like a beacon on a fog-shrouded shore. As with any other book idea, you need to do your homework, in terms of both potential readers and potential publishers.

Researching the Market

The two most effective ways to research the children's market are to visit your local bookstore and chat with your local librarian. In the bookstore, you can get a good handle on what types of books are—and, equally important, are not—available for your chosen age group. Reading children's books gives you an idea of the tone and style appropriate for your target readership. You also can make a note of which publishers have produced these books.

QUESTION?

Do I need an agent to represent my children's book?
No. In fact, many agents won't handle children's books because the pay, both in advances and royalty rates, is so low compared with other genres. Most publishers of children's books understand this business reality, and they are content to work directly with writers and illustrators.

Your local librarian also can be a good resource for finding out what children are reading. He should be able to tell you what books are most in demand for boys and girls of different ages, what parents seem to look for when choosing books for their children, and so on. The library also should be able to supply information on upcoming books, either through the personnel's knowledge or through resources like *Books in Print.*

Submitting Your Manuscript

As with other types of book projects, you will need to research submission guidelines and contact information to make sure your idea gets into the right hands. Target publishers who have a hole on their lists that your book will fill, or publishers who have produced books similar to yours. Direct your submission to the correct editor, and be sure to spell the editor's name correctly on all correspondence.

Your submission package will differ depending on what type of children's book you're writing. For picture books, most publishers prefer to see the entire manuscript, with a brief cover letter. Your cover letter should include the title of your book, the age group it's intended for, and the story's word count. As always, include a SASE for the publisher's response.

For longer fiction and nonfiction, start with a query letter. Make sure you have sample chapters, or, better yet, the complete manuscript, ready to send if you get a positive response to your query. Occasionally, a publisher may ask for a complete proposal, usually for YA projects. This would include discussions of potential readers and competing books, as well as your author's bio.

Even when writing for children, you need to present a professional image. Avoid gimmicks like sending toys or candy with your proposal, or writing your text in crayon. This kind of thing immediately marks you as an amateur. Let your writing demonstrate how much you care about and understand children.

Writing for children presents unique challenges for the beginning writer, but there also are plentiful opportunities. Although advances and royalty earnings usually are smaller than those for adult books, children's books tend to stay in print longer than many adult books, so they can produce long-term income for you. Just as important, children are loyal fans of their favorite authors, and once you capture that fan base, they will seek out everything you write for them.

Chapter 10

The Query Letter

Many writers tend to focus on their manuscripts and dismiss the query letter as a mere formality. In fact, the query letter is the most important piece you'll write because it's the only piece guaranteed to be read by an agent or an editor—or at least by their assistants, who often have the authority to accept or reject. A poorly written query will get you a quick trip to the dead file. A well-written, well-presented query makes you look professional and knowledgeable, a promising candidate for publication.

Start on the Right Foot

A query letter is like the first phase of a job application. You want to make a good impression so that the agent or editor will give you an opportunity to submit your proposal—the equivalent of a first interview in a job hunt. Normally, there are certain questions every agent and editor expects will be answered in your query letter:

- What is the subject and slant for your book?
- Why is your book needed?
- Who will read your book?
- How are you qualified to write the book?
- How enthusiastic are you about your book?
- How professional is your presentation?

Also, a query letter must include your name, address, telephone number, and e-mail address (if applicable). And if you'd like a response, be sure to include a self-addressed stamped envelope, labeled with your name and address.

Dear Sir or Madam

The query letter is a business letter and should project a clean, professional image. You're trying to convince an agent or editor to take a look at your work. The query letter is the entire basis for that agent's or editor's decision, so it's important that you pay attention to details like proper business-letter formatting, readability, and the correct name and title of the person you're writing to.

Business Letter Format

Business letters are typically single-spaced, with flush-left paragraphs and an extra line between paragraphs. Your name, address, telephone number, and e-mail address should appear at the top of the page, either in letterhead format or flush right. The addressee's name, title, company, and address should be flush left, two lines below the last line of your contact information. The date should be two lines below the addressee's information, flush right.

FACT

These days, virtually all word-processing software includes a variety of templates for creating your own letterhead. Some of these are visually impressive but difficult to read. When creating your personal stationery, select a straightforward format, font, and type-size; Times New Roman, or a similar typewriter-like font, is easiest on the eyes.

In most cases, you should keep your query to one page. Agents and editors receive dozens of queries every day, and they make yea-or-nay decisions quickly, sometimes after reading the first paragraph. If you make them slog through a rambling, five-page query letter, chances are you'll end up in the reject pile.

A two-page query is acceptable only if your idea is exceptionally complex or meaty. Even so, if your first draft is two pages, see what you can eliminate or rephrase to whittle it down to one page. Remember that brevity is a virtue here; make your point quickly and get out of the reader's way. Of course, it's also possible to be *too* brief. One would-be client sent a one-sentence query to an agent, asking if she would like to see his manuscript. She said no; the writer didn't give her any reason to say yes.

Readability and Convenience

Choose a 12-point type size for easy reading. Smaller type can be difficult to read; agents and editors spend many long hours reviewing query letters, and they don't want to look at yours with a magnifying glass. Larger type, on the other hand, will look odd and unprofessional. Likewise, you should stick with a classic font like Times New Roman for greatest readability; other fonts can be hard on the eyes.

Avoid colored paper and inks. Black ink on white paper is the easiest to read and gives a classic, professional appearance to your letter. Select a good-quality paper; a 20-pound paper with rag or linen content is heavy enough to feel substantial in the hand without being too heavy to fold neatly.

Your envelope, too, should be of a good quality. If you're sending a one- or two-page query letter, fold the pages in thirds and mail it in a standard #10 business envelope. If you're mailing anything with more than three pages, use a 9" x 12" manila envelope, preferably with a typed or computer-generated mailing label. You should enclose the same type of envelope as a SASE (self-addressed stamped envelope). Fold a business-size envelope in thirds and paper-clip it to the top of your query letter; the 9" x 12" envelopes can be folded in half and paper-clipped to your material. Make sure your SASE has your address and the correct postage on it. The SASE is essential if you want a response to your query, so make it as easy as possible for an agent or editor to use it.

Most word-processing software includes a function for addressing envelopes, and a typed address adds to the professional appearance of your material. However, if you have to hand-write the address on the envelope, print it with block letters to make it as easy as possible to read.

Always affix the proper postage to your SASE; do not paper-clip stamps or attach a check or money order for postage. The only exception to this is when you're contacting agents or editors overseas; in that case, clip International Reply Coupons (IRCs) in the proper amount to your return envelope.

Name and Title

Your query is a sales pitch, and any sales professional will tell you that one of the keys to success is knowing your customer. That means knowing an agent's or editor's name and correct title, and spelling them correctly in your letter. Check the most recent directories of agents and publishers; if you're sending a query to a magazine, pick up a copy and check the masthead. If the agent or publishing house has a Web site, you may be able to check contact information there as well.

Occasionally you'll run across writing coaches or teachers who advise you to address your query generically to "Dear Agent," "Dear Editor," or "To

Whom It May Concern." While this may save you some time and effort, it's a lazy approach, and agents and editors will recognize it as such. A generic salutation gives one of two impressions: that you're mass-mailing form letters, or that you couldn't be bothered to look up an individual's name.

Your salutation should be businesslike, not overly familiar or casual. Don't use just the agent's or editor's first name; business etiquette demands courtesy titles until you are invited to address the other by his or her first name. Use Mr. or Ms. in the greeting; if you aren't sure of the gender, use the full name, as in, "Dear K. C. Jones" or "Dear Jan Smith." Don't guess at gender; if your guess is wrong, you'll make a lousy first impression.

Organization

A standard query is organized into four or five paragraphs. The first paragraph, discussed in the next section, is your lead. The second paragraph names your book and describes it briefly, as well as identifying potential markets for your book; in some cases, this might take two paragraphs. The next paragraph sells the agent or editor on you as the writer, and the last paragraph wraps up your letter.

Although the format is the same for virtually every query, be sure to inject your queries with your own style and personality. Agents and editors receive far too many "cookie-cutter" queries that were obviously copied from some how-to book. When you demonstrate your talent, professionalism, and creativity in your query letter, you're really showing that you are capable of coming up with original and exciting material.

The Call to Action

Any business letter, including your query, should end with a polite call to action. In this case, the call to action usually is expressed as a simple expectation of further communication. Do not specify the type of response you expect; obviously, you hope for a positive response, and every agent and editor knows that.

A standard closing paragraph for a query reads like this: "Thank you for your time and consideration. I look forward to hearing from you." This is brief, polite, and professional, and it doesn't place any undue demands on the agent or editor. You have acknowledged the value of the recipient's time and attention in reading your query—a simple but important inclusion that many would-be writers ignore, surprisingly. You also have stated your expectation of a response without pressuring the recipient.

Selling Your Idea

The objective of your query is to show why your book is needed, how it differs from other books on the topic, and that there is a large potential readership for your book. The best book idea in the world will languish in your desk drawer if you can't sell an agent or editor on these key points.

The first paragraph of your query is the hook; it should grab the attention of the agent or editor and compel him or her to read on. Anecdotes, questions, or comparisons can be effective techniques to evoke interest. Sometimes you can even adapt the first paragraph of your book to create an effective lead for your query letter.

The News Angle

Next time you read your daily newspaper or favorite magazine, pay attention to the first paragraph. Notice how the writer seeks to capture your interest and draw you into the story. There are several widely used techniques in this type of writing, any of which can form the basis of your query lead.

ESSENTIAL

While on the alert for effective leads, also pay attention to those stories where your interest slumps before you reach the end of the article. By analyzing others' writing, you can identify styles and techniques that work and separate them from styles and techniques that don't.

News stories tend to have straightforward leads, with the broad message up front and the promise of details later on: "The state legislature yesterday passed a budget that will lower income tax rates but raise fees for everything from vehicle inspections to fishing licenses." If you own a car or like to fish, chances are you'll keep reading to find out how the new budget affects you.

Feature stories in both newspapers and magazines are usually more circumspect in their approach. They may begin with a close-up and give you the broader picture later: "Mary Jones can tell you anything you want to know about her childhood. As with so many people who suffer from Alzheimer's, the details of her life on a small farm 80 years ago are far clearer in her memory than what she had for lunch today."

Facts and Figures

Sometimes the quickest way to make your point is to cite impressive statistics or juxtapose seemingly contradictory facts, like this: "Two-thirds of American adults are overweight, even as private gyms report a 42 percent increase in memberships and fast-food chains stumble over each other to tout their new, healthier menu options."

With this kind of lead, you give a factual representation of an issue and raise a question in the reader's mind. If Americans are exercising more and eating more healthy foods, why are they still overweight? You can answer this question in your query letter.

You also can spark interest by summarizing a problem or issue: "Recent public health crises over SARS and avian flu show that modern medicine has neither the arsenal nor an effective strategy to control dangerous and often drug-resistant viruses." With this kind of lead, the reader infers that you have the solution to the problem. Of course, your query (and ultimately your proposal) must live up to that expectation.

ALERT!

Avoid passive sentence constructions; they are clumsy and they slow down the pace of your writing. An active voice lets your writing sing, and that is music to an agent's or editor's ears.

What's Most Important?

If you're stuck on how to begin your query, try thinking like a reporter. Without looking at your manuscript or proposal, ask yourself this question: "What sticks out in my mind about this project?" The answer is your lead.

The thing that you remember best, without a fresh look at your own notes, most likely is the most important thing to share with others, and it belongs at the beginning of your query letter.

Selling Yourself

In today's publishing climate, it's not enough to have a great idea for a book. Your query letter also must tell the agent or editor why you are the best person to write your book. Point out your credentials, your experience, and your published credits, if any. If you're fortunate enough to have high-profile endorsements from a celebrity, a well-known author, or an expert in the field about which you're writing, be sure to include those, as well.

Toot Your Own Horn

Your query letter is no place to be modest. You don't want to come off as arrogant or cocky, but you do want an agent or editor to have a good grasp of your qualifications. Cite awards you've received that relate either to your writing or to the topic of your book. If your book is about creating winning public relations strategies and you've won awards from the Public Relations Society of America, for example, mention that in your query letter.

Life experience can count as a qualification, too, but don't overdo it. If you're pitching a murder mystery set in a fictional Southwestern artists' colony, let the agent or editor know that you lived in Taos, New Mexico, for two years. You don't have to give your life story; in fact, most times it's better not to, unless you're pitching your autobiography. Choose what's most relevant to your topic and eliminate unnecessary details.

Emphasize the Positive

First-time authors sometimes make the mistake of calling attention to their lack of publishing credits or to previous rejections of a proposal. Statements like "I have never written a book before . . ." or "Seventeen other agents have declined to consider my proposal . . . " make you sound defensive and amateurish. Remember, the impression you want to make on the agent or editor is one of a positive, energetic, and talented author—even if this is your first venture into the world of publishing.

Instead of highlighting the shortcomings, rework your query to focus attention on the positive. If you don't have any book credits, list your magazine or newspaper credits instead. If you don't have any published credits to cite, tell the agent or editor about your years of experience in the field covered in your proposal. Talk about what you have done, not about what you haven't done.

Take honest stock of what you have to offer and find the best light in which to cast your assets as a writer. For example, if you want to write a cookbook for working mothers, your query letter might mention how you devised your tasty new recipes in between sales meetings and school plays, or how your family's favorite dish was created by accident one day when your youngest child dumped a bowl of grapes into the stew pot. With this approach, you highlight your expertise as a working mother trying to make sure your family gets fed without calling undue attention to the fact that this would be your first book.

ALERT!

Using humor in queries can be tricky; sometimes what is meant to be funny comes off as flip and will turn off the reader. If you aren't sure whether humor is appropriate in your query letter, leave it out and stick to a more straightforward approach.

Select Appropriate Endorsements

Agents and editors don't care whether your mother, college roommate, coworker, or best friend thinks you're a terrific writer, unless your mother, college roommate, coworker, or best friend also happens to be a well-known author or expert. However, the right third-party endorsement can give an extra boost to your query. Even a one-line recommendation can carry much weight with agents and editors who are leery of signing up untried authors.

Who is that "right" endorser? It depends on your project. If your book deals with constitutional freedoms, for example, you might ask a prominent constitutional law professor to write a line or two as a recommendation. For the cookbook example, a dietician's endorsement can add heft to your proposal.

For your fiction proposal, you might seek a recommendation from a published author of the same genre. You also can mention that your novel is written in a certain style—"after the manner of Danielle Steele," for instance, or "in the vein of James Thurber." Be careful with phrasing here; you don't want to claim to be imitating another writer, only that your style is similar.

Sometimes agents or editors will agree to review your material if you've been referred by an existing client; in fact, some agencies only consider new authors if they come with such a recommendation. Be sure you have the referring party's explicit permission to use his or her name.

It can be tempting, especially when we want to impress someone, to overstate or exaggerate things. Resist this temptation in your query letters. Put your work and yourself in the best light, but never lie about endorsements or referrals; it will catch up with you, and you'll end your writing career before it even starts.

Sleep on It

Always wait at least one day between writing your query letter and dropping it in the mail. This gives you a mental break and allows you to look at your query with fresh eyes and a fresh viewpoint. You might come up with a better lead or a more effective approach altogether. You may discover that the tone of your query isn't quite right, or that your attempt at humor has fallen flat. Of course, you also might discover that the query is better than you thought it was when you were struggling to compose it.

The Mind's Editor

A read-through twenty-four hours later also might reveal typos or missing or extra words that you just didn't see the first time around. By giving yourself a waiting period, you can correct any errors before you send your query off. Remember, you're hoping to impress an agent or editor with your writing ability, and careless errors will only tarnish your image. While most people will overlook minor goofs, you owe it to yourself and your writing career to make your query the best it can be, both in concept and in mechanics.

When we read our own copy, and especially when we read the same thing several times, our brains can act like editors, transmitting what we *meant* to write rather than what we actually typed. As we hone and polish our query letters, we might insert different words but fail to delete the original words. Sometimes we misspell a word, or make a grammatical error that we don't catch at the time. But because we know what we wanted to say, our eyes sometimes just skip over these mistakes. That's why a final read-through, preferably after you've taken a good, long break from working on your query, is critical; you're more likely to catch those kinds of mistakes after a rest.

A Second Opinion

If you have a friend or relative who is willing to critique your query and whose judgment you respect, you might ask for her input. This can be especially valuable if you're concerned about whether you've made your query sufficiently clear or interesting. Ideally, a friend or relative who reads your query will understand the broad outlines of your proposal and will be interested in learning more; that's the reaction you want from an agent or editor, too. A second set of eyes also can help identify typos and other errors in your query.

If you use this technique, don't give the reader any extra information about your manuscript or book idea. Your query letter has to stand on its own; you won't be there in person to fill in the blanks when the agent or editor reads it. Again, the fact that you know what you meant to say doesn't necessarily mean you did a good job of explaining it on paper, and the outside reader can give you valuable feedback on that point.

ALERT!

Friends or relatives who are unfamiliar with the way agents and editors work might urge you to include much more detail in your query than is warranted. The goal of a query is to pique an agent or editor's interest so he will invite you to submit your proposal, and your proposal is the proper place for those details.

The Follow-Up

Virtually all literary agencies and publishing houses will take at least one to two weeks to respond to a query and six weeks or more to respond to a proposal or full manuscript. There's a very good reason for this: Literary agencies and publishing houses are extraordinarily busy places. Business hours are devoted to existing projects and clients. The stacks of queries and piles of proposals from potential new talent are at or near the bottom of the list of priorities, waiting for those rare free moments in an agent's or editor's day.

Directories of publishers and agents, such as *Writer's Market*, include average reporting times for each establishment. Whenever you send out a query, mark it on your calendar, as well as the approximate date you can expect to hear back from that agent or publisher. This not only helps you keep track of your submissions; it also reminds you not to get too anxious when you go several days, or even weeks, without a response.

No Reply

Even if you expected a response to your query in two weeks, give the agent or editor a total of six weeks to get back to you. If you haven't heard anything by then, chances are you forgot to include your SASE, or your SASE did not have your address and the proper postage affixed. Book queries usually receive a yes or a no response right away; rarely is one held as "maybe."

If you like, you can assume that your query got lost in the mail—it does happen, though not often—and resubmit your query. If you do this, make sure you include a complete SASE and tell the agent or editor, tactfully, that you are resending your query because you haven't received a response from your first try. Don't demand that the agent or editor look at your query immediately, and don't demand any special treatment, such as a phone call confirming receipt. If you still don't hear anything, or if you decide not to resubmit, move on to another agent or editor.

Send More

When you get a positive response to your query, the agent or editor will ask you to send more material—usually a proposal or partial manuscript.

Read the instructions and follow them carefully. If you're asked to send the first three chapters of your book, send the first three chapters; don't send the second, fifth, and twelfth chapters, and definitely don't send the entire manuscript.

Pay attention to the tone and mechanics of the response. Just as an agent or editor makes judgments about your professionalism based on your query, you can get an idea about the professionalism of the agent or editor by the response. A poorly written letter, or one with lots of errors, doesn't bode well for your project.

Sometimes agents and editors will call and ask you to send more material. When this happens, take notes to make sure you know exactly what you're supposed to send. Don't rely on memory; write things down during the conversation and, before you hang up, go over the list one more time. Ask if there's anything else the agent or editor needs, and tell her when you plan to send the material. Also ask when you can expect to hear back on the additional material, and make a note of it so you can mark your calendar.

Don't, Don't, Don't

No author—not even a published pro—receives a positive response to every query he sends out. But, like all of us, agents and editors have pet peeves that almost automatically disqualify certain queries from consideration. These are some of the more common pitfalls to avoid in your quest for publication.

Telephone Queries

If you're not John Grisham or Amy Tan, you should not attempt to make a query over the telephone. Agents and editors devote their business hours to existing projects and clients. Telephone calls from unknown hopefuls are intrusive and annoying, and you are far less likely to get a warm reception for your idea from someone who is irritated and just wants to get off the phone. Besides, you want to impress an agent or editor with your writing ability, and that cannot be done over the phone.

Some would-be writers feel that their ideas are so hot and so time-sensitive that a telephone query is warranted. That is never the case. Remember that it can be up to two years between the signing of a book contract and the appearance of that book on the store shelves; even rush jobs will take several months. You can afford the three or four days it will take the post office to deliver your killer query letter.

E-mail Queries

E-mail submissions are only slightly less intrusive than telephone calls. Most agents and editors devote significant portions of their days to responding to e-mails from colleagues, known authors, and existing clients. Insistent e-mails from would-be writers can interfere with the demands of the business day; in addition, it is far too tempting for the writer to expect an immediate response to an e-mail and fire off unnecessary and unsuitable replies to any response he might receive. Unless an agent or editor specifically requests e-mail queries or states that she prefers e-mail over other methods, stick with the regular mail.

Another reason to avoid e-mail queries: With spamming and debilitating computer viruses so prevalent, most agents and editors have powerful e-mail filters on their computers. If you are an unknown writer, there's a good chance your e-mail won't get through to the agent or editor you want to reach. The old-fashioned postal service may be slower than e-mail, but snail-mail queries stand a much better chance of being opened and read.

Premature Demands

The process for acquiring new writers and new material is almost universal. It starts with the query and an agent or editor deciding, based on the query, that he wants to see more. Virtually no literary agency or publishing house will offer you a contract based solely on your query letter; that decision won't be made until after the proposal or partial manuscript has been submitted and reviewed.

Unfortunately, some would-be writers are so excited with a positive response to their query that they leap ahead to contract negotiations. Some demand to know what kind of advance they can expect; others expect to "interview" the agent or editor before sending requested materials. This is a huge turnoff for agents and editors, who are far too busy with their existing projects and clients to answer inappropriate or premature questions.

ALERT!

It's in your best interest to resist pushing agents and editors too much. If you insist on making all kinds of demands before you agree to send your proposal, the agent or editor may decide you're more trouble than you're worth.

Some writers might chafe at the molasses-like pace of the publishing industry and feel constricted by the seemingly picayune requirements of the process. But professional writers—whether well established or just starting out—know that these are the rules of the game, for better or worse. If you ignore them, chances are you'll spend your entire writing career watching from the sidelines. But if you follow them, you give yourself an edge from the start.

Chapter 11

Elements of the Fiction Proposal

Often, authors of a new work of fiction, even those on their second or third novels, have to complete their manuscripts before they begin marketing their work. Agents and editors generally won't even consider your novel unless they know it's finished. However, when you're ready to begin submitting your fiction, you might want to put together a proposal package to entice an agent or editor to request your complete manuscript. As always, check submission guidelines to find out whether an agent or editor requires a query letter first.

The Cover Letter

Whether you're sending an unsolicited proposal or responding to a request for material, your proposal package should include a cover letter. This letter should never be longer than one page. Its sole purpose is to introduce you and your work to the agent or editor, or, if the agent or editor has asked for your proposal, to remind him that he asked to see your material.

FACT

At many publishing houses, one editor may be in charge of more than one line or series of fiction. If you're sending a book proposal with a specific line or series in mind, make sure you specify this in your cover letter. Otherwise, you might end up with an undeserved rejection.

If the agent or editor asked for your proposal in response to a query, you might include a copy of your original query in your proposal package. This helps remind the agent or editor why her interest in your project was piqued, and it saves her the trouble of searching through her files to find your original query. However, don't let a copy of your query act as a substitute; you still need a separate cover letter.

Required Information

Your cover letter should include the following:

- Your contact information, including telephone number with area code and e-mail address
- The genre and target audience for your novel
- The word count of your entire manuscript
- A very brief description of your story, no more than two paragraphs
- A thank you and call to action in the closing

As always, make sure you have the correct name and title of the person you're sending the proposal to, and keep the tone of your cover letter professional and businesslike. Also check the mailing address for the agent or editor. Large firms often have more than one office; make sure the person you're sending your proposal to works in the office you're addressing it to.

Don't tell a prospective agent or editor that "everyone" will want to read your book. If you're writing for a specific type of reader, identify the reader's key characteristics—whether the audience is likely to be women, Latinos and Hispanics, and so on. If you can't narrow your target audience, simply state that your novel is intended for a general audience.

Markets and Competition

Unlike the nonfiction proposal, you don't have to include separate discussions of your potential readership or competing books in your fiction proposal. However, your cover letter should indicate the genre or category of your novel; you can even say your novel is "similar to" the works of Dick Francis or "along the lines" of Toni Morrison's novels. This helps the agent or editor see where your book would fit on a bookstore shelf. If your novel defies conventional categorization, try to identify a similar quirky novel the agent or editor might be familiar with.

The Synopsis

Many writers hate the concept of the synopsis. They would rather let their work speak for itself, and they resent the fact that nearly all agents and editors expect to see an abbreviated overview of their masterpiece in a proposal package. Sometimes writers will "forget" to include the synopsis in their proposal packages, hoping the agent or editor won't notice. This never works; all it does is show the agent or editor that you can't or won't follow their guidelines. Sometimes writers even write long explanations as to why they can't possibly condense their novel into a synopsis. This doesn't work, either. You must include a synopsis if you want to be taken seriously as a fiction writer.

Remember that your proposal is a marketing tool. The synopsis is a key selling element in your package. Agents and editors are inundated with material every single day, and many of them use the synopsis to decide whether they want to read the rest of your proposal—or at least how much time and attention they want to give when reading. A well-written synopsis can mean the difference between a close reading and a casual perusal.

Your synopsis is a descriptive narrative that covers the main plot points in your story, usually two to three pages long. It never should be longer than five pages. It is always written in the third person and in the present tense: "Jane Smith is a bookseller in a small Midwestern town." Cover the important scenes, but don't stray into subplots or minor characters.

QUESTION?

Should I write my synopsis before or after I write my manuscript?
There are advantages to both methods. If you write your synopsis beforehand, it can serve as a roadmap while you're writing the actual story. However, keep in mind that you'll probably change key points of your plot as you write, so you'll have to rewrite your synopsis accordingly.

Engage the Reader

The opening sentence of your synopsis is at least as important as the opening sentence of your novel, and it deserves as much of your energy in crafting it. If your first sentence is blah, the reaction of the agent or editor will be blah, too. Just as your novel has to engage the reader, so does your synopsis; the only difference here is that the reader you're targeting is an agent or editor. Play around with your synopsis until you find the proper approach to keep that person reading.

Keep a Narrow Focus

Beginning writers often have a hard time writing a synopsis because they want to veer off into unnecessary exposition about their stories. The agent or editor just wants to know the main points of your plot and get a feel for your lead characters. Save the details for your manuscript, where you can give them the proper attention.

The narrow focus also applies to the mechanics of your writing. Stay in the present tense. Use the active voice. Eliminate adjectives wherever possible. The tighter your writing in your synopsis, the better your chances of impressing an agent or editor. And, if she's impressed, she'll want to read more.

One advantage to writing your synopsis first is that you won't get bogged down in details; you haven't thought of all the details yet. The synopsis tells you what your story is about. The details, subplots, secondary characters, and so on tell you *how* your story happens.

Avoid Amateur Devices

Your synopsis needs to be lively, descriptive, and, ideally, written in the same style you use in your manuscript. It does not need to be cutesy or gimmicky. Avoid glib, review-like comments, like this: "The best murder mystery since Agatha Christie!" Self-aggrandizing hype tends to turn agents and editors off. They may read your proposal, but they're likely to do so with an even more critical eye; they'll be looking for reasons why your work is not what you claimed it was.

Another amateur device is asking unnecessary questions, such as, "Will Jane find the real killer before it's too late?" The synopsis must tell exactly what happens in your story. Stopping your narrative to ask questions interrupts the flow for the reader and wastes valuable space for you. You only have two to five pages to sell your story; make sure every word in your synopsis gets you closer to that goal.

Reveal the Ending

Failing to reveal the ending is one of the most common mistakes beginning writers make in their synopses. They believe they'll entice the agent or editor to ask for the entire manuscript by ending their synopsis right before the climax. In fact, you'll probably irritate the agent or editor beyond belief. At the very least, you'll mark yourself as a rank amateur who isn't ready to start marketing her novel.

One of the purposes of your synopsis is to show that you can dream up an interesting plot, build suspense and drama, and resolve the issues of your story in a convincing and satisfying way. If you withhold the ending in your synopsis, the agent or editor might jump to the conclusion that you don't know how your story ends, which may mean that the agent or editor will have to help you devise a good ending. And that will only jeopardize your chances of selling your novel.

The Outline

Agents and editors differ on whether a chapter-by-chapter outline is necessary when you're marketing a work of fiction. Because chapter descriptions are so short, they tend to be dry and boring to read, and they don't do much to help your marketing efforts. However, even if you don't include an outline in your proposal package, it's a good idea to write one when you first start gearing up to write your novel. First, an agent or editor may ask for an outline after reading your proposal, and it's more convenient if you already have one ready to go. Second, an outline can be useful to you as you start writing.

Tracking Plots and Subplots

A chapter-by-chapter outline has several benefits for the writer. It forces you to plan out each step of your novel and keep track of your main plot and subplots. It can help you resolve issues with pacing—a problem many beginning writers encounter, particularly in the middle chapters—and it can even keep you focused as you finish your manuscript. If you already know what needs to happen in each chapter to move your story along, you're less likely to become sidetracked or mired in nonessential scenes.

Outline Format

Your outline, like your synopsis, should be written in a present-tense narrative style. Describe the major action for each chapter, and any important developments in your subplots. You can go into slightly more detail in your chapter outline, but you should keep each chapter's description to one or two sentences.

Your outline should be single-spaced, with an extra line between chapter descriptions and with no indentations. Chapter numbers (and headings, if you use them) should be all uppercase. A typical chapter description might read this way: "In CHAPTER ONE: THE DISCOVERY, a dead man is found in Madeleine Trevor's locked office, with a spray of rosemary clutched in his hand and a notebook full of unintelligible letters, numbers, and drawings in his jacket pocket."

FACT

For your own use, you might want to create a more detailed outline that covers each scene or lists specific events in every chapter. However, a broader outline is more useful and more appropriate for submitting to agents and editors.

The Characters

Many fiction-writing coaches advise you to craft biographies of your characters before you begin writing your story. Where your character was born, what her family was like, educational background, significant experiences during childhood—all these things help you see your character as a three-dimensional person, someone who existed before your story begins and who will continue to exist after your novel ends. This technique is helpful even when you don't use all the biographical information in your story.

A short "cast of characters" description can also be helpful to the agent or editor who is reading your proposal. It acts as a sort of scorecard for the reader (who, for a variety of reasons, may be merely skimming your sample chapters) and allows him to keep track of the players in your story. Gripping character descriptions also can be a useful selling tool to pique the interest of an agent or editor.

If you decide to include this element in your proposal, keep your character bios brief. Devote no more than a short paragraph to each main character, and list them in order of importance. Include minor characters only when they are essential to the plot, and give these characters only a one-sentence bio.

About the Author

Your proposal package should contain a separate sheet about you and your writing qualifications. This should be no more than four paragraphs, written in the third person and in the style you find on book jackets. Again, avoid hype; your author's bio should be a positive but straightforward summary of your qualifications. If your novel is a collaboration, include separate bios for you and your coauthor.

The points you emphasize in your bio can change depending on the project you're trying to sell. Your published credits always are most important and belong in the first paragraph. Education and work experience might be included if they relate to your book. If you're a retired police investigator and your novel is a murder mystery, you would include your work experience in your bio because it lends authenticity to your writing. If you're writing a historical romance, however, your police experience isn't relevant; leave it out.

Published Credits

The best selling point for you as a new author is published credits, even if you haven't yet published a book. Bylined articles in magazines and newspapers, even large-circulation newsletters or respected Internet sites, demonstrate that you have professional writing experience. (Chapter 15 discusses in detail ways you can build your portfolio and thus beef up your bio.) The key here is showing an agent or editor that you really are serious about your writing, not just someone who thought it would be neat to write a book.

Your writing credits should be listed in descending order of importance: book credits first, then national magazine or newspaper credits, followed by regional or local periodical credits, and, finally, alternative media credits. You should list well-known periodicals by name—*Redbook, Newsweek,* etc.—but you can lump lesser-known publications together.

If you've published a nonfiction book, be sure to include that credit when you're marketing your fiction. The important point for an agent or editor is that you're a published book author; genre is secondary at this stage.

A typical "About the Author" bio might begin like this: "Joe Jones's short stories have appeared in several literary magazines, including *Frank* and *Nostalgia*. His commentaries on life as a single father have been published in *Reader's Digest, Family Circle,* and various local and regional publications." Note that the "big names"—those most likely to catch the agent's or editor's attention—are highlighted. The smaller credits can be combined to reinforce your position as a published author.

Awards and Honors

If you won the *Writer's Digest* short story competition this year or won a national college fiction competition ten years ago, include that in your bio. Even if you didn't take the top prize, you can claim bragging rights in your bio. Don't make more of an award than it is, but let the agent or editor know that others have recognized your talent. Saying you "placed in the top twenty-five in the annual *Writer's Digest* short fiction contest" gets your point across without going into unnecessary detail.

Awards and honors that aren't directly related to your writing might be useful to include, depending on the circumstances. Speaking awards and public appearances can help demonstrate that you would be comfortable promoting your book publicly. Academic honors related to the genre of your book can help establish your qualifications as an authority.

Other Experience

The difficulty facing new authors is what to discuss in the author's bio if you don't have any published credits or relevant awards to include. The first rule, of course, is never to call attention to the fact that you're an unpublished author. Keep your bio positive and focused on what you have accomplished. Highlight your writing credits or other experience in the first paragraph, and expand on these things in your second paragraph. The last paragraph should be a one-sentence summary of personal information.

Here's how an unpublished author's bio might read in full:

Ellen Brown is an architect and mother of four who spends her spare moments reading and writing of more romantic times and people, whose adventuresome spirits were free from the clutching tendrils of meetings, soccer practice, ballet lessons, cellular phones, faxes, and frozen dinners. Her own stories incorporate the architectural grandeur and stability of the antebellum South, which serves as the backdrop and counterpoint to the turbulent times and tumultuous passions of her characters.

Brown is a member of the American Institute of Architects, the Society of Architectural Historians, and the American Cultural Resources Association. She has won several awards for design excellence and for historical preservation and restoration projects.

Brown is a native of South Carolina and lives there today with her family and a large assortment of pets.

ESSENTIAL

If your writing has received acclaim or endorsements from celebrities or well-known authors, mention it in your author's bio. Words of praise from a judge of a fiction contest would be appropriate, for example, as would a recommendation from a well-known author or celebrity. Include these in the second paragraph of your bio.

Sample Chapters

For your nonfiction proposals (see Chapter 12), you can send random sample chapters. But in your fiction proposals, it's crucial that you include the beginning chapters, ideally the first three or four. If you prefer, you can include the first fifty pages of your novel.

The following is one of the most common mistakes beginning fiction writers make in preparing their proposals. They send Chapter 3, Chapter 15, and Chapter 22, often because they think those are the most action-packed, the most dramatic, or the best-written parts of their manuscript. But agents and editors want to see how you set up a story. They want you to demonstrate your ability to draw the reader in and keep him engaged in the opening chapters. At this stage, agents and editors don't care about your fabulous ending; if you don't engage the reader from the very first sentence of the very first page, he isn't going to stick around for the ending anyway.

Another point to consider is this: If you feel that your third chapter is stronger than your first chapter, *why* do you feel that way? Your first chapter must compel the reader to keep reading. If you're not convinced an agent or editor will want to keep reading, then you're not ready to send out your proposal. Rework your beginning chapters until you're satisfied that they represent your best writing and storytelling skills.

Final Tips

Your proposal, like all your other communications with agents and editors, should project a clean, professional image. Stay away from colored papers and inks; black ink on a good white paper is the most professional combination. Package your material in a padded mailer or, in the case of a full manuscript, in a sturdy box. Don't go overboard with tape or packing materials.

A professional fiction proposal includes the following elements:

1. A cover letter, complete with your contact information.
2. A copy of your query letter, if appropriate.
3. A title page for your proposal.
4. A table of contents for your proposal.
5. Your "About the Author" page.
6. The synopsis of your novel.
7. The outline and/or "cast of characters" for your novel, if appropriate.
8. Your sample chapters.
9. Supplemental materials, such as reviews or endorsements.
10. Your SASE.

You can use a large binder clip or a large rubber band to keep your pages neat and in order during shipping, but don't staple, glue, or otherwise bind your material. Agents and editors prefer loose pages. Using three-ring binders, plastic covers, or other devices to "package" your work marks you as an amateur.

Title Page and Table of Contents

The title page for your proposal should include your name, contact information, genre or category of your novel, and word count for the complete manuscript in the upper left corner. If you want your novel published under a pen name, that should be noted here, too. Type the title of your novel in the center of the page; type the word "By" two lines below the title, and your name or your pen name two lines below that, also centered. If you have an agent, put her name and contact information below your byline, or leave space for her to do it.

The table of contents is for your proposal package, not for the entire manuscript. Your author's bio will be Page 1. From there, consecutively number each page of your proposal.

ESSENTIAL

Some beginning writers like to use desktop publishing software to create a "mock-up" of their books. The logic behind this is that it helps the agent or editor visualize your manuscript as a finished book. This is a fallacy. Agents and editors will not be positively influenced by fancy packaging; their job is to find good stories that are written well and likely to be purchased by readers, and they much prefer to read manuscripts in standard format.

Formatting

Use a standard, 12-point, typewriter-like font for your proposal and manuscript, such as Times New Roman. Leave one-inch margins on all pages. Give each page a header that includes either your name or the title of your book and the page number; this is critical in case your proposal is accidentally knocked to the floor or mixed up with pages from other proposals.

Your cover letter, author's bio, synopsis, and outline should be single-spaced, with an extra line between paragraphs and no indentations. Your sample chapters should be double-spaced, with indented paragraphs. Begin each chapter on a new page, and leave a three- or four-inch top margin on the first page of each chapter. Use italics, underlining, and bold type sparingly.

SASE

As always, include a business-sized self-addressed, stamped envelope for the agent's or editor's response. This can be paper-clipped to your cover letter. Also be sure to include the proper-sized mailer if you want your proposal returned to you. Always affix the correct postage. If you're sending material outside the United States, paper-clip International Reply Coupons (IRCs) in the correct amount to your mailer. Your return mailer must be addressed to you; put the agent's or publisher's address in the upper left corner so you can track who is returning your proposal.

Never send your only copy of your proposal or manuscript. It's a good idea to keep at least one hard copy for your files, as well as a back-up computer disk. That way, if one version gets damaged or lost, you'll still have a complete copy to work from.

Double-Check Everything

Before you drop your proposal in the mail, double-check the agent's or editor's name, title, and mailing address. Make sure your name and contact information is on your cover letter and on the title page of your proposal. Give every page a final read-through to check for typos, missing or extra words, and grammatical errors. If possible, have someone else read through your proposal to check for these things: A fresh set of eyes often can spot mistakes that you overlook.

Eagerness to get your work out to an interested agent or editor can tempt you to cut these last corners in your submissions. Remember, though, that the agent or editor will form an impression of you based on what you send. Clean, professional copy won't guarantee you an acceptance, but it will give your work its best showcase.

Requests for More

If your proposal is successful, the agent or editor will contact you and ask to see (usually) your complete manuscript. This is exciting, but don't let your excitement overshadow your good judgment. Remember to take the process one step at a time. Don't interpret a request for your manuscript as an invitation to call the agent or editor; that will come later, if your manuscript lives up to the promise of your proposal. Similarly, don't expect a critique of your proposal. If an agent or editor asks for your manuscript, your proposal has done its job; be satisfied with that.

When you are asked for your manuscript, send the entire manuscript and another copy of your synopsis. You'll also need to send another cover letter, this time reminding the agent or editor that he asked for your manuscript after reading your proposal. You also can include new, pertinent information, such as a new endorsement from a celebrity or changes in current events that make your book more salable.

Be sure to answer any questions the agent or editor had after reading your proposal, too. Don't avoid answering such questions because you fear the answer might reflect poorly on you. Evasiveness eventually will catch up with you and can do you more harm than telling the truth in the first place. Being honest in your answers always is better for your career.

Finally, after you've sent your manuscript, don't pester the agent or editor for her response. If you don't hear anything, it's because she isn't finished reviewing it yet. You'll know when she's done because you'll receive a rejection in the mail, or an e-mail or phone call saying she wants to talk to you. Nothing makes waiting any easier, but in the publishing world, no news really is good news until you get some definite news.

Chapter 12

Elements of the Nonfiction Proposal

The nonfiction proposal is a combination marketing tool and showcase for your work. A well-crafted proposal not only gives an agent or editor a clear grasp of the project itself, it marshals all the pertinent facts and arguments in its favor. By including the following elements in your proposal, you'll be able to demonstrate a need and market for your book as well as your ability to write it.

The Cover Letter

Every proposal needs a cover letter, though it should be brief—no longer than half a page in most instances. If you're sending your proposal at the request of an agent or editor, remind the recipient of that at the beginning of your letter. Then give a brief description of your proposal, reiterating the important points, particularly about potential readership and sales. Close with a thank-you and a call to action. As in your query letter, you should express simply an expectation of further communication, nothing more.

FACT

If there is anything new—changes in current events that make your topic even more timely, for instance—note this information in your cover letter. It shows an agent or editor that you're on top of the things that affect your proposal, and it can be an additional selling point.

Many authors include their original query letters with their proposals. This isn't a bad idea; some agents and editors find it handy in reminding them of why they were interested in seeing the proposal to begin with. However, if you choose to do this, you also need to include a cover letter, and the wording of your cover letter should be different than the wording of your query.

As with your query letter, make sure you have the agent's or editor's name and title correct in your cover letter. Use a standard business salutation; you're still in the wanting-to-impress stage, and you don't want to turn off the agent or editor by getting too familiar too quickly. Reserve the first-name-only greeting for when you've got the contract.

The Overview

The overview gives an agent or editor a quick glance at the nonfiction project as a whole. It should be a one- to two-page synopsis, written in narrative form, that gives a clear view of the purpose and need for your book. An agent will use the overview to help market your book to publishers; an editor will use it as an internal sales pitch when he thinks a project deserves a contract offer.

The Lead

The lead paragraph of your overview is the "hook." This is where you explain why readers (and publishers) will be interested in your book. If you're writing an inspirational book on living with diabetes, for example, you might lead with statistics on how many American adults develop diabetes. You also could point out that, while there are countless cookbooks and health manuals aimed at diabetics, there is a shortage of material that focuses on positive anecdotes and inspirational tales of people living with the disease.

If your project is, or could be, part of a series, mention that in your lead, too. More and more agents and publishers these days are looking for multiple-book deals rather than so-called one-shotters. This makes sense from a business standpoint; successful agents want authors who are interested in building careers, and publishing houses are interested in landing potentially successful series that can generate ongoing profits.

The Pitch

The pitch is a brief statement (one or two sentences at most) that tells the agent or editor what your book is about. You should be able to adapt a sentence or two from your query letter to include here. Think of it as a blurb on a book jacket: a clear, concise statement of the overall concept of your book.

After you've offered the pitch, you can elaborate further on the book's contents, but don't get tangled up in too much detail. Your overview should be lively and engaging, leaving the agent or editor with a clear understanding of what your book covers, the point of view it offers, and so on. If your project includes research or interviews with prominent experts, include that in your overview.

Finally, let the agent or editor know an approximate word count for your project. Most nonfiction books are a minimum of 60,000 words, but this is just an offer. An editor may later ask for a different length if your project is accepted.

ALERT!

Literary agencies and publishers often have their own guidelines for formatting various elements of a book proposal, including the outline. If such guidelines are available, follow them. If there are no guidelines, or if the guidelines are silent on formatting, the format offered here will serve you well.

Sample Overview

Your overview should be no more than two pages, and, in most cases, one will suffice. The title of your book is always uppercase. On first reference, use the full title and subtitle of your book; on second reference, you can use just the main title if appropriate. For example, if the working title of your book is *THE FORGOTTEN WAR: A MEMOIR OF THE KOREAN CONFLICT*, you would use the full title on first reference, but you would use *THE FORGOTTEN WAR* in all subsequent references.

The overview should be single-spaced, with an extra line between paragraphs. Do not indent paragraphs when using this format.

Here's how an overview for this book might read:

You've just come up with a killer idea for the Great American Book, and you can't wait to see it on the shelves of your local Barnes & Noble Booksellers. But how do you get there from here?

THE EVERYTHING GUIDE TO WRITING A BOOK PROPOSAL answers every first-time writer's questions about how to craft a professional book proposal. Filled with useful tips about collecting credentials and managing projects, as well as inside information about how literary agencies and publishing houses work, *THE EVERYTHING GUIDE TO WRITING A BOOK PROPOSAL* gives step-by-step instruction on studying the markets, researching readership, and packaging proposals for fiction and nonfiction in today's competitive publishing industry.

THE EVERYTHING GUIDE TO WRITING A BOOK PROPOSAL is a collaborative effort between a published author of several books and a respected literary agent with more than 15 years of experience in the field. Designed to be an essential guide for both the beginning writer and the published pro, this book delivers the "unwritten rules" of publishing in a friendly, easy-to-follow format that allows its readers to create professional, targeted, and attention-getting proposals, no matter what their subject or genre may be.

THE EVERYTHING GUIDE TO WRITING A BOOK PROPOSAL is approximately 85,000 words.

Note that this sample overview is just four paragraphs, including the proposed word count. But it tells agents and editors everything they need to know about the book idea, including the main points the book will cover and how the information is presented. Ideally, an agent or editor should be able to tell from this one page whether your book idea fits into her line, whom the target audience is, and what is new or different about your idea.

About the Author

Your author's information is a brief bio—not a resume—that highlights your qualifications to write your book. It should include your career experience or education only if these factors are relevant to the topic of your book. If you have twenty years of experience in dealing with diabetic patients as a doctor, for example, or if you have a degree in psychology, you would include that in your proposal for the inspirational living-with-diabetes book. If you have your degree and work experience in computer science, it wouldn't be relevant for this project, so it's best to omit them.

Highlight Your Writing Experience

If you have published writing credits, put those first in your bio. This lets the agent or editor know right away that you have some writing experience, even if this is your first book. If your published credits include national newspapers or magazines, mention them by name; if your work has been for smaller organizations, mention that your work has appeared in these publications, but don't go into specifics. If you're a regular contributor to a newsletter with a decent readership, a respected and well-known Internet site, or similar outlets, you can mention that experience, too.

List your most impressive writing credits first. Published credits should be listed in the following order: book credits, magazine and national newspaper credits, local and regional media credits, and alternative media credits. Here's how a bio for a reporter might begin: "Jane Brown is an award-winning writer with more than a decade of experience in print journalism. Her work has appeared in *Adoption* magazine and *USA Today*, as well as in several local and regional publications."

If Jane Brown already has a book credit to her name, her bio might start like this: "Jane Brown, author of *The Great American Nonfiction Book* (ABC Publishing, 1998), is an award-winning writer with more than a decade of experience in print journalism."

ESSENTIAL

If you've received awards for your writing, be sure to include that information, with the most prestigious award listed first. Don't worry about including dates or other details; you can say you received an award from the California Business Writers Association without specifying which article or series of articles the award was for or when you won it.

If Jane Brown is trying to sell her first book, and if she hasn't won any awards or been published in national media, her bio might begin this way: "Jane Brown has more than a decade of experience in print journalism. Her work has appeared in numerous daily and weekly newspapers and regional magazines throughout the Midwest."

Notice that the emphasis always is on Jane Brown's writing experience, regardless of the scope of that experience. The message to an agent or editor is that Jane Brown is a published writer, which helps her sell herself as being qualified to write her book.

Other Experience

If you don't have any published credits, do *not* say so in your bio. Instead, talk about other experience you have that relates to your book topic. Say you're the doctor writing the book about living with diabetes, but you don't have any writing credits to boast of. Here's one way to begin your bio: "John Black, M.D., has spent twenty years treating diabetic patients of all ages, economic strata, and ethnic backgrounds. Throughout his years of practice, he has collected anecdotes and tales of individuals who have transcended the physical effects of their disease to lead lives full of accomplishment and inspiration."

In this case, the emphasis is on John Black's extensive experience and familiarity with the subject of his book. The first paragraph of his bio highlights his medical degree, which adds heft to his credentials as an authority on diabetes. It also shows how he came up with the idea for his subject and subtly emphasizes that his topic is based on years of experience with real-life diabetic patients. The one thing it doesn't say is that John Black is an unpublished writer.

Additional Information

In general, your author's bio should be no more than three or four paragraphs. It's not meant to be a list of your accomplishments, but a brief introduction of yourself. The bio always is written in the third person.

The first paragraph highlights your writing experience and/or other ways in which you are qualified to write your book. The second paragraph expands on your first paragraph, listing the organizations from which you've received writing awards, favorable quotes from reviews of your work, or other relevant experience, such as radio or television appearances. If necessary, this might extend to the third paragraph. The last paragraph should include brief personal information.

Here's how a typical author's bio might read in full:

Jane Brown is an award-winning writer with more than a decade of experience in television, radio, and print journalism. She has appeared on C-SPAN's *Washington Journal* and has served as a story consultant for the CBS newsmagazine *60 Minutes.*

Her journalism honors include awards from the Montana Associated Press Managing Editors, Women in Communications, and the Maryland-Delaware-D.C. Press Association.

A native of Oregon, Brown now lives outside Washington, D.C., with her husband.

What if I'm collaborating with another person on a book?
Include "About the Author" information for each person, on separate pages. Don't worry here about how the work and responsibility will be divided; if both your names will appear on the book's cover, you need a bio for each of you.

The Outline

The outline is particularly useful for nonfiction proposals because it clearly shows an agent or editor what you intend to cover in your book and how you've arranged the information. It's also useful to you when it comes time to write your book; a good outline keeps you focused, ordered, and organized, and it helps diminish the feeling of being overwhelmed when you're starting on a big project. With some publishers, an outline even becomes part of the contract.

The outline is a chapter-by-chapter breakdown of your book, with a brief description of what each chapter covers; each description is usually one or two sentences long. Think of it as a road map that shows you where you're going and how you'll get there, but which doesn't tell much of what you'll see along the way. For most nonfiction projects, the outline will be at least two pages.

Write your outline in the present tense, and avoid overly detailed explanations. Each chapter description is a mini-overview of that chapter; hit the high points, and leave the rest for the actual manuscript. Here's how an outline for the first two chapters of this book might read:

CHAPTER ONE: WHAT DO YOU WANT TO WRITE? discusses setting goals, career-planning, the difference between projects you feel passionate about and projects that will further your career, how to find and develop ideas, and managing your time as a writer.

CHAPTER TWO: THE BUSINESS OF PUBLISHING offers an insider's view of how publishers seek out and evaluate book ideas, how a typical editor's day goes, and how a project is transformed from query letter to published book.

As with your book's title in the overview, your chapter numbers and headings are all uppercase in the outline. Chapter descriptions should be single-spaced, with an extra line between chapter descriptions, and no indentations.

FACT

Agents and editors sometimes will request changes in an outline to better organize the information, to include missing topics or subtopics, or to eliminate repetition. Be open to suggestions when this happens; the agent or editor is trying to make your proposal stronger, not weaker.

The Market

An important part of a nonfiction book proposal is providing information about your target audience. Hard numbers are most useful and most persuasive in convincing an agent or editor that there's a need for your book, so do some demographic research. If you're targeting homeowners, for instance, the U.S. Census Bureau can tell you how many people own their homes and how many people rent.

Your goal is to show that there's a large potential audience out there, just itching to pick up and purchase your book. Most publishers want to see a demonstrable market of at least 100,000 people. You can reasonably expect that between 1 percent and 10 percent of your potential readership will become aware of your book; for actual sales, assume that, at best, about 1 percent of your potential readers will buy your book.

Organizations and Associations

There are hundreds of thousands of social and professional organizations, and many of them might encompass the audience you're looking for.

If your book is aimed at accountants, for example, you can point out that there are about 400,000 certified public accountants in the United States, according to the American Institute of Certified Public Accountants, and that 328,000 of these CPAs are members of the institute.

Look at the Bigger Picture

In researching the potential market for your book, consider all the populations to whom your book might be of interest or use. That inspirational book on living with diabetes naturally will be of interest to diabetics; who else would benefit from reading it? Doctors, nurses, and home health aides, for example, might be able to use it in their dealings with diabetic patients. Friends and relatives of diabetics might find it useful to understand what their loved one is coping with. Reporters who cover health issues might be able to use it in developing stories.

All of these potential markets should be included in your proposal. Quantify each of these markets as much as possible. For example, if you can find out how many doctors, nurses, and home health aides deal with diabetic patients, include that in your market discussion. Also include the source of your numbers, even if the numbers are only estimates: "The American Diabetes Association estimates that more than 18 million people suffer from diabetes, including more than 5 million people who are unaware they have the disease."

The Competition

When you do your market research (see Chapter 5 for more information on researching the market), you'll probably find other books in print that cover the same topic or a similar topic. It's usually in your best interest to find titles on the same or similar topics that are doing well in publication. If a similar book is in its tenth print run, that's a pretty good sign that there's a market out there for this topic. Check bestseller lists and book reviews for this kind of information. In fact, it's a good idea to start a folder of these kinds of clips when you first get your idea; they can help you fine-tune your proposal to fill a void not covered by already-published books, as well as help you build your case that there's a market for your topic.

Focus your market research on books only; don't talk about nonbook rights in your proposal. Publishers are primarily concerned with book rights. They don't care about movie rights, for instance, unless a studio has already taken an option on those rights, in which case that might be a selling point for you.

The "competition" section of the book proposal is the place where you point out the weaknesses in those other books and the strengths in your book. Highlight differences in point of view, research, approach—anything that makes your book stand out from the crowd. If your book deals with financial independence, you can point out that other books on that subject tend to target the upper-middle class, while yours focuses on the things individuals making $20,000 a year can do to improve their financial health.

Do not be snide or overly disparaging in your discussion of the competition. In the first place, it's unprofessional. In the second place, the agent or editor you are dealing with might have worked on the competing book you're criticizing. Be detached and as objective as possible in your analysis of the competition; a matter-of-fact explanation of what these other books lack will carry much more weight than an angry or belligerent tone.

No Competition

What if your idea never has been covered in book form? What if the books that have been done on your topic are no longer in print? Do you still need a discussion of the competition in your proposal? The answer is yes, definitely. This is a splendid opportunity to reinforce the newness and innovation of your proposal, so take advantage of it.

Agents and editors are always on the lookout for something that hasn't been done before, or something that hasn't been done for quite a while and therefore is due for an update, if not a complete overhaul. If your book deals with genealogy, for example, and the most recent book on the topic was published before the home computer and the Internet came into common use, you've got a great opening—as long as your proposal includes information on using the Internet to trace family histories.

You don't have to mention out-of-print books when talking about the competition, but make sure you check the latest book lists for soon-to-be-published titles. If you're writing for a mass market, you don't have to talk about technical books on your topic or those that are aimed specifically at professionals.

Too Much Competition

Sometimes you'll find lots of books, still in print, that cover some, or even most, of what you intend to cover in your book. When that happens, sometimes the thing that makes your book proposal unique is the packaging—that is, how the information is organized and presented.

Let's use this book as an example again. There are dozens of books for writers. Some of them deal with writing query letters; some cover formatting manuscripts; some offer tips on the craft of writing itself; some supply information about markets and research; and some talk about the writer's relationship with editors and publishers. How do you sell an agent or editor on yet another book about trying to get published?

In this case, the selling point—and what differentiates this book from all those others—is the entire package. An agent or editor would be able to tell from the outline that this book covers all the essential topics that those dozens of other books cover, in one convenient volume. In the discussion about the competition, then, the proposal for this book would talk about pulling all of these elements together under the *Everything*® umbrella to create an all-in-one, useful reference for a writer at any stage of his career.

Promotional Possibilities

Your discussion of promotional possibilities should highlight any ideas you have for promoting your book and what you are willing to do to help in promotion. Keep in mind, though, that promotion is not the same as sales. The publisher's job is to place your book where it will sell: in bookstores, catalogs, book clubs, online retailers, and so on. The publisher will also send news releases and copies of your book to select media outlets. Your job is to focus on the things that you can do, not what you think the publisher should do.

If you're available for book signings, speaking engagements, media interviews, and so on, say so here. If you have experience in writing news releases or public speaking, mention that as well. The idea is to show the agent or editor that you have thought about ways to reach your readers and that you are willing to take an active role in the book's success.

As with any type of selling, word-of-mouth is the best form of advertisement in publishing. Readers often buy books because they've heard good things from reviews, friends, or coworkers, or because they've heard, seen, or read an interview with the author. When you're brainstorming promotion ideas, try asking yourself these questions:

- Do I have any contacts with local, regional, or national media who might be willing to interview me?
- Do bookstores in my area offer signing dates, "meet the author" events, or lecture series?
- Do the organizations and associations that might be interested in my book have regular newsletters or mailings to members?
- Are there local or regional chapters of those organizations and associations that might like me to speak at one of their events?
- Do local colleges or universities offer extension or adult education programs that might be interested in a lecture or seminar based on my book?

Not all of your promotion ideas will be suitable for your particular proposal, and very likely not all of them will come to fruition. But you'll impress an agent or editor with your enthusiasm and professionalism when you come up with thoughtful, sensible ways to market your book to the reading public.

Sample Chapters

A typical nonfiction proposal includes three sample chapters. Writers who already have book credits may be able to sell their proposals with fewer sample chapters, but first-time authors should strive for three. This gives an agent or editor a good idea of both your writing ability and your vision for your project. Sample chapters should always be double-spaced, with one-inch margins all around. The first page of each chapter should have a three- or four-inch top margin.

Your sample chapters don't have to be the first three chapters in your outline, or even consecutive chapters. Write the chapters that will best show-case your talent and your subject. For example, if your book is about a new way to plan your career, you would include the chapter that explains why this new way works better, and two chapters that detail the steps involved in your method.

If you're sending a proposal to an agent or editor who has requested materials from you based on a query letter, make sure you send exactly what she asked for. In most cases, the agent or editor simply will ask to see your proposal. But if the agent or editor specifically asks to see your first three chapters, send the first three; if you're asked for any two chapters, send only two. In any case, don't send your entire manuscript unless it's requested.

If you're sending a solicited proposal—that is, a proposal that has been requested by an agent or editor—write "Requested Materials" on the mailer to alert the recipient that he asked to see your proposal. This is especially important for agencies or publishers that don't read unsolicited materials.

Final Tips

A typical nonfiction proposal runs about fifty pages when all the information discussed here is included. Your proposal package, like anything else you send to an agent or editor, should present a polished, professional image.

In addition to the main elements discussed above, your proposal will need a title page that lists the title and subtitle of your book, and your name, address, e-mail address, and day and evening telephone numbers. If you're collaborating with another person whose name will appear on the book's cover, include her name and contact information on the title page, too.

Don't staple or otherwise bind your proposal package; most agents and editors prefer loose sheets. Because of this preference, it's vital that you include either your name or the book's title at the top of each page of your proposal; loose pages can get mixed up with other papers or otherwise disarranged. Each page also should be numbered, with the overview being page one of your proposal. Most word-processing programs have a function to add headers and page numbers to documents.

FACT

If you already have an agent, leave your contact information off the title page of your proposal. The agent's contact information will go there instead; you can either include it yourself, or leave it for the agent to stamp.

You'll also need a table of contents for your proposal (not to be confused with the outline for your book) to list each section and its page number. This lets the agent or editor see at a glance what is included in your package.

When you prepare your package, the pages should go in this order:

- Cover letter
- Copy of query letter (if you decide to include it)
- Title page
- Table of Contents (for the proposal)
- Overview
- About the Author(s)
- The Market
- Promotion
- Competition
- Outline
- Sample chapters
- Supplemental material

Supplemental material should be used only if it adds another selling point for your proposal. Articles about you or by you might be appropriate if it helps demonstrate your qualifications to write your book. Articles that support the need for your book also might be useful in swaying the agent or editor in favor of your project.

Finally, remember to include a self-addressed, stamped mailer if you want your material returned. Most proposals will fit comfortably in a 9" x 12" envelope; fold the return mailer (with proper postage affixed) in half and paper-clip it to your cover letter. UPS, FedEx, and the post office also have cardboard document mailers that work well for virtually every proposal.

With UPS, FedEx, or priority mail, you can track your submissions through delivery and be sure that an agent or editor received them. This can be especially valuable if your package is misplaced, as sometimes happens, either by the shipper or by the recipient.

For your own tracking purposes, you can include a self-addressed, stamped postcard so the agent or editor can let you know your material was received and when he expects to get back to you. Type on the postcard: "Proposal was received by XYZ Publishers on _____. Estimated reporting time is _____ weeks."

As always, the decision to pick up or pass on a given nonfiction proposal is fundamentally a business decision, based on whether the agent or publisher thinks readers will buy the book. By preparing a comprehensive proposal, you give yourself the best possible chance of convincing the publishing professionals that your work is salable.

Chapter 13

Common Proposal Mistakes

Agents and editors slog through thousands of queries and proposals every year. The majority of them get sent back ignominiously to the author, accompanied by a form rejection letter, because they don't come anywhere near the standards required for a salable project. Many of these writers repeatedly make the same errors—the ones that mark them as amateurs. You can make your book proposal stand out from the crowd by avoiding some of the most common proposal mistakes.

What's Your Purpose?

An unclear purpose is perhaps the most common, and most glaring, error in proposals and manuscripts from beginning authors. Your book project, whether it's fiction or nonfiction, should have a definite end in view. If you don't have a clear idea of what that objective is, you can't sell an agent or editor on it.

ALERT!

You can send your query or proposal to several agents *or* to several editors at the same time, but don't send to both agents and editors. This just causes confusion and hard feelings; once you've been rejected by editors, agents will find it difficult to market your work. Before you get ready to send out your material, decide whether you want to find an agent or whether you want to solicit editors on your own.

Your Book's Purpose

Every book ever written, fiction or nonfiction, has had a purpose that goes beyond the author's need to write. Some writers, like Kafka, Dickens, and Orwell, used their fiction to write social commentary. Others, like Hemingway, explored basic human needs and desires in exotic locales and unusual situations. Still others, like P. G. Wodehouse and Douglas Adams, aimed to entertain with humor and left it to others to derive any deeper meaning from their works.

Your book needs a purpose, too. Imagine a conversation between you and your readers. What do you want your readers to feel after reading your book? Do you want them to view your topic from a different angle? Do you want them to learn something specific from your book? How do you want your readers to feel and think after they get to the end? Your purpose doesn't have to be noble or majestic; it can be as simple as wanting to share information or giving your reader a pleasant escape from the mundane. But knowing the answers to these questions will help you focus your writing to satisfy that purpose.

Your Proposal's Purpose

The purpose of your proposal is to show an agent or editor that you have a salable manuscript. That means you have a great story to tell, and you have told it well. It also means doing your homework: finding out who and where your readers are, and matching your book with appropriate agents and editors. Both these elements are critical to your success, but many beginning authors skip these steps.

Many writers claim "everyone" will want to read their book, thinking, perhaps, that an agent or editor will be impressed with such universal appeal. In fact, this claim tells an agent or editor that you don't know who your readers are. They'll be much more impressed if you give them specific information about who will be interested in your book.

The more specific information you can give about potential readers, the better. Agents and editors want to know whether you're targeting a certain age or socioeconomic group, for instance. Find out as much as you can about your potential audience (see Chapter 5) and include it in your proposal.

The other half of your homework involves matching your book proposal with an agent or editor who works in the same genre or general category. So many beginning writers send their queries and proposals out blindly that this has become one of the leading frustrations for agents and editors. Take the time to find agents or editors who seem like a good match for your book.

Use the market guides and your local library or bookstore. See who is publishing your type of book, and check the acknowledgments for names of agents and editors. Make a list of ten potential agents or editors who handle your genre. Then rank those ten and begin your marketing with the top one on your list.

Get Organized

Poor organization is a common failing in both proposals and manuscripts. When you get a comment from an agent or editor saying your material seems unclear, unfocused, or rambling, lack of organization usually is the culprit. You may have the seed of a great idea in your book, but you have to put the various shoots of that idea in the proper order to make it thrive. Likewise, your proposal package has to be in the right order to show off your book idea to its best advantage.

Organize Your Book

Think of your writing as a game of follow-the-leader, with you as the leader. Your reader doesn't know where you're going, but he trusts you to take him through this territory because you know the way. As the writer, you have to act as guide, pointing out the things of interest along the trail, instilling your reader with confidence in your knowledge and experience.

If you don't lead your reader well, he loses that confidence. He begins to feel that you're wandering in circles, far afield from the real action, and that maybe you don't know where you're going after all. He becomes impatient and critical, and, in the worst case, he goes off to find another guide, one who is better able to share the wonders of the journey with him.

FACT

Leaping ahead of the process is a common mistake for new authors. Don't talk about advances or deadlines or production schedules during the proposal stage. Those things will come about naturally through the acquisition process, and broaching them too early will leave a sour taste in the agent's or editor's mouth.

At the proposal stage, the reader is the agent or editor, and the risk of being abandoned because of poor organization is actually the risk of rejection. When planning and executing your story, do it with the reader (or agent or editor) in mind. What does the reader need to know first? If you leave out something early, does that build suspense, or does it leave the reader confused? What needs to be explained, and when, so that the reader can easily follow you through the story? Plan the reader's itinerary so that each leg of the trip builds upon the last, and you'll find that lack of organization no longer is an issue in your writing.

Organize Your Proposal

Your submission should be as user-friendly as possible. Good organization in your proposal demonstrates that you have a firm grasp on your book and on your potential readership. The proposal is the selling tool, so its presentation influences the agent's or editor's perception of your book. Organize your proposal logically, and make sure everythin', the agent or editor needs is included in your package. The following chart shows what your nonfiction and fiction proposal packages should include.

Checklist for Proposal Package	
Nonfiction proposal	**Fiction proposal**
Cover letter	Cover letter
Copy of query letter	Copy of query letter
Title page	Title page
Table of Contents (for the proposal)	Table of Contents (for the proposal)
About the Author	About the Author
Overview (of the book)	Synopsis (of the book)
The Market	Outline/character bios
Promotion	Sample chapters (first three or four)
The Competition	Reviews or endorsements
Outline	SASE
Sample chapters (any three)	
Reviews or endorsements	
SASE	

Occasionally an agent or editor will ask for something different than what's listed here. She might ask to see a synopsis and the first fifty pages of your novel, for example, rather than the first three chapters. For your non-fiction book, she may want only one sample chapter. It's important to follow instructions when you receive them. If the request for material leaves any doubt in your mind about what to send, use the lists here; you won't run the risk of leaving anything out, and your package will look professional and inviting.

Never print any part of your proposal package on both sides of the paper. From your query letter to your sample chapters, print on one side only.

Too Much Information

Beginning writers often inundate agents and editors with information they neither need nor want. Remember that publishing professionals deal with reams of paper from hopeful new authors every day, and too much information can be as much a turnoff as too little. Be merciless in editing your proposal—and your manuscript, for that matter—and cut away anything that doesn't directly advance your cause.

About You

Agents and editors want to know why you're qualified to write your book. They don't care that you spent your twenties drifting from job to job, trying to find your niche, and finally decided to try your hand at writing—unless that's what your book is about. If your book is a science fiction masterpiece, they don't need to know about your bachelor's degree in economics. If you're marketing a cookbook for college students, you don't have to mention that you have a private pilot's license. Only give the information that relates to your book and your qualifications to write it, and save the rest for your autobiography.

About Your Book

Some beginning writers write on and on and on about their book, going into excruciating detail in their query letters and even in their overviews or synopses. This wastes your energy and the agent's or editor's time. More important, if you try to cram all that information into a one- or two-page query or synopsis, you risk presenting a distorted picture of your book.

Think of the elements of your proposal as the skeleton for your book. Your query and your synopsis should trace only the big bones of your story. Your character bios add the major muscles. The rest—the vital organs, the veins and arteries, and so on—belong in the manuscript. Your sample chapters will give a glimpse of the whole body, where it can breathe freely; you don't have to jam it all into the confined space of your synopsis.

Good writing is tight writing, in your manuscript and in your communications with agents and editors. Don't let yourself ramble. Get in, make your point, and get out. You'll impress both publishing professionals and your readers with the power and economy of your writing.

About Your Marketing

Hopeful writers do themselves untold damage by announcing how many "no confidence" votes their work has received from others. Often, they'll open their query with something like this: "I have sent my novel to twenty editors, and none of them have seen fit to publish it yet. I'm hoping I'll have more luck with you."

The pity-me approach never works. It makes you sound unprofessional, and it implies that the recipient of your query isn't at the top of her field— not a very flattering supposition to make, and not the way to win an ally in the publishing business. Agents and editors who receive this kind of query letter usually have the same reaction: They wonder why, after so many failures, you haven't made some changes to your manuscript to improve its salability.

If you're asked whether you've received any other responses on your project, be honest about the who, when, and why of any rejections. An agent needs to know whether your project has been rejected by editors, because she either may be able to find a way around that rejection or will omit that particular editor or publishing house from her marketing plan for your book.

But don't volunteer your setbacks in your query letter or cover letter. As discouraged as you may be privately, keep your correspondence with potential agents and editors positive and enthusiastic.

FACT

It's virtually impossible to sell a first novel before you've finished it, because too many publishers have been burned by aspiring novelists who couldn't complete the job. Be sure to tell the agent or editor, in your query letter and again in the cover letter for your proposal, that the complete manuscript is available, and provide a precise word count.

The Sin of Omission

Beginning writers commonly leave out key information in their proposals. Often, they leave out their own contact information. Equally as often, they forget to include a SASE, which means they'll never hear back from the agent or editor, and they'll never know why.

Just as frustrating for agents and editors, many aspiring authors omit some of the basic elements of a proposal package. Sometimes they "forget" to send a synopsis of their novel because they don't know how to write one. Sometimes nonfiction writers will leave out the discussion of competing books simply because they don't know how to frame that discussion. And, all too often, the writer will fail to deliver something the agent or editor specifically asks for.

Agents and editors are intimately familiar with writers who "accidentally" leave out important information, and they tend to view it as a sign that the writer isn't ready for publication. Whatever the reason behind the omission, the result is to make you look unpolished and amateurish.

Check It Off

The easiest way to make sure your proposal includes everything it needs is to make a list and check items off as you assemble the package (use the chart provided earlier in this chapter and add anything else you think you might be prone to forget). If you moved recently, you might want to double-check your contact information, for instance. If you don't usually keep stamps in the house, a checklist can remind you not to seal your package until you get to the post office, so you can stick a stamp on your SASE.

Many published authors use a checklist for each of their projects, to make sure they don't inadvertently leave anything out of their proposals. This is a good habit to get into. It relieves stress for you, because you can see at a glance what you need, and it promotes a professional image.

Follow Instructions

If an agent or editor asks you for a synopsis and your first two chapters, send her what she asks for. Don't send her your complete manuscript; don't send the last two chapters. Follow the instructions you're given as closely as you can.

Never tell an agent or editor that he already has a copy of whatever he asked for, even if you've already sent it. Chances are your material is buried in a precariously balanced stack of loose papers somewhere, and the agent or editor generally is not inclined to go pawing through that stack to look for your initial submission. Instead of being irritated that you have to send something twice, take the request as a compliment. It means the agent or editor is interested, and that's what you're aiming for.

Le Mot Juste

Professional writers are never satisfied with their first drafts. Though it may be close to perfect, there are always loose places to be tightened, plot points to be strengthened, dialogue to be jazzed up, and the occasional phrase to be retooled. The more work you put into your manuscript before you begin marketing it, the better condition it will be in to catch the eye of an agent or editor.

Rest and Revise

Once it's in the hands of an agent or editor, your work has to stand on its own, so give yourself time to polish it. Let the manuscript or proposal cool for a bit before you get ready to market it. Coming back to it after a few days or a week gives you a fresh perspective, and you'll be able to spot—and correct—weaknesses before you send it out. Have a trusted friend or relative read your manuscript, and listen objectively to the feedback. Look at the redrafting process as an opportunity to turn a good project into a better project.

ALERT!

When you're polishing your manuscript and your proposal package, think about what you can leave out. Cut scenes that don't advance the story. Eliminate details in the synopsis that take the focus off the bigger picture. Be your own severest critic, and your writing will shine.

Watch Your Tone

If you're like many people, you may labor under the notion that your writing, whether in your query letter or in your manuscript, has to be extraordinarily formal. But few readers find formal writing interesting or engaging. In fact, most readers (including agents and editors) find that kind of style stilted and awkward.

Your writing tone has to be appropriate for your subject. If you're writing a scholarly treatise on butterflies, your tone and vocabulary will be scientific and structured. If you're writing a passage about butterflies in your romance novel, your tone and vocabulary will be more lyrical and conversational. Again, think about your reader when you're writing, and choose a tone and style designed to involve the reader in your story.

And once you pick your tone, stick to it when writing each of the elements of your proposal package. Your synopsis, character bios, and other proposal elements should reflect your complete manuscript. Remember, an agent or editor will be judging your writing ability, if only subconsciously, even when she's reading your cover letter. Take every opportunity to show off the quality of your work.

Stamp out Clichés

According to a recent survey by the United Kingdom–based Plain English Campaign, clichés are not only annoying, they actually cause people to tune out. Among the most tired of tired phrases, according to the Plain English Campaign:

- "Touch base"
- "Bottom line"
- "On the same page"
- "Between a rock and a hard place"
- "I hear what you're saying"
- "To be honest with you"
- "Bear with me"
- "24/7"

Unless you have a compelling reason to use clichés in your writing, don't. Pretend these phrases are evil aliens bent on ripping the heart out of meaningful communication and thus destroying our civilization. Then put a stop to the invasion by vigilant and ruthless self-editing.

Mechanics of Writing

Far too many beginning writers send their material out without paying proper attention to the mechanics of writing. Certainly, rules of grammar and syntax can be broken occasionally, especially if that's part of your style and appropriate to your story. But a proposal full of misspellings or apparently random punctuation casts a long shadow over even the best of plots or topics. Agents and editors expect writers to pay attention to the basics of their craft. Those writers who permit such sloppiness during marketing are likely to be the same ones who cause copyeditors to flinch at the sight of their manuscripts.

If spelling, grammar, syntax, and punctuation cause problems for you, get a good set of reference books. If you prefer not to use those, hire someone to proofread your copy. Your community college might be a good place to start; students often earn extra money doing such work. If there isn't a community college in your region, check the business listings in the telephone book. Some resume-writing bureaus offer proofreading services as well, and the prices usually are reasonable.

Agents and editors tend to be detail-oriented people. They'll cut newcomers some slack, but the responsibility for making a professional presentation rests on you. If you're serious about building a writing career, it's worth the extra time and energy to make your proposal as polished as it can be.

Chapter 14

Your Professional Image

Publishing is not a business for amateurs or hobbyists. Agents and editors are professionals, and they like to work with writers who are professional in their attitudes and presentations. Many a promising manuscript has landed in the dead file because the writer demonstrated in some way that he wasn't prepared to play in the big leagues. Even if you haven't been published yet, you can reinforce your written work with a polished, professional approach.

Following the Rules

Many aspiring writers feel constrained by the array of apparently arcane rules agents and publishers impose on the publishing process. Sometimes the query letter seems like a waste of time and energy; wouldn't it be more efficient just to send your entire manuscript? Sometimes impatience gains the upper hand; you'd rather call an agent or editor about your project than wait a month for a response to your query. The myriad steps of submission, requests, and replies can seem like unnecessary obstacles to the eager writer, and the temptation to skip one or two is undoubtedly strong. But, believe it or not, these rules are designed to help both you and the agent or editor, not to keep you from getting your work published.

The sheer volume of material that crosses their desks every day makes it impossible for agents and editors to give prime consideration to every proposal or manuscript. This is why many won't read unsolicited proposals or manuscripts; they will only read material they requested on the basis of a query letter. Queries serve as a quick prescreening tool, allowing agents and editors to apportion their limited time most effectively.

FACT

Many publishers have tightened security in the past few years, and some of them even destroy unsolicited proposal packages these days rather than opening them or returning them to the sender. Your best bet is always to send out query letters, and save your proposal for those agents or editors who ask to see it.

Most agents and editors have a preferred method for receiving all your materials, from your query to your complete manuscript. These preferences are readily available in various directories, such as *Writer's Market*. Some agencies and most publishers also have writer's guidelines that detail their submission policies. Electronic submissions are becoming more common, but they are by no means universally preferred. So-called snail mail is still preferred by most agents and editors, and this should be your default submission method if you're ever in doubt.

Other common rules you should follow include the following:

- Never call an agent or editor with a query or to find out what she thought of your proposal.
- Always include a self-addressed, stamped envelope with any material you send.
- Never send "gifts" (candy, money, flowers, etc.) with your queries or proposals.
- Always respect the agent's or editor's time and experience.

When you break the rules, you do call attention to yourself, but not in a good way. Usually, you'll succeed only in irritating an agent or editor by failing to follow their guidelines, and that irritation can linger even if they like your work. Agents and editors are only human, after all, and their impression of a person can easily color their perception of that person's work. Following the rules may feel boring, but it will never hurt your image.

Your Image on Paper

The first impression you make on any agent or editor is made through your writing—your query letter, proposal, or manuscript. The accoutrements that go with your writing, such as envelopes and packing materials, also contribute to that first impression. There are some critical steps you must take to make your on-paper image the best it can be.

Contact Information

Include your name, address, telephone number (with area code), and e-mail address on every piece of correspondence with an agent or editor. This is about as basic as it gets in publishing, but you'd be astonished to learn how many aspiring authors forget this essential ingredient. When an agent or editor likes your work and wants to see more, he wants to be able to contact you easily; he certainly doesn't want to have to call Directory Assistance to get your phone number, or to get the area code for your city.

ESSENTIAL

If you're prone to forget things, and many of us are in these busy days, make a checklist for each query or proposal you send out that includes things like the stamp on the SASE and your contact information. This will force you to take the time to double-check your material, and you'll avoid errors made in haste.

Occasionally, a writer will enclose a stamped envelope with the agency's or publisher's return address, but omit to put his own address on the envelope. Since agents and editors usually separate material into piles as they read, chances are this writer never will receive a response to his query or proposal—and he'll probably complain about the lack of response to others, never knowing what the problem was. The moral: Before you seal your package, double-check everything, including your SASE, to make sure all the relevant information is included.

Clean Copy

Remember the continual admonishments from your junior-high English teacher that neatness counts? Agents and editors subscribe to that philosophy, too, and you would do well to become a devout follower. Handwritten pages, pages with weird margins, or pages riddled with typos, crossed-out words, or spelling, punctuation, and grammatical mistakes can do more to harm your image as a professional writer than almost anything else.

Handwritten pages are a big no-no, whether you're writing a query letter, a cover letter, or a sample chapter. Even if your handwriting is neat and legible, it still is more difficult to read than a page of typescript. The only time a handwritten note is appropriate is when it's a very short note attached to typed material—one or two sentences at most. In the query and proposal stages, the only time your handwriting should appear on your pages is on the signature line of your query or cover letter.

Manuscript formats are standardized because they're easy to read, and that's important to agents and editors who spend so much of their time reading. No matter what genre you're writing in, your manuscript pages always should be double-spaced, with one-inch margins. Each new chapter should begin on a fresh page, with a three- or four-inch top margin.

Finally, proofreading is an important element in polishing your professional image. If you aren't confident that you'll spot mistakes in your copy, ask someone else to check it for spelling, punctuation, and grammatical errors. If your word-processing program has a spell-check feature, use it regularly, but be aware of the limitations of such programs. Invest in a good dictionary and a good stylebook to supplement your resources.

ALERT!

Don't trust your proofreading entirely to the spell-check function on your computer. Few, if any, of these programs can recognize incorrect usage of correctly spelled words: They won't alert you to "effect" when you should use "affect," for example. Always keep a good dictionary and a good style guide close at hand and use them when proofing your work.

Shipping and Handling

Most proposals will fit in padded 9" x 12" or 10" x 14" mailers. If you're sending your entire manuscript, use a sturdy box. You won't usually need additional packing materials, such as bubble-wrap or foam nuggets, but if you do use them, use them sparingly. The same rule applies to taping your package. You want your package to be secure, but you also want the recipient to be able to open it without a blowtorch.

In most instances, you don't need to insure your proposal or send it via registered mail. The main exception is when you include photo slides with your proposal, but even then it's unnecessary if you keep copies of the slides. Most agents and editors find it annoying when they have to sign for your package, and you don't want them annoyed when they read your material.

If you want an acknowledgment that your proposal has been received, use priority mail, UPS, or FedEx; these services provide tracking and delivery information without unduly disturbing the recipient. Another option is to include a self-addressed, stamped postcard that states your proposal was received by so-and-so on such-and-such a date and the estimated reporting time is so many weeks.

If you have an agent, he may request several copies of your proposal for his marketing efforts. You can use a large rubber band or binder clip to separate your copies, or you can place a blank sheet of colored paper between each of your copies. Either way makes it easier for the agent to quickly grab a copy of your proposal to send to an interested editor.

Your Image on the Telephone

These days, when authors, agents, and editors can be located pretty much anywhere, much of your communication will take place over the telephone. Professionalism—or the lack of it—can come across on the phone as clearly as it does on paper or in person. Tone of voice, language, even distractions like coworkers, children, or pets can affect your image and influence an agent's or editor's impression of you. Knowing when to call and when not to call is important, too. Agents and editors spend much of their business days on the phone, and unnecessary phone calls are both an intrusion and an annoyance.

Professional Etiquette

Any customer service representative will tell you how important proper telephone etiquette is. You need to speak loud enough to be heard, but not so loud that the other person has to yank the phone away from his ear. Smile when you speak; this makes you sound cheerful and interested, and it's impossible to sound bored or irritated when you smile. Never eat or chew gum while you're on the phone. Those noises are amplified through the handset and are incredibly annoying to the person on the other end. Watch your language when you're talking with an agent or editor. A phone call is still a business communication. There is no room for swearing or vulgarity.

Try to avoid distractions while you're on the phone with an agent or editor. Turn off the television or radio. If you have children or pets at home, go into another room and, if possible, close the door during your conversation. Don't try to multitask while you're on the phone; if you're trying to cook dinner or sort the mail or do the laundry, you'll inevitably give the agent or editor the impression that she doesn't have your full attention.

When to Call

Phone calls between authors and agents or authors and editors are relatively rare, especially now that nearly everyone has an e-mail address. There are times when phone calls are appropriate and even preferred. However, e-mail has proven itself a very efficient medium for asking and answering questions, trading information, and clarifying issues. It is also less intrusive than a phone call, and it provides a record for later use if necessary. If you need to call your agent or editor, it's a good idea to first send an e-mail explaining what you want to talk to her about.

If you absolutely must talk directly with your agent or editor, keep your conversation brief and to the point. Especially during business hours, agents and editors rarely have time for chitchat. Since you never know what is on his plate, always ask upfront if he has a few minutes to spare. If he says no, ask when it would be convenient for you to call back. Except in the most dire emergencies—you are being admitted to the hospital for emergency surgery, for instance, and won't be able to meet next Tuesday's deadline— don't insist on talking right now if the agent or editor is busy.

Because their schedules are so full, most agents and editors prefer to set up "phone dates" whenever possible. This lets them schedule a convenient time to talk to you when they aren't rushing off to meetings or working furiously to meet a deadline. Some agents and editors prefer to schedule phone dates for evenings or weekends, when they are less likely to be sidetracked by business-related crises.

Agents and editors might have to break a phone date if something urgent comes up, as it often does in the publishing world. You'll typically get a phone call or an e-mail as soon as possible, explaining why the agent or editor wasn't available at the original time and asking to reschedule. Although it can be frustrating when things don't go as planned, don't take it personally. It's just the nature of the business.

When Not to Call

Some writers make positive pests of themselves on the phone, continually calling their agent or editor to nag about their material, to deliver unnecessary updates on the progress of their manuscripts, or even just to say "hello." Aspiring authors—those who don't yet have an agent or editor—will sometimes use the pretense of checking names or addresses and, once they have an agent or editor on the line, will seize the opportunity to pitch their project. Rejected authors have been known to call the rejecting agent or editor and either demand an explanation or berate the agent or editor—or both.

It shouldn't need to be said, but this sort of behavior continues, so the caution is warranted. Do not call an agent or editor to make your sales pitch. Do not call an agent or editor to complain about a rejection. Do not call an agent or editor to find out if she has read your proposal.

A good rule of thumb is this: If you aren't sure whether you should call, don't. Use e-mail or snail mail instead. If the agent or editor wants to talk to you, he'll call.

Delivering What You Promise

In the publishing business, your word is your bond. You're expected to tell the truth about your published credits and any endorsements you might have received; you're expected to deliver original work, with nothing plagiarized or otherwise lifted from another work without the appropriate permissions; you're expected to deliver your work in the time you agree to. Do all these things, and agents and editors will regard you as a pleasure to work with. Keeping your promises is a key element of building a professional image.

Being Honest

You've probably heard stories about college "professors" who turned out to have fake credentials, airline "pilots" who obtained a uniform and managed to take off in a Boeing 747 with no previous training, and "doctors" who performed surgery without ever setting foot on a medical school campus. Likewise, there have been authors who flesh out their bios with false credits or who claim to be experts in a field when they really have no expertise. Often, these pretenders justify their actions by saying it was the only way they could get an agent or editor to take their work seriously. But in the end, the damage to a dishonest writer's career far outweighs any gain they might have received thanks to these tactics.

Agents and editors appreciate honesty in writers as much as any other quality because it saves them enormous difficulties down the road. An agent can always talk up a client's talent and potential, even if the client hasn't yet been published. An editor can make allowances for an unpublished author who doesn't know what to expect out of the publishing process. But neither will be inclined to help or work with someone who has misled them.

Being honest extends to your own concerns and worries, too. If a deadline in a proposed contract seems too tight, tell your agent or editor why you think you'll need more time. If, in the middle of a project, you run into a problem that will affect your ability to complete the work on time, tell your agent or editor right away. If you're stuck on a chapter or scene, let your agent or editor know; they might (and usually do) have some useful advice that will free you and keep your book on track.

FACT

Agents and editors have heard every imaginable excuse from writers who just can't seem to meet their deadlines. But they also know that life can interfere with the best-laid plans. The earlier they know about problems, the better; early warning gives both of you time to work out a solution.

Being Responsive

Just as writers get frustrated and sometimes cranky about going weeks or even months without hearing from an agent or editor, agents and editors get justifiably edgy when their authors suddenly go incommunicado for indefinite periods. Consistent failure to reply to e-mails or return phone calls causes needless anxiety. You always should respond as quickly as possible, even if it's just to say that you're swamped right now and will get back to the agent or editor as soon as you can. Of course, you have to do that second follow-up; that's part of keeping your promises.

If you're going on vacation or a business trip, let your agent or editor know that you'll be unavailable during that time. It can be as simple as sending an e-mail to that effect, or using the "auto-reply" function if your e-mail program offers it. If you can't let your agent or editor know about your absence beforehand—if, for example, you have to fly to your parents' hometown because your father suffered a heart attack—make sure you notify your agent or editor once the crisis is past.

If you just can't get in touch with your agent or editor, and you come back to find e-mail or phone messages, explain why you didn't respond earlier. Agents and editors have vivid imaginations, just like the rest of us, and unexplained silence from an author can conjure up all sorts of awful scenarios. A simple explanation, even after the fact, is an antidote to those imaginings.

Building a Reputation

As your writing career progresses, you'll build a reputation with your agent and with editors inside your own publishing house and even in other houses. Editors, like all of us, talk among each other. With your first book, word will get around the publishing house about both the quality of your writing and how easy or difficult you are to work with. Because editors often switch publishing houses, your reputation can spread around easily, and this can either help or hinder your future writing efforts.

How You Deal with Rejection

Even published pros receive rejections. How you handle rejection is just as important as how you handle acceptance. Agents and editors generally don't like to turn down authors. When they have to do it, most of them try to do it gently, and many of them, through experience, consciously or unconsciously, brace themselves for the potential maelstrom of ill feeling from the author.

If you can develop a philosophical attitude toward rejection, understanding that it's a business decision and not a rejection of you personally, you'll polish your image as a professional in the business. No matter what your private reaction is, a calm and reasoned reaction to the agent or editor preserves your image and relieves a lot of stress for those who have to tell you "no."

How You Handle Criticism

Agents and editors offer suggestions and constructive criticism with the goal of improving your work, of making it more salable and more likely to succeed in the marketplace. Certainly, you can—indeed, you are expected to—defend your point of view. But it is unprofessional to resort to insults or abuse when you disagree with the criticism. Step back from your writing and make a genuine effort to see the issue from the other's perspective. If you still disagree, take care to focus your arguments on the criticism, not on the agent's or editor's taste, style, or personality.

How You Cope with Problems

Like that of true love, the course of publishing rarely runs smoothly. Inevitably, there will be delays, questions, disagreements, and misunderstandings. Whether you're a beginning writer or well-established, one of the most useful survival skills you'll learn is how to roll with the punches. Be patient with delays, even if they make you crazy inside. Answer questions quickly, honestly, and kindly, even if you think they're silly. Detach yourself from your emotional investment in your work and try to resolve disagreements amicably. Do what you can to clear up misunderstandings quickly and with minimal unpleasant residue. These skills not only will enhance your image as a professional writer, they will help you avoid the more extreme lows that come to every author sooner or later.

How You Deal with the Deal

Negotiating a contract is a delicate business, and many new authors expose their inexperience and egos with the demands they make. Some will try to horn in on the publisher's rightful territory, wanting the authority to choose trim size (the size of the book), paper stock, even the font for their book. Professionals know these things are the proper purview of the publisher and are willing to let the publishing house apply its expertise. Professionals also know that there are other things that are more important from their perspective, such as billing, payment terms, which rights are covered, and maybe even having a say in choosing cover art.

When you're ready to negotiate a book contract, either yourself or through an agent, organize your requests and present them all at the same time. Know which items are non-negotiable and which have some wiggle room. Know, also, which items are deal-breakers for you, and which are perks that you would like but don't need in order to sign the contract. A professional approach during the negotiations makes life easier for everyone involved and is far more conducive to a deal everyone is happy with.

Protecting Your Professional Image

When you're seen as a professional, you're treated as a professional, so your image is worth protecting. The simplest way to do this is to make sure you're well organized, able to focus on the project at hand, and, perhaps most critical, protected against common potential problems.

Nearly everyone who has ever worked on a computer has experienced the horror of a system crash, virus, or other technical problem that irretrievably erases days or even months of work. One writer, two days before she was due to turn in several chapters to her editor, found that the diskette she had been using to store her work had been damaged somehow, and all those beautifully written chapters were inaccessible. Fortunately, she was able to retrieve her work before the deadline, but she suffered several heart-stopping hours in the meantime.

FACT

You always need backup. If you work from your computer's hard drive, make copies on diskettes. Print out each chapter or scene as you finish it and file it safely away. E-mail your chapters to yourself, to a friend, to your agent. If you always make sure there's more than one copy of your work, you'll save yourself a lot of panic when technology suddenly fails to perform.

Imagine how the professional image of the writer noted above would have suffered if she had had to call her agent or her editor and explain that she had, indeed, completed the work required under the contract, but couldn't deliver it because she didn't take the elementary precaution of backing up her files. Missing the deadline throws the publisher's schedule off, which can affect the publisher's catalog, which affects the sales and publicity departments, and so on. And, aside from all these things, the writer would have looked immensely foolish.

We aren't suggesting that you have to be perfect, or that you should devote an inordinate amount of time and energy to polishing your image. But, just as you want to make the best possible impression at, say, a job interview, it is in your interest to present the best side of your writing self as consistently as you can. Your image as a professional is an intangible asset, but it can be surprisingly influential in your writing career.

Chapter 15

E Collecting Credentials

Unpublished authors are in much the same position as new high school or college graduates looking for their first full-time job. Like many employers, publishers seem to prefer working with authors who have a track record, but how do you get a track record if no one will publish your book? Fortunately for the unpublished, there are myriad ways to build your portfolio and improve your chances of landing that first book contract.

Publishing Credits

The first thing agents and editors look for in an author's bio is publishing credits. Book credits are best, of course, because they show that you've done the heavy lifting required for a book-length manuscript. But there are lots of opportunities to get your shorter works published, and these can add up to an impressive resume of credentials.

FACT

Nonfiction tends to be easier to break into than fiction for first-time authors. If you can turn a hobby or area of interest into a salable nonfiction book, that publishing credit will be a point in your favor when the time comes to market your novel.

Magazine Credits

Everyone's impressed when you get an article published in a national magazine like *Redbook* or *Cosmopolitan*, and prospective agents and editors are no exception. Unfortunately, these markets can be just as difficult to break into as book publishing, and you might serve yourself better by looking at smaller publications when you're starting out.

The best place to start may be in your own geographical area. Most medium and large cities have at least a few publications—local business magazines, entertainment magazines, and the like—that are very specific in their coverage area and may be open to "contributing writers" who aren't on their staff. You probably won't make a lot of money submitting your articles to these periodicals, but you should be able to earn some clips for your credentials folder.

There are all kinds of magazines, each of them a potential market for your articles. Trade journals target highly specific audiences—meeting and event planners, for example, or coffee distributors, or chiefs of police, or youth soccer coaches. Can you turn one of your interests or hobbies into a bylined article for one of these publications? These types of magazines vary in their policies about accepting freelance articles, but it's worth doing some research to see if there's an opening for you.

ALERT!

Many small-circulation and literary magazines pay contributors only in copies; no money changes hands. Don't turn up your nose at these opportunities, especially if you're just beginning your writing career. They still count as publishing credits, and many authors have used these opportunities as springboards to more lucrative projects.

Some of the national magazines are open to freelance submissions as well. Often they reserve feature articles for their staff writers or for freelancers they've worked with before, but many have departments that are open to newcomers. Usually these are for shorter pieces, and pay rates run the spectrum from a very few dollars to several hundred—or even $1,000 or more. When you're just starting out, you might have to weigh the advantages of a published byline against the disadvantage of little or no pay.

Newspaper Credits

Daily and weekly newspapers can be gardens of opportunity for the freelancer. Many hire "stringers" to help cover local sports, review concerts or plays, or to submit periodic columns with a specific theme such as "The Outdoor Life." Again, pay rates vary widely.

The amount of time and effort you have to put in for such work also will vary. You have to decide whether it's worth the hours and (probably) low pay to be able to tell a prospective agent or editor that you've been a weekly columnist for the Rochester, N.Y., *Democrat and Chronicle* for the past eighteen months.

National newspapers are much more difficult to break into, but you might be able to get a clip from a high-profile publication by writing a killer opinion piece. Letters to the editor, which are quite short (usually no more than 150 words), especially for newspapers like *The New York Times*, have the best chance of getting published. Still, remember that competition is quite stiff; the *Times* receives thousands of letters a week, and only a highly select few ever make it to print. Guest editorials are longer pieces, usually around 600 to 800 words; these provide great clips, but they are even more intensely competitive than letters to the editor.

Some newspapers have "community columnists"—people who don't work for the paper but who are leaders in the community. Often these guest columnists are invited to write a monthly column for, say, a year; then a new crop of guest columnists is brought in. Contact the opinion page editor at your local newspaper to see if this is a possibility for you.

Newsletter Credits

Newsletters can provide different kinds of opportunities for the aspiring writer. Most companies, even relatively small ones, have newsletters for their employees; while some of them are done in-house, some regularly hire free-lancers. A few outsource everything, from the writing and editing to design and production. A gig with a strong newsletter can give you a boost when it comes time to pitch your book idea, especially if the main topic of the news-letter relates in some way to the topic of your book.

If you have the time and ambition, you can start your own newsletter. Most home computers include some variety of self-publishing software, but a newsletter doesn't have to be fancy. Choose a topic you're interested in—a social cause, for example, or a fascinating hobby—and build a subscriber base. If you can tell an agent or editor that you're the founder and writer of the "Thrill of Falling" newsletter for skydiving enthusiasts, with 300 subscribers in the Pacific Northwest, you're demonstrating that you have experience in writing and in marketing what you write.

FACT

Magazines and newspapers require the same kind of research you'll do for your book proposal. Offer the editor something so perfectly tailored to his publication's readership and style that he'd be crazy to pass it up, and you'll have the best odds of getting your article published.

Brochures, Fliers, and Reports

Many companies and organizations hire freelancers to write copy for promotional brochures, fliers for special offers or events, and even for their quarterly or annual reports to shareholders. Some of these projects are more involved than others, of course, but any kind of writing project will add to your experience, and a three-fold brochure is easy enough to include with your query letter as a sample of your work.

Web Sites

The Internet has made it easier than ever for aspiring writers to get their works into the public eye. Keep in mind that all Web-related publishing credits are not created equal; no agent or editor will be impressed if all your material has been published solely on your own homepage and the only people who read it are your second cousins in Osceola.

ALERT!

Posting articles on the Internet counts as publication, which means you can't sell first serial rights to a conventional publication for the same article. However, depending on the readership of the Web site, you might be able to convince a magazine to reprint your Internet article, and such reprints count as additional publishing credits when you market your book.

However, big numbers are impressive. If you publish a weekly blog (a Web log, or online journal) about your dogs, for example, and you can truthfully say you get an average of 100,000 unique visitors to your site each month, you have a selling point that will impress agents and editors. Not only does it demonstrate your writing ability, it gives you a platform to announce your newly published book to an interested audience. Starting your own Web site isn't difficult, and it's inexpensive if you learn to do it yourself. Readers will find your site if you provide valuable, interesting content, and you can build a following that can translate into book readership.

Many established authors have personal Web sites that serve as monthly newsletters to their readers. The content may include informative articles, free tips or advice, and announcements of new products, including books and magazine articles and where they can be found. Setting up your own Web site now can serve you well as you embark on your writing career.

Areas of Expertise

Most people tend to define their own areas of expertise too narrowly. Most commonly, we think of ourselves as experts in whatever our profession happens to be—doctor, plumber, waitress, account executive—and professional experience certainly is an important part of your roster of credentials. But there are other areas that also deserve consideration as you work on building your author bio. We all have interests outside our work, and these interests can help when it comes to rounding out author credentials.

Professional Experience

If your education and professional experience are related to your book topic, they can be turned into nice, hefty credentials as you market your book. This is true for both fiction and nonfiction. Scott Turow and John Grisham are both attorneys who turned their experience in the legal system into novels; their education and experience as lawyers added credibility to their law-based stories. Likewise, most self-help books you see on the bookstore shelves are written by professional counselors, psychotherapists, or psychiatrists. Their methods have been used in person with hundreds or even thousands of clients before being put into book form, and that makes their books more credible.

Life Experience

Life experience adds depth and richness—not to mention a sense of authenticity—to writing. Many of us can imagine what it might be like to be homeless and broke, but think how much more genuine a novel about being homeless and broke feels when it's written by someone who has lived through that experience. Your guide to living with adult children resonates more with agents and editors when they know you were forced to move back in with your parents after college because of the poor economy. An inspirational book about what autistic children can teach us carries more weight if you're a teacher's aide at a special school for autistic children.

Personal Resources

Family and friends can be useful in bolstering your credentials, too. Perhaps you have a friend who has told you about the months he and his family spent on the road, looking for work and living in homeless shelters after the steel mills closed in Pennsylvania. Maybe it was your sister, not you, who had to move back in with Mom and Dad after college because she couldn't find a job in her field. If you don't have firsthand experience related to your book topic, having access to people who do have that experience is the next best thing.

Honors and Awards

Recognition of your outstanding performance in writing—or in other fields that are related to your book topic—could make you more attractive to prospective agents and publishers. If you won a national short story competition when you were in college, that's a talking point for your book-length fiction (or even nonfiction) project, especially if the contest was judged by a bestselling author. If you've been named salesman of the year three consecutive times for a *Fortune* 500 company and you're pitching a book on winning sales strategies, the awards give you additional credibility as an authority on that topic.

Carefully pick your awards and honors to match your book proposal, calling attention to those that are most relevant. An employee-of-the-year award won't do much to elevate your standing in the eyes of an agent or editor if your book is a historical romance novel. But if you received a scholarly honor for your historical research, especially if your research covers the same period or historical events that form the backdrop for your novel, that information is certainly relevant.

Try putting a twist on some of the less serious awards you've received. If you were voted "Most Likely to Succeed" in high school, for instance, you can use it as an ironic highlight in marketing your book about young entrepreneurs and their business failures.

Think of your book's genre in its broadest sense, then think of other things you've done that match or complement that broad heading. Say you're writing a humor book on growing up Protestant in a predominantly Catholic town. You once won a statewide competition for a humorous speech you delivered on moronic drivers. One topic doesn't have anything to do with the other, but they both come under the heading of humor. Letting agents or editors know that you won a humorous speech contest shows them that you have a track record of being funny.

Professional and Social Memberships

Memberships in professional and social organizations can also add to your credibility as author. If you want to write a book on business networking or community building, membership in your local Rotary, Kiwanis, or Optimists Club can help you establish yourself as an expert. Such memberships also give you networking opportunities, with additional access to other well-credentialed sources.

Don't mention membership in local writers' groups, unless your local group is very well known or is a chapter of a national organization. Too many writers' groups are so informal as to be considered amateur, and this alone can turn off editors and agents.

Memberships don't have to relate directly to your book topic. If you're a member of Toastmasters International, that tells agents and editors you're getting practice with speaking in public, and that means you can help promote your book with personal appearances, speaking engagements, and the like.

Personal Appearances

Agents and editors tend to look favorably on authors who are promotable. You don't have to be an international authority on your subject, but it helps if you can demonstrate some experience in making a name for yourself. There are lots of ways to heighten your profile, even if just on a local level.

Radio Commentary

Local radio stations—particularly those with an all-news or all-talk format, and local affiliates of National Public Radio—often produce weekly shows on topics of interest to their listeners: local sports, parenting and relationships, music, food, and so on. You might be able to get a spot as a guest on one of these local programs, or even as a cohost or a member of a panel of experts. Sometimes local radio stations also allow listeners to record commentary—sort of an audio opinion piece—for broadcast. These appearances can be one-time deals or regular gigs. Think about what you might have to offer for the station's listeners, then contact the program director with a proposal.

Don't believe something like this can make a difference? Several years ago, an agented author had an editor interested in his book proposal, but the publication board (the committee that decides whether to buy manuscripts) was waffling. The agent asked the author if he had any credential that might tip the scale in his favor. After a lengthy conversation, the author mentioned that he taped regular short radio pieces that were aired across the country. Because they were public service announcements and he didn't get paid for them, he hadn't thought them worth mentioning before. The agent took this information back to the editor, who told the pub board, and the book was sold—all based on this "minor" credential.

Media Expertise

Reporters for newspapers, magazines, radio, and television always are looking for "talking heads," jargon for experts who provide context and analysis in news stories. If you're an authority on anything from political polls to personal fitness, get your name in the Rolodex of every reporter in your area. Keep clips of articles in which you are quoted and tapes of your radio or television appearances, and keep track of stories that might be picked up by statewide or national media. Most local newspapers are members of the Associated Press and other wire services, and if the story is of sufficient importance or general interest, chances are good your quote for the *Small Town Daily News* might appear a day or two later in the *Big City Gazette.*

FACT

The more often you appear in news stories before your first book is published, the better impression you'll make on agents and editors, who'll see you as a promotable author. Once your first book is on the market, you will be automatically considered an expert and will get even more media requests. Each news story that quotes you will identify you as the author of your book, making you even more attractive as an author.

Speaking Engagements

Can you write a fifteen-minute speech on your favorite hobby, social cause, or even an aspect of your job? Local civic, business, and social organizations might be interested in hearing it. Organizations like the YMCA and YWCA, Rotary clubs, and even Girl Scouts and Boy Scouts troops often invite outsiders to give short presentations to their members. You probably won't get paid for making these appearances, but you can make valuable contacts, gain experience in public speaking, and raise your profile as a player in your community. At the very least, this kind of experience tells agents and editors that you are comfortable in promotional situations. If you're able to build a large attendance for your engagements, you can give each participant a copy of your book (the cost being included in the price of admission, of course), which gives you another platform for promoting yourself and your work.

Teaching Gigs

Another way to establish your credentials is to teach your book topic to others. You don't always need a teaching certificate; requirements vary according to the type of course you teach. Check with your community college or school district to see if they offer community education courses. These are generally offered as not-for-credit classes, so the requirements for teachers are much less stringent. Find out how to submit a proposal for a class on your pet subject. Ideally, you should teach a class that strongly relates to your book topic to bolster your qualifications to write your book. Again, once you get published, you can include a copy of your book in the fee for students who take your class.

Getting Endorsed

Name-dropping might be frowned upon in some circles, but an endorsement from the right person can work wonders in publishing. Such endorsements don't have to be lengthy. Even a one-sentence note of praise from a celebrity, expert, or published author can convince an agent or editor to take a good look at your material.

FACT

Cold-calling celebrities or high-profile experts and asking them to endorse your book proposal most likely will result in depressing failure. Instead, look for an "in" among your acquaintances, or seek out lesser-known people who have similar expertise in the field your book covers.

Networking Opportunities

So where do you find these celebrities, experts, and published authors? First, take stock of your own circle of family, friends, and colleagues. Do your parents, siblings, or other relatives work with someone who might be a qualified endorser? Do you have a friend who works with (or is related to) an expert in the field covered by your book? Is there someone in your church or Rotary Club who might be willing to help you, either personally or through her own contacts? Publishing is in essence a networking business, and you can get valuable experience in networking by starting on a small scale.

Colleges and Universities

Community colleges, four-year colleges, and universities are treasure troves of potential endorsements, as well as resources to improve your writing and research skills. College professors who teach writing courses probably have to publish a certain number of articles or books as a condition of their tenure, and they may have impressive writing credentials. For example, Jane Smiley, who won the 1992 fiction Pulitzer Prize for her novel *A Thousand Acres*, taught creative writing at Iowa State University for several years.

There are two potential benefits to taking college writing courses, no matter what age you are. The first benefit is obvious—you get to practice your craft and hone your skills. But there's also a second benefit—your professor might be willing to review your book proposal or manuscript and give you valuable feedback, or even a brief recommendation that you can cite in your query letter. Be sure to get your professor's permission before you use his name in soliciting agents and editors; this kind of request from students is quite common, and some professors have policies against issuing such endorsements.

Colleges and universities also have experts in many other fields, one of which might be suitable for your project. Again, tread carefully and politely when seeking a review or endorsement from a professor or researcher, and learn to accept whatever answer you get with grace. If they turn you down, you're not any worse off than you were before.

School districts and community colleges often have community education programs where adults can take classes on a broad spectrum of subjects. Look for writing classes or seminars that are taught by published authors; this may turn out to be an opportunity for getting an endorsement.

Many first-time authors get discouraged as they begin to market their book proposals or manuscripts, feeling trapped on the I-can't-get-published-until-I-get-published merry-go-round. But agents and editors always are on the alert for new, talented writers. With a little effort and a little creativity, you can mold your bio into a tool that will help convince an agent or editor to give you that all-important first publishing contract.

Chapter 16

Writer, Beware!

The process of getting published can be excruciatingly slow, especially for first-time authors, and it's no wonder so many writers look eagerly for shortcuts. Unfortunately, that eagerness to see your name in print can make you an easy target for scams. Some of these schemes have been around for decades; others have proliferated via the Internet, where writers' sites swarm with potential prey. A healthy skepticism will help you protect both your bank account and your dream of being a published author.

Reading Fees

At first glance, the idea of literary agents charging fees to read unsolicited manuscripts appears to make sense. The volume of submissions from hopeful writers is so great that it seems reasonable, even logical, for the agent to charge a nominal fee for his time and expertise in reading and evaluating material. Besides, the opportunity to get valuable feedback from someone on the inside of the publishing business is so rare that many aspiring writers are glad to pay $75, $150, or even $500 or more for a professional evaluation of their manuscript.

Unfortunately, writers seldom—if ever—get what they pay for when they submit their material and their personal checks to fee-charging agents. The practice is so ripe for abuse that the Association of Authors' Representatives prohibits its members from charging clients or potential clients any upfront fees for any purpose.

FACT

In the 1960s, agent Scott Meredith began charging reading fees to consider the works of unpublished writers. Today, his agency continues the practice with its "Discovery Program," which charges $450 to assess a manuscript. There are several hundred fee-charging agencies in the United States, and not all of them are dishonest. However, you need to be aware that most reputable agents will not charge upfront fees.

By Any Other Name

The backlash against reading fees has led some creative and less-than-scrupulous agents to rename their upfront fees. They may call it a marketing fee, a retainer, or a fee to cover office expenses. Whatever they call it, it's still upfront money that you are expected to pay the agent, and that's a bad deal for you.

Reputable agents make their money from the 15 percent commission they get when they sell a manuscript to a publisher. Reading submissions and determining which are most likely to sell is an integral part of an agent's job. In fact, the possibility of discovering a great new writing talent is what keeps most agents motivated to pore over the piles and piles of manuscripts and proposals they receive.

Agents do have costs associated with marketing a manuscript to potential publishers. They have long-distance phone bills and overnight shipping costs and expenses for office equipment like computers and copiers and fax machines. These are all part of the agent's cost of doing business. The 15 percent commission should cover those costs and leave the agent with a fair profit. There is no good reason to charge an author for these routine expenses.

Occasionally, an agent will pass extraordinary costs on to her clients. For example, if your agent has an unusual number of international telephone calls when she's trying to sell the foreign rights to your book, you might be asked to foot the bill for that expense. Your agent should always discuss these extra costs with you beforehand.

Follow the Money

The easiest way to figure out if you're on the right path in the publishing business is to follow the flow of money. As a writer, you should get paid for what you produce. You should not have to pay for the privilege of being represented or published. Any setup that involves you writing checks instead of cashing them is likely to lead to financial hardship and bitter disappointment.

Unfortunately, scam artists are adept at making these sorts of arrangements sound plausible. Suppose an agent charges a $200 "contract" fee for new clients. If you question that fee, the agent might explain that this is how much it costs to have her attorney draw up the contract for representing you. Sounds reasonable, right? It isn't. Most good agents have a boilerplate (standard) contract they offer to all clients. If, for some reason, they need an attorney to change something in the boilerplate contract, that expense should be factored into the agent's overhead.

Money should come to you, not from you. An agent who charges any upfront fees from new or potential clients is likely making her living from those fees, not from selling manuscripts to bona fide publishers. If you run across one of these fee-charging agents, get as far away as you can and continue your search for a reputable agent.

ALERT!

Any request for money upfront should set off your internal alarm. Reputable agents do not charge upfront fees; they get paid only if they sell their clients' work. Royalty-paying publishers pay the author; they do not charge the author for the expenses of producing, marketing, and delivering the book.

Book Doctors

There's a fine line between legitimate freelance editors and self-styled "book doctors," and it's not always easy for writers to tell the difference until it's too late. A good editor will evaluate your manuscript or proposal and give you a thorough critique that covers everything from plot points to tone and style notes. A "book doctor" will claim to provide the same service, but usually delivers only generic commentary that could apply to any piece of writing. Both will charge significant amounts of money for their services.

Professional Editing Services

There are times when it can make sense for writers to seek out the services of a professional editor. If you are unable to find people to read and give honest feedback on your work, or if you don't trust that feedback, you might consider hiring a professional editor. If you've received several rejections, all citing more or less the same problems with your manuscript, it might be worthwhile to get help from someone experienced in your genre. The main point to consider is whether you understand what you're buying and whether what you get in return justifies the cost.

There are no licensing or regulatory organizations that oversee freelance editors, so you'll need to do some research if you want to hire one. Perhaps the most important factor is finding an editor who has experience working in your genre. Someone who has spent his career editing technical journals might be able to offer constructive advice on your fantasy novel, but the odds aren't good. Likewise, an editor with experience in fantasy novels might not be the best choice to critique your historical fiction.

Also make sure you know what you're paying for. Will the editor give you advice on plot and character construction? Will she provide a line-by-line critique, suggesting a different word here or phrase there? Will she proofread for errors in spelling, punctuation, syntax, and grammar? Generally, the less involved the service, the cheaper it should be.

Remember, too, that no editor can guarantee anything except his own service. There are no magic formulas for plots or characters or even style that will assure publication of your work. Even the best editor can't turn a bad manuscript into a stellar one, and no one can guarantee a bestseller. If a potential editor is making unrealistic promises in exchange for your money, run far, far away.

Kickback Schemes

Referrals to paid editing services can signal a kickback scheme between the agent and the editing service. Here's how it works: An agent reads your manuscript, then contacts you, usually via letter or e-mail, praising your work. It needs editing, the letter or e-mail will say, and then you'll be directed to a specific person or company, which will provide the necessary critique—for a fee. Almost universally, the agent strongly implies that he will accept your manuscript for representation if you use the service he recommends.

Many new writers are so elated to find someone who likes their work that they are blind to the implications of this kind of offer. In many cases, the agent either owns the service being recommended, or he receives a kickback for referring writers. And, all too often, even after you pay for the service and implement their suggestions, the referring agent will reject your manuscript; very likely, other agents will reject it, too.

Even a reputable agent may suggest that you seek out a professional freelance editor to review your manuscript. The difference is that reputable agents will not recommend a specific editor or firm. They may provide a short list of companies that do this kind of work, or they may give you pointers on where you can find a professional editor. The real red flag should rise if the agent recommends a particular person or company, especially if the agent indicates he'd be willing to represent you after you use the service he recommends.

There are good professional editors who will critique your work for a fee, which is usually fairly high—maybe $10 or more per page. However, when an agent or publisher recommends a specific editor or editing service, this should raise a warning flag for you. You're better off seeking out these services on your own.

If you come across this situation, ask questions. Is the agent affiliated with any of the recommended people or services? Does the agent or editor guarantee that your manuscript will be publishable after the critique? Is using the recommended service a condition of representation? If the answer to any of these questions is yes, thank the agent for his time and look elsewhere.

Agent Finders

There are lots of businesses, in all fields, that charge you for information you could get yourself for free. Publishing is no exception. There are firms that will research potential agents or even potential publishers whose interests match your manuscript; you pay for their list of recommended places to submit your work. These businesses aren't necessarily scams. Sometimes it's easier and more effective to pay someone else to do the research for you, especially if you have more money than time. But it's important to understand that you could get this information on your own.

It's also important to know what you're purchasing. Does the person offering this service have experience and contacts in publishing? Does she know what the current trends in publishing are? How many potential agents or publishers will she identify for you? Does she have access to resources that are not available to you?

As always, be wary of any person or business that "guarantees" results. There are no guarantees in publishing; even publishers don't know what the hot title or genre will be in any given season. Also be on the lookout for a possible scam. An agent finder may claim a 90 percent success rate in matching writers with agents, but if all those matches are with the same agent, this easily could be a clever mining operation for an unscrupulous agent, designed to lure unsuspecting writers into a fee-charging scheme.

Contests and Searches

Contests and calls for submissions have recently become a favored technique for a variety of scams. Certainly, there are legitimate writing contests and legitimate agents who may put out a broad request for materials as a way of priming the pump, especially if they are just starting out and are eager to build their client base. But these methods are often used by dubious people and companies to separate writers from their cash.

"Contest" Scams

Contest scams are most prevalent in the poetry and short story fields. They may look legitimate on the surface, and they aren't generally illegal, but they can lead to disappointment—not to mention wasted money—all the same. Usually, these contests will be advertised in writers' magazines or on writers' Web sites. To the winners, they may offer cash prizes and/or publication in a magazine or anthology.

The disappointment comes after you've entered the contest. You receive a letter or e-mail praising your work and saying that, although it didn't win a prize, it does merit inclusion in the published collection. However, to guarantee publication of your story or poem, you need to purchase a copy of the book. That's your tipoff that this isn't a genuine contest driven by the quality of the submitted work. Anyone who forks over the cash can get his poem or story "published." But this is vanity publishing, and it doesn't count as a real publishing credit for legitimate agents and editors. Worse, using this "achievement" in your author bio may brand you as hopelessly naive.

Legitimate contests do often charge nominal entry fees—generally between $5 and $15 per submission. These fees are used to cover the contest's expenses and to create the prize pool. An entry fee doesn't automatically identify a contest as a scam. The scam comes in when you're asked to pay an additional fee for your work to be included in the published version. When you consider entering a contest, find out first if your work will be published in a known and respected periodical; if the publication is a book, find out who the publisher is and whether the book will be available in libraries and bookstores. If not, you're better off applying the entry fee toward the cost of mailing your proposal to agents and editors.

FACT

Writers who are desperate to get published are easy prey for scam artists. While it's impossible to tell how many would-be authors get fleeced, one estimate from the Science Fiction Writers of America puts the tally at 10,000 victims, who shell out as much as $50 million each year to bogus agents, publishers, book doctors, and other scam artists.

"We're Looking For . . . "

Sometimes you'll run across advertisements in writers' magazines and on various Web sites posted by literary agents who are seeking submissions. Not all of these ads are scams, but you should exercise reasonable care in responding to them. The main element in distinguishing a potential scam is the kind of material requested.

Beginning agents might ask for proposals or manuscripts for romance novels, nonfiction, or whatever their specialty is. But no reputable agent will ask for anything other than book-length work. Legitimate agents don't handle short stories, magazine articles, or poetry, especially for new clients, because the pay rates for these things are too low to make the commission worth the agent's time. Be wary of anyone claiming to be an agent who wants to see your short stories, poems, or nonfiction magazine articles.

ALERT!

Be suspicious of any agent, book doctor, or publisher who solicits you via a mass mailing, spam e-mail, or canned phone campaign. Scam artists often search for victims by purchasing mailing lists from writers' magazines, trolling writers' Web sites and message boards, even tracking copyright registrations. A legitimate agent or editor may contact you if they've read an article of yours, for example, but generic solicitations usually signal a scam.

Book Packagers

Book packagers provide all the elements that go into a final book. They design the front and back covers, arrange for artists (who may be in-house employees or independent contractors) to provide illustrations for the cover and for the book itself, and organize the typesetting and placement of graphs and illustrations in the text. The major difference between a book packager and a book publisher is that the publisher handles the logistics of marketing, distribution, warehousing, and so on, while the packager does not offer those services.

Freelance Opportunities

Book packagers often work with major publishers to create specific projects or lines, and this can provide opportunities for aspiring writers. For example, a publisher might want a series of educational books on astronomy aimed at middle-school readers. The book packager takes on the responsibility for designing the series and finding qualified authors to write the books. In most cases, these opportunities will be work-for-hire deals, meaning you'll be paid a flat fee, won't collect royalties, and won't retain any rights in the work. But if you are billed as the author, it can count as a publishing credit, which helps boost your chances of getting your own work published.

Directories like *Writer's Market* now list book packagers along with traditional publishers, including the same kind of market information that is listed for other types of publishing opportunities. You can also find names of book packagers by checking out titles at your library or bookstore. On the copyright page, there will be a line that says the work was "prepared for" the publisher by the packager.

FACT

Most often, publishers hire book packagers for projects that demand a lot of research, are highly technical, or require lots of graphs and illustrations. To become an author for one of these projects, your credentials must be impeccable or you must have unusual access to experts and authorities on the topic.

Hiring a Book Packager

If you're self-publishing your book, you may want to consider hiring a professional packager to design the cover, illustrations, and pages; many book packagers also offer editing services. These services are sometimes offered by book printers, but more often you'll have to either do these things yourself or find someone else to do them. Usually, a book packager will see a project through to delivery of the final product, working with the printer to ensure a quality book. The packager's fees will vary according to how much work you need done.

Self-publishing is the only reason you would consider working with a book packager on your own project. You don't need their services to approach agents or royalty-paying commercial publishers. When you get a contract from HarperCollins, for example, they'll handle the editing and design work. Agents and editors are not impressed with fancy packaging, so it's a waste of your money to pay a book packager when you're following the traditional publishing route. The key to getting a publishing contract still lies in the quality of your manuscript.

Self-Publishing

The world of self-publishing has become increasingly complicated as disreputable companies have sprung up to take advantage of credulous authors desperate to see their work in print. Part of the confusion stems from the variety of terms surrounding nontraditional publishing; these terms, though different in meaning, have been used interchangeably, often deliberately, to delude and deceive unsuspecting victims. Before you consider any self publishing scheme, you must understand the differences among self-publishing, vanity presses, and copublishing arrangements.

Self-publishing means you, the author, take on all the responsibilities of writing, designing, printing, marketing, and distributing your book. It's a respectable option, and some authors have even used self-publishing to launch careers with royalty-paying commercial publishers. Self-publishing also can be a good choice if your book is specifically tailored to a very narrow audience, and if you know how to reach that audience. If your book has more general appeal, you should exhaust your traditional publishing options first; a commercial publisher is much better equipped to reach a mass readership.

Self-publishing also is an expensive proposition. Even in the world of e-books and print-on-demand, you can expect to spend several thousand dollars to create, market, and distribute your book. That doesn't include the time and energy you'll spend on those tasks. Weigh all these factors carefully before you decide to take the plunge into self-publishing.

The biggest disadvantage to any form of self-publishing is that these types of books never make it onto traditional bookstore shelves, and they are rarely, if ever, reviewed by the media. A well-designed self-published book might catch the eye of an agent or commercial publisher, especially if you can show that you sold 1,000 or more copies. But for most book projects, your best bet is to keep trying to land a contract by the usual means.

Vanity Publishers

Vanity publishers and their ilk have given self-publishing a bad reputation, because so many people confuse the two. A self-publisher typically already has his market in mind, knows how to reach that market, and is prepared to do the work necessary to get his book out to interested readers. Vanity publishers—also called subsidy publishers—have no interest in a book's potential market, and they don't care whether you know anything about marketing your book. Anybody who comes up with the cash can get a book printed through these outfits.

ALERT!

Dishonest vanity publishers specialize in pushing writers' emotional buttons. They'll appeal to your ego by telling you that they accept very few projects every year. They'll feed your fears by making traditional publishing sound like a hopeless cause. The truth is, these publishers will take anybody's money, no matter how good or bad their work is. Don't be fooled by the flattery or the fear-mongering.

Often, there is no quality control with vanity presses. That means you may end up with a poorly designed book or one riddled with typos and other errors. You might get to see proofs of your book before it goes to press, but as often as not you won't have that opportunity. You'll get stuck with whatever the so-called publisher delivers to you.

Vanity presses have migrated to the Internet, promoting e-books and print-on-demand services. This can raise some legal nightmares for you depending on how the contract is worded, because you may not have the right to sell your work to another publisher if it's considered "in print" by an e-book or print-on-demand service. Before signing with a vanity publisher, make sure you know exactly what the contract entails. If you have any doubts, take the contract to an attorney who specializes in copyright law or who works extensively with writers and artists.

Copublishing

Copublishing is a relatively new wrinkle in the vanity publishing business, designed, perhaps, to sidestep the natural caution of writers who are familiar with the risks of vanity or subsidy publishers. In a copublishing situation, the publishing company draws a picture of author and publisher sharing both the risks and rewards of putting out a book. Unfortunately, many copublishing arrangements have the same drawbacks as more conventional subsidy arrangements. The author ends up paying, with no guarantees of a salable product, and some writers have found themselves without a product at all, after paying thousands of dollars in a copublishing scheme.

There are countless sharks circling the backwaters of publishing. They prey upon a writer's natural anxieties, confirming your fears about the industry and the difficulty of breaking in, then buoying your hopes with outlandish promises and blatant ego-stroking. Your best defense is a combination of realistic expectations, skepticism of offers that seem too good to be true, and faith in your own abilities.

Chapter 17

Thanks, but No Thanks

For every manuscript that gets published, there are hundreds, and perhaps even thousands, that are received with a marked absence of interest and enthusiasm. These manuscripts may spend their entire existence wandering from agent to agent, from editor to editor, collecting nothing but dust and rejection letters. Learning how to handle rejection is one of the most critical skills you'll need in your writing career; you'll come up against it more often than any writer wants to admit.

Rejection Is a Fact of Life

If you've been writing for more than a month or two, you probably have run across this admonition from agents and editors: Don't take rejection personally. And, if you're like most writers, you thought to yourself, "Who are they kidding?" You've spent heaven knows how many hours writing, rewriting, thinking, rethinking, polishing, and perfecting. There's a tiny piece of your soul right there on every double-spaced page. And some heartless Philistine of an agent or editor sends you a smug, generic form letter saying your masterpiece "doesn't suit our needs at the present time." *Of course* it feels personal.

FACT

Some writers look at their rejections as an indication of progress. You can't get a rejection if you don't submit your work to agents and editors, and if you submit your work often, chances are you'll get lots of rejections. By submitting your work even once, you've taken a step that scads of would-be writers never will attempt.

So where do agents and editors get off telling you not to take it personally? Hard as this is for many writers to believe, agents and editors base their decisions on the business interests of publishing. There are dozens of reasons why your proposal or manuscript may not fit the business needs of an agent or publisher. Here are some of the most common:

- There are similar books on the market or on the publisher's list that haven't sold well.
- There is not a demonstrable market of potential readers for your book.
- Your book idea doesn't fit in with an agent's or publisher's usual line.
- Your angle or slant is not distinctive enough to make your book stand out from other, similar books, even if those similar books are selling well.

- There are weaknesses in your proposal or manuscript that make it unsalable.

The first three reasons are business conditions; you don't have any control over these, but sometimes you can make adjustments for them. The last two reasons are creative conditions, and those are entirely within your control.

Business Conditions

Rejections very often have nothing to do with the quality of your writing or even of your idea. An editor who loves your proposal might discover that her publishing house already has one or more books on your topic and doesn't need another; another editor at the same house might have recently acquired a similar or related title. High-level executives may have issued a directive that the house is no longer accepting the type of book you're pitching, or the pub board may have put a moratorium on new acquisitions while it considers a new direction for its catalog.

Agents can have similar issues. They may have recently sold a similar title, or they may be shopping a similar title for another client and getting little response. They may know of soon-to-be-published books on your topic, which will dim the prospects of selling your book.

Agents and editors consistently complain of receiving inappropriate material from writers. A publisher specializing in how-to books is not and never will be interested in historical fiction, no matter how good it is. You can cut your rejection rate significantly by submitting your material only to agents and editors who handle your type of book.

Those are business conditions that you might not even be aware of when you receive a rejection, and there isn't anything you can do about them. But you can take into account other business considerations to give your project its best chance. For example, adopt the mantra of agents and editors and study the market. Come up with a unique angle, shop your stuff to the people and publishers who handle your genre, and explore every avenue to show there's a large potential audience for your book.

Creative Conditions

Creative conditions are the ones you have the most control over. You come up with the initial idea. You work that idea into a well-constructed, finely detailed book project. You choose your perspective and your style, and you string the right words together in the right order to give your idea life.

When your idea comes back to you, rejected by an agent or editor, most likely it will come back without any hint as to the reason it was rejected. For most writers, the haunting fear is that their work was rejected because it just isn't good enough, and that means, in the writer's mind, that the writer isn't good enough. This is why rejection feels so personal—it feels like an attack on your creative ability, the core of your identity as a writer.

Professional writers—published or unpublished—feel that creative pressure, too; they just handle it differently. They get frustrated and discouraged just like the rest of us, but they don't give in. Instead, they learn to use that negative energy to better purpose, to generate new ideas and new perspectives that can help them improve their projects. Professional writers know that their responsibility is to create the best possible proposals and manuscripts, and, after that, it's out of their hands.

Professionalism is as much about attitude as it is about getting paid for the words you write. Published writers can have unprofessional attitudes, and unpublished writers can have professional attitudes. A professional attitude won't guarantee you a book contract, but it goes a long way toward convincing agents and editors that they want to work with you.

That's what agents and editors really mean when they tell aspiring writers not to take rejection personally. When you do your homework on the business end and submit your best work on the creative end, you have the comfort of knowing that a rejection really is nothing more than a business decision, not an indictment of you or your writing.

The Professional Response

Agents and editors have an amazing capacity to remember which writers gave them a hard time when their work was rejected and which accepted the decision with every appearance of aplomb. Not surprisingly, the ones who make a fuss are the ones those same agents and editors will, if possible, avoid working with in the future. And because the publishing world is a relatively small community, built as much on an individual's reputation as anything else, word of an irate and unprofessional response to a rejection letter can make the rounds alarmingly fast.

Your Private Response

On receipt of a rejection letter, the temptation to sit down and write a stinker of a response is undoubtedly strong. Writers who have put so much of themselves into their manuscript understandably want to defend their creation and point out all the wonderful qualities the rejecting agent or editor overlooked. Some even go so far as to point out all the undesirable qualities the agent or editor must have, an assumption based on the sole fact that the agent or editor rejected the wonderful manuscript.

There's no question that writing such a response can be therapeutic. It lets you purge yourself of all the negative energy that nearly all of us experience when we receive a rejection, and there is a certain satisfaction in finding just the right words to tell the person who rejected us exactly what we think of him. And, truthfully, there's nothing wrong with writing that scathing response—*as long as you never send it*. If it helps you reach a calmer frame of mind, that's fine. But, as soon as you cool down, put that piece of vitriol in the shredder.

Remember the Network

If you give in to temptation and send that nasty response, don't expect it to remain private for long. Agents and editors talk to each other; it's a huge part of their jobs. Even if your name isn't mentioned, your unprofessional response is likely to become a topic of conversation.

Another thing to keep in mind is that editors, and sometimes agents, move around. Today, the editor who rejected you is working for Smallest of the Small Presses. In a year or two, he may be working for MegaPublishers Inc., where you're trying to market your next bestseller. He may not remember the nasty note you sent him when he was back at Smallest, but do you really want to bet your career on it?

The same applies to agents. The one who rejects you today may be working for a different agency—or may even have ventured out to open her own business—next year. She might not tell her coworkers about the unpublished amateur who called up to holler at her because she had the temerity to send a rejection. On the other hand, it's a great conversation-starter around the water cooler, and everybody likes a good war story. And you can imagine the kind of reception you'll get when you try to solicit this agent, or even her new employers, for your next project.

Your Public Response

Most writers never respond to rejection letters, and that's fine. If you've received the standard form rejection with no personal note from the agent or editor, there's no reason for you to reply; no one expects you to. But if your form rejection slip is accompanied by even a brief comment, you should consider sending a polite reply thanking the agent or editor for his input.

The key here is the word "polite." No matter what you privately think or say about the validity of the comments, your public response—that is, the one you actually post or e-mail to the agent or editor—must be polite in order to be professional. That's the image you want to convey in any case, and it's just as important in these kinds of communications as it is in your query, proposal, or manuscript.

Here's an example of the difference between a private and a public response. A writer was asked to submit an outline for a potential book project on a subject he wasn't familiar with. He talked with the editor to get an idea of what he wanted, then he spent several days doing some research on the topic. He came up with a preliminary outline and was in the process of polishing it when he received an e-mail from the editor, saying the publishing house had found another author to do the project and apologizing for the inconvenience.

The writer, naturally, was disappointed. He also was angry that he had spent so much of the past week working on a project that had been passed on to someone else. His first impulse was to express his frustration in a snide reply. But, wisely, he waited an hour or so before responding. When he did respond, he did so politely and graciously, asking the editor to keep him in mind for other projects. This writer may never work with this editor again, but you never know what the future might bring. His restraint in dealing with the situation guarantees that the editor won't blacklist him as more trouble than he's worth.

FACT

Some writers feel it's dishonest to maintain a polite and detached façade when you're seething with fury at a rejection. It's not dishonest; it's the standard of decorum that is expected of you. Agents and editors know that rejection is tough to deal with, but they expect you to deal with it on your time, not on theirs.

Welcoming Comments

There's a reason most agents and editors send out form letters when they're rejecting material. It's not just because form letters save time. It's because most of them have learned, through bitter experience, that even the most tactful suggestions and the most constructive criticisms are too likely to earn them a nasty note—or, worse, a nasty phone call—from the writer.

This is unfortunate, because it sets up a Catch-22 for everyone. Agents and editors rarely offer genuine critiques because they don't want to waste their time giving advice to someone who may not appreciate it and who, likely as not, will take offense at it. Writers collect a pile of rejection letters, all saying more or less the same thing, and have no idea why their book idea isn't going anywhere. Without the input of professionals in the publishing business, writers don't know what to change in their proposal or manuscript to make it more salable, and agents and editors don't get the quality projects that might be worthwhile because writers don't get that input.

When you do receive comments along with a rejection, you have to decide first whether you think the criticism is valid and then whether you want to make changes based on the comments. These are entirely your decisions, and that can provide some balm when the soul is bruised.

The Value of Comments

Many writers expect personalized comments from agents and editors and are offended when they receive a form rejection letter. Worse, many writers who do receive comments don't understand the true value of those few words penned at the bottom of the standard rejection. An agent or editor who has taken the time to jot you a note about your material—assuming, of course, that the note is constructive and helpful—has given you a rare gift that most aspiring writers never will receive. To take this gift in the spirit in which it is intended, place yourself in the agent's or editor's chair for a moment.

Agents and editors receive an astounding volume of submissions every day. Because their business hours are consumed with the myriad duties surrounding existing clients and pending projects, the typical agent or editor spends her evenings and weekends going through the never-shrinking stacks of proposals and manuscripts from unknown, would-be authors. Probably 99 percent of those submissions will receive the standard rejection. But it is that 1 percent that keeps agents and editors reading; they are forever looking for that promising proposal by a talented new writer that merits further consideration. The ones that show potential but aren't quite ready for the market yet are the ones that receive personalized comments.

What an agent or editor is really telling you in her comments is that you have caught her attention, enough to make her take a break from the routine of reading and rejecting and write you a note. She's offering you her professional advice, at no cost or obligation to you, and most likely she's doing it on her personal time. Even if you don't like what she has to say about your work, it's important to understand the generosity she has shown in sharing her time and her experience with you.

Analyzing Criticism

Most of us slide headfirst into defensive mode when we receive criticism of any kind, whether it's about how we fix dinner or how we write; it's a natural human reaction. Some forms of criticism are harder to take than others, of course. Constructive criticism, which offers suggestions for improvement, usually is less emotionally provocative than criticism that doesn't include such helpful advice. In the course of your writing career, you're likely to run into both kinds, so the first step in dealing with criticism is to learn the difference between the helpful and the not-so-helpful kind.

ALERT!

It's one thing to say you should shrug off unhelpful criticism, and it's another to put it into practice. Try thinking of it this way: Agents and editors who make sweeping, unhelpful remarks are not the agents and editors you want to work with anyway. Keep searching until you find one willing to offer constructive suggestions.

Unhelpful criticism comes in the form of broad, nonspecific statements attacking either the project or you: "This idea is terrible," or, "You'll never be published." You can't respond to this kind of criticism because there's nothing to grab hold of. If the critic doesn't give you an inkling of exactly what he thinks is wrong with your material, you have no roadmap for making changes. Your best option in this case is to shrug it off and move on to other agents or editors.

Constructive criticism does give you something to grab hold of. If an editor rejects your novel with a note that the beginning chapters don't do enough to draw in the reader and set up the rest of the story, that's something you can examine and, perhaps, change. If an agent says your nonfiction proposal needs to be more tightly focused for a specific market, that's advice you can act on if you choose.

To Change or Not to Change

You are the final judge of whether the changes suggested to you should be implemented. The proposal or manuscript, after all, is your work. Sometimes writers feel that the very essence of their work would be destroyed if they made changes according to an agent's or editor's fancy. That's a valid point of view, but sometimes it carries a high price: failure to get published.

QUESTION?

How can I tell if criticism is valid?
Lots of constructive criticism is subjective; you may run into an agent or editor whose tastes simply don't match yours. However, if you receive the same type of comment time after time, this is a good indication that the criticism has merit, and you should take another look.

The trick is figuring out what is important to you and to what degree. Think about the discussion in Chapter 1 about the passionate project versus the business project. If you're like most writers, there will be situations where protecting the integrity of your work is more important to you than getting published, and there will be situations where the opposite is true. The good news is that this determination is entirely yours, and it will be entirely yours for every single project throughout your career.

No Arguments, Please

Sometimes writers want to debate the merits of a rejection, or even specific criticisms. They'll accuse the agent or editor of not reading the proposal or manuscript carefully; sometimes they'll even accuse the rejecting person of not reading it at all. They'll do their best to turn the process into something akin to a presidential debate and use their considerable skills to convince the agent or editor that she is wrong and the writer is right.

Certainly, agents and editors make mistakes from time to time. They see a lump of carbon instead of a diamond in the making, or they underestimate the market for a particular project. If someone has made this kind of mistake with you and your work, you might find solace in the thought of future vindication. The agent who today decided she didn't want to handle your project may someday writhe in self-abasing agony for failing to recognize your incredible talent. The editor who rejects your manuscript today might kick himself repeatedly in a year or two when he sees your book climbing the bestseller list with another publisher. But you will never convince either an agent or an editor to reconsider his decision by arguing with him.

Arguing over a rejection or constructive criticism has the same effect as sending a nasty note in response to a rejection. It marks you as immature and amateur, and that mark can grow into an inky cloud capable of blotting out any potential sunshine in your writing career. No matter how mistaken or unfair you think an agent or editor has been in judging your work, do not try to make her see the error of her ways. If you need to vent your spleen, do it in your journal, to your family, or to your writer's group.

Reassessing Your Project

Many writers become so attached to their projects that they can't look at them objectively. They are unshakably convinced they have a terrific idea, superbly organized and written, and they genuinely cannot understand why they haven't been able to find a buyer. These writers have developed mental blinders that prevent them from seeing their work from any perspective but their own. It takes some practice and a good bit of introspective courage to remove those blinders so you can reassess your work honestly and objectively.

Question Your Beliefs

It's a common gripe for writers: "I've got a killer query and a great manuscript, but I keep getting rejection letters." The one making the complaint rarely recognizes the inherent illogic in the two halves of this statement, but for agents and editors, and even outside observers, it's obvious: A killer query and a great manuscript do not add up to rejection. If that's the equation for your project, something is wrong.

Rejection letters are tangible facts, so start there. Who are the letters from? Are they from agents and editors who specialize in your genre? If not, that could be the explanation of your out-of-balance equation. If you have targeted the appropriate agents and editors, however, you need to look further for the answer to your problem.

Is your query really of "killer" quality? If it isn't getting results, it might not be as good as you think it is. Read it again with a critical eye; imagine yourself as an agent or editor reading it for the first time. Scrutinize everything in your query, from your angle to your lead to your tone to your mechanics. It might need tweaking, or even a full rewrite.

It's easy to get discouraged if you discover that your query or manuscript isn't as wonderful as you thought it was. Instead of looking at it as a mistake or a failure, though, look at it as an opportunity to improve your writing. Remember, the quality of your work is the one element you have complete control over in publishing.

The same principle applies to your proposal and your manuscript. Does it live up to what you promised in your query letter? Is your angle sufficiently different from existing books to set yours apart? For nonfiction books, look for key information you might have omitted or better ways to organize the material. Your subject might be too narrow or too broad, too common or too obscure. For fiction, think critically about your plot and character development, as well as organization and mechanics.

Find a Good Critic

Yes-men and sycophants do you no good if your aim is to improve your writing and correct the things that keep you from getting published. You need constructive feedback from a critic who can be trusted to tell you the truth about what your writing has and what it lacks. Family members and friends may be more motivated to appear supportive than to give you an honest appraisal of your writing, so it's a good idea to look for an unbiased third party.

You might be able to find what you need in a writers' group, as long as the group is focused on moving its members closer to salable projects and not mired in self-defeating negativity. A group that spends all its time carping about the short-sightedness of agents and editors is no more useful to your writing career than the relative who thinks everything you write is fantastic. Look for a writers' group that is positive and energized, but not shy about giving honest feedback.

You also might be able to find a good critic at your local community college. These institutions often offer classes on a variety of topics that are open to the general public, typically under the umbrella of "community education" or something similar. Enroll in a creative writing class and ask the instructor if she would be willing to read your proposal or manuscript and give you a critique.

ALERT!

When you ask for an honest critique, be prepared to hear some things you probably won't like. As with any criticism, you decide what is and what is not valid, but you must be willing to listen to another's opinion before you can make that decision, and you must treat the person offering you advice with respect—especially if you expect him to come to your aid again.

Resubmitting Your Project

Richard Bach once said that a professional writer is an amateur who didn't quit. Many would-be writers cap their pens after receiving a single rejection slip. Some writers set timelines or submission quotas to meet; they give themselves a year to market their book, for instance, or they decide to send their proposal to twenty-five agents or editors. If they reach the end of the year or the twenty-fifth agent without scoring an acceptance, at least they know they've given their work a fair shot.

These kinds of goals also are useful in motivating you to re-evaluate your book idea. If you're getting constructive criticism with your rejections, you can pool the notes from agents and editors to see if a pattern emerges, and you can decide whether it's worthwhile to continue with your original work or whether it's time for a rewrite. Alternatively, you can decide to give yourself a rest from this particular project and file it in a drawer until you're ready to retool it or start a new round of marketing.

FACT

Sometimes the timing just isn't right for a particular book idea, but that doesn't mean the right time won't come around. *Jonathan Livingston Seagull* was rejected more than a dozen times before it found a publisher. Ironically, the publisher that eventually picked it up had rejected the manuscript a year earlier.

If you get significant feedback from a specific agent or editor and decide to take the advice offered, it's a good idea to resubmit your proposal to that agent or editor. There are two good reasons for this. One is that you already know the agent or editor is interested, so you start with that advantage. The other is professional courtesy. An agent or editor who gives you his expert advice at no charge deserves the first chance to look at how you applied his advice. This doesn't guarantee that you'll land a contract. But it does show the agent or editor that you appreciate his time and his comments, and that polishes your image as a professional, whether you're published yet or not.

Chapter 18

The Business of Writing

W hen the subject of writing as a business comes up, lots of writers groan like a tenth-grade history class being given a pop quiz on the Monroe Doctrine. Creative personalities like to be paid for their art, but seldom do they have any real interest in the details of business. Even published authors can find the business side of writing to be a nuisance, but they know it's a necessary irritation if they take their writing seriously.

Tools of the Trade

Theoretically, writing can be done anywhere, any time, with any implement that will make a mark on any kind of surface. But if you hope to turn your talent into a revenue-generating career, you need the proper equipment. A few diehards still use typewriters and carbon paper, but most of us prefer the easier, cleaner, and faster methods afforded by today's technology.

Personal Computer

A personal computer with a good word-processing program is virtually indispensable for today's aspiring writer. Many publishers accept electronic submissions, either via e-mail or computer disk, and some even prefer electronic versions of complete manuscripts. Some publishers will accept manuscripts created in a variety of programs, but Microsoft Word is the most common word-processing software that publishers accept. Some publishers even stipulate in their contracts that the manuscript must be prepared in Word.

FACT

Software packages sold with home computers often include word-processing programs other than Word, such as WordPerfect or WordPad. You may have to buy the Word program separately and install it on your computer, or upgrade the software package when you purchase your computer.

Your computer system must include a good quality printer. The old dot-matrix printers that were common fifteen to twenty years ago are frowned upon today because the quality of the printout is so poor. Some agents and editors have gone so far as to explicitly prohibit dot-matrix copy from consideration. Fortunately, printer prices have dropped significantly in recent years, and you don't have to spend a lot of money to get a printer that will give your copy a fresh, readable, and professional look.

Internet Access

These days, Internet access is standard equipment for writers. Agents and editors like to communicate with their authors via e-mail because it's quick and less intrusive than telephone calls, and e-mails don't have to be sent during regular business hours. For writers, the Internet provides an instant research tool. You can do a lot of your market research online, and even research for your book project; you can connect with other writers and take online classes or seminars; you can check out other books in your genre and keep up with industry news.

In most areas of the United States, you can find an Internet service plan to fit almost any budget, from as little as $10 a month in some cases. If you use your Internet service solely in pursuit of your writing and not for any other purpose, you may be able to claim it as a deductible expense on your income tax return; check with your accountant or tax preparer.

Though quick and convenient, e-mail isn't always reliable. A large test conducted by *InformationWeek* columnist Fred Langa revealed that up to 40 percent of valid, nonspam e-mails never make it to their intended recipients, presumably because of overactive antispam filters. This is another reason why snail mail remains the preferred method for submitting queries and proposals.

Filing System

Every professional writer needs an efficient filing system. What constitutes "efficient" varies widely from one writer to the next. You might like to keep your records, notes, first drafts, and so on neatly organized in a file cabinet, alphabetized, and clearly labeled. You might use shoeboxes on a bookshelf, one box devoted to each of your projects. Or you might divide your papers under more general headings, like research, rejection slips, and receipts, and stack them around your office.

It doesn't matter what sort of system you use or how odd your system might seem to outsiders. The important thing is that you know where to lay your hands on what you need when you need it. That's the real key to efficiency.

Reference Materials

Even the most talented and technically skilled writers need to look up a word or a punctuation rule now and then. The tools of your trade include a personalized library of useful reference materials. A good dictionary, a good thesaurus, and a good style and usage guide form the foundation of your reference shelf. Some publishers will specify which references they use to resolve questions of spelling, grammar, and style.

FACT

Most publishers use the *Chicago Manual of Style* as the general copy-editing bible for their books, but some have their own style guides that supersede the CMS on certain points. Other common style guides include Strunk & White's *Elements of Style* and the *Associated Press Stylebook,* both of which should be available through your local bookstore.

Your reference shelf also should include directories of potential agents and publishers. Guides like *Writer's Market* provide essential information, ranging from mailing and Internet addresses to pay rates and policies. Many directories, including *Writer's Market*, now come on CD-ROM or have Web sites where you can browse listings by a variety of search criteria; these sites typically charge an annual fee for full access.

The rest of the materials in your personal library depend largely on what you write or aspire to write. There are countless how-to books aimed at writers of specific genres. There are reference books about poison and weapons for the mystery writer and about life in the eighteenth century for the historical fiction writer. There are books meant to inspire you and keep you motivated to write, and there are books that show you how to format your manuscript for children's books, short stories, screenplays, and book-length work. Keep the books you find most useful within arm's reach so it's convenient to refer to them as you practice your craft.

Tracking Your Projects

Some writers prefer to block out everything but their current project, but most of us have several ideas kicking around at once, and may even be shopping more than one project to agents and editors. This can get confusing if you don't have a system in place for tracking your projects. You need to be able to follow the details of your projects—where you sent it, when you sent it, who's next on your list to send it to, and so on. For projects that aren't ready to be marketed yet, your tracking system will help you identify what you need to do to get to that point.

Overview Tracking

The easiest way to keep track of all your submissions at once is with a calendar—desktop, wall, or computerized. Calendars let you see at a glance when you mailed your materials and when you can reasonably expect a response. They let you highlight upcoming events and deadlines. They can even serve as writing logs, showing what you accomplished in a given day, week, or month. Using a calendar in this way also can be a motivational tool; when you get discouraged, as all of us do from time to time, your calendar can remind you what you have done to fan the spark of your writing career.

Some writers prefer to track their projects on a database, using the spreadsheet program on their computers. The advantage is that you can adapt the format to suit your style, including as much or as little information as you wish. The disadvantage is that databases can become unwieldy, and you may find yourself falling behind in updating your tracking.

Individual Tracking

While a calendar gives you an overview of your work, you also need a way to track each of your projects individually. Each project should have its own file folder, shoebox, or stack, in which you keep every piece of paper related to that project. When you receive a rejection slip for a project, staple or paper-clip a copy of it to your query letter. Print out any related e-mail and place it with that project. This lets you follow a project's specific history, making it easier to find patterns in rejection comments, for example, or to determine how far along you are in your marketing strategy.

The very rejection slips that make you so mad when you receive them can help you when tax time rolls around. They serve as proof of your submissions and document that you are actively attempting to earn income from your writing. Keep them on hand to show that your writing is not merely a hobby.

What Comes Next?

Experienced writers almost always advise beginners to start their next project the same day they begin marketing their current project. There's no feeling of helplessness quite as poignant as the one that engulfs you when you've dropped your query or proposal into the mail. It's like sending your child off to college: You can only tell yourself that you've done your best and hope your best is good enough for the rest of the world.

The only antidote for that feeling, at least when it comes to writing, is to start a new project. Directing your energy into another book—or even an article or short story—prevents you from fretting unnecessarily about your first project's eventual fate. It even can help ease some of the pressure beginning writers inevitably experience. Starting a new project right away quiets the demon voice that whispers in your mind, saying your first project was a fluke. It also helps build your confidence. After all, if you have a new project to work on, you have a whole new world of possibilities.

Working on a steady stream of projects also is part of building your career. As discussed in Chapter 1, most published authors have at least three writing projects in development at any given time—one that has been written and acquired by a publisher, one that is in the query or proposal stage, and one that is in the "dreaming-up" stage. As an aspiring author, you also can have at least three projects going at once: one that you're marketing to agents and editors, one that you're researching and polishing, and one that's on your list to do next.

Tracking Income and Expenses

Good bookkeeping is just as important as good book writing. You can use bookkeeping software to record your writing revenue and expenses; you can develop your own spreadsheet on your computer; you can even use a ledger book, available at most office supply stores. Whatever method you use, you also should keep copies of checks and receipts. When receipts aren't available, log the expense in a diary, with a note about what the expense was for.

Advances and Royalties

Whenever you receive a check for a magazine article, a book advance, or royalties, log it in your books and keep a copy of it for your files. Doing this provides some measure of encouragement, because you can see the monetary results of your writing efforts. And, at tax time, you can use your own records to double-check the year-end statements from your agent or publisher.

If you earn $600 or more from a single publishing source, you'll receive IRS Form 1099 at the end of the year. The 1099 will state all your earnings from that particular source. If you are fortunate enough to have sold articles or received advance or royalty checks for $600 or more from more than one publisher, you'll receive a 1099 from each one.

If you have an agent, she will issue one 1099 that states all the earnings you received through her office. Since many agents don't handle magazine articles, you could receive a 1099 from your agent that covers your book revenues, and other 1099s from magazine publishers to whom you sold articles.

Expenses

Most beginning writers rack up expenses long before they earn any income from their writing. It's easy to get lax about your record keeping when the prospect of profits seems but a distant dream. Even if you don't end up claiming your writing expenses as deductions at tax time, it's helpful to give yourself a picture of the monetary investment you're making in your writing career. Besides, the earlier you get into the habit of tracking your expenses, the better prepared you'll be when it becomes a necessity.

Expenses you should keep track of include:

- Office supplies, such as paper, ink cartridges, envelopes, and stationery
- Equipment, such as computers, fax machines, and copiers
- Mailing expenses
- Telephone expenses, especially long-distance calls or a second line devoted solely to your writing business
- Travel expenses, including mileage, tolls, and parking fees
- Membership fees and dues for writers' organizations
- Admission fees for writers' conferences and seminars
- Book purchases related to writing or to your genre
- Magazine and newsletter subscriptions related to your writing

ESSENTIAL

The IRS loves a paper trail, so make sure you hang onto receipts and keep a log of your mileage, meal, entertainment, and other expenses. Most experts advise retaining these records for at least ten years in case you get audited. If space is a concern, you can store digital copies of your records on CDs.

For income tax purposes, all these expenses must be related to your writing. You can claim mileage when you drive to the post office to mail your proposal, for example, but not when you send out your Christmas gifts. If you're a budding romance novelist, your membership in Romance Writers of America is a legitimate writing-related expense; your membership in a science fiction writers' organization may not be, unless you also are trying to break into that market.

Don't cheat yourself out of potential tax savings. If you're in doubt about whether an expense will qualify as a deduction, keep a record of it anyway. When tax time comes, ask your accountant or tax preparer about it; if it doesn't qualify, you're no worse off for having logged it.

Business Structures

There are several ways to structure your writing business. Most writers, and especially those just starting out, are considered "sole proprietors." You also can set up a limited liability company, or LLC, with yourself as the only member, or you can structure your business as a partnership with someone else, or as a corporation. Laws governing these and other business structures vary widely from state to state, and each business structure has its own advantages and disadvantages. You might want to do some research about the laws in your state, or consult an attorney about your situation.

The "sole proprietor" structure is the least formal, and it's the one most writers use. As a sole proprietor, your income, expenses, depreciation, and losses from your writing are included on Schedule C in your personal income tax return. Other business structures require separate tax returns.

FACT

Bestselling authors often set up limited liability companies, or LLCs, for each of their titles to protect other assets in the event of a lawsuit. Beginning writers usually don't have to worry about this, but you might want to consult an attorney experienced in both business law and in working with writers and artists.

Tax Issues

Even if you're struggling to make a living with your writing, the government wants its cut of your revenue. That's why keeping good records is so important. You can offset at least some of your income tax liability by claiming deductible expenses related to your writing. But there are some rules you need to be aware of as you prepare your tax return.

The "Hobby Rule"

If you show losses from your writing endeavors—that is, your expenses are more than your income—in three out of five years, the IRS may determine that your writing is a hobby rather than a business. The difference is important for tax reasons. Hobby expenses can be deducted only as long as they don't exceed the income from the hobby; any expenses above the income don't count. If your writing is classified as a business, however, you can carry over the extra expenses into future years (or even prior years if you want to file an amended return).

The hobby rule has been challenged successfully in court, so it may not be as big an issue for writers in the future. However, most tax professionals recommend that writers try to show at least a small profit in three years out of every five, just to be safe.

QUESTION?

Do I have to delay deductions until I get income from my writing?
No. Since 1988, writers and other artists have been exempt from the general rule that requires most businesses to match their expenses and income. The law recognizes that you might spend several years working—and incurring expenses—on a project before you earn any income from it. However, the "hobby rule" may come into play here.

Deductible Expenses

The expenses listed above can be deducted on your income tax return, as least up to the amount you earned from your writing. If you earned $3,000 from a book sale, you can claim writing-related deductions up to $3,000. If your expenses for that year were $4,000, you can only claim $3,000; however, you might be able to carry the extra $1,000 forward and deduct it the next year.

Although you should request and keep receipts whenever possible, the IRS may allow small expenses—under $75—without receipts. Things like taxi fare, lunch at a hot dog stand, and other expenses might fall into this category. You should keep a diary or log to record those nonreceipted expenses, including such information as the date, the purpose of the expense, who was with you, where you were, and how much the expense was. The IRS generally allows such properly recorded expenses for travel, meals, and entertainment.

Keep in mind that you don't report income until you actually receive it. If you sign a book contract in December 2004, for example, you probably won't receive the advance check until January 2005. In that case, you wouldn't report any income from the book contract on your 2004 tax return.

What if you sell a project but never receive payment from the publisher? This sometimes happens when magazines go out of business, and there's a popular misconception among writers that they can write off the monies they are owed but have not been paid. This isn't true. As far as the IRS is concerned, that payment is just income you haven't received yet; it doesn't count as income until you get it, so there's no loss for you to claim if you don't receive it.

Home Office

IRS guidelines on home offices are fairly strict. Your home office has to be a separate part of your residence—a separate room or part of a room, or even a separate building—and used "regularly and exclusively" for your business. Your home office doesn't have to have doors, or even permanent partitions, but it does have to be off-limits for other activities. You can't use your office to watch television with the kids, and you can't call the dining room your office if you use it for dining. Whatever the set-up for your home office, it qualifies for tax purposes only if the area is used exclusively for your writing.

If you can claim a home office deduction, the dollar value is based on the ratio of your office space to your entire residence. If your office is 120 square feet and your home is 1,200 square feet, your home office represents 10 percent of your home. Therefore, you can claim 10 percent of all household expenses—utilities, rent or mortgage, property taxes, insurance, maintenance, even tips for the newspaper mail carrier—as a deduction.

ALERT!

You can only claim the home office deduction in years when your income from writing is greater than your expenses. If your expenses are higher than your income, you may be able to carry the home-office deduction forward into a year when you earn more money from your writing.

The business side of writing can be confusing, and many writers have a hard time motivating themselves to keep good records and do the research to take care of the financial side. But it's well worth your efforts, both in terms of averting headaches in the future and in terms of preparing for the day when most of your income comes from your writing.

Chapter 19

Inking the Deal

Most writers aren't especially interested in the details of publishing contracts, beyond the central issue of money. An agent is much better equipped than the typical author to negotiate with publishers. However, since a contract is basically a set of written promises between you and the publisher, you need to be familiar with at least the main points of the agreement.

What's for Sale

The first clause in virtually every publishing contract will cover the "grant of rights." As the author of your book, you own the copyright to it; the copyright covers a broad range of specific rights that you can sell, or license, to a publisher, a film company, a merchandiser, and so on. Your contract with a publisher spells out which rights you're granting to the publisher and which rights you are reserving for yourself.

FACT

Copyright is an intellectual property right that you can lease, sell, and even pass on to your heirs. The U.S. copyright law extends copyright protection for works created on or after January 1, 1978, for the life of the author, plus seventy years. Copyright protection for works-for-hire lasts between ninety-five and 120 years, depending on the circumstances.

Publishers can vary so much in the types of rights they purchase that it's almost misleading to characterize any given publishing contract as "standard." The one element that is truly standard is that, whatever specific rights you give the publisher, you will be giving those rights on an exclusive basis. For example, the contract may call for the publisher to have the exclusive right to publish and distribute your book anywhere in the world, but only in the English language; translations might not be covered by your contract. In this instance, you wouldn't be able to sell the English-language rights to another buyer until the current grant of rights expires, but you would be free to find another buyer for translations.

There are so many possible combinations of granted and reserved rights that it is impossible to cover them all here. However, most contracts these days will touch on three main categories of rights: print-related rights, electronic rights, and licensing and merchandising rights.

Print-Related Rights

Print-related rights cover everything from book club sales to reprints and revised editions. Your publisher might sell your book to a book club either "as is" or as a special reprint. Reprint rights cover the various formats for books—hardcover, trade paperback, and mass-market paperback. After a couple of years, the publisher may issue an updated edition of your book; you'll make some changes to the original, but not many. Revised editions require substantial changes—at least 30 percent new material—and are issued with new ISBNs and new marketing campaigns.

> Royalty rates differ according to the type of rights covered. You might get a 50 percent royalty rate for book club rights, 60 percent for reprint rights, and 90 percent for first serial rights, for example. Publishers might expect 50 percent of film rights, on the grounds that its book sales help promote a film based on your book.

These rights almost always are included as a package with the overall grant of rights. Publishers want them because they increase the profit potential for a book. It also makes sense to keep these rights together from the author's standpoint, because your primary publisher is in the best position to exploit these rights, and that means higher royalty checks for you.

Other print-related rights include serial or excerpt rights, in which portions of your book are published verbatim in magazines or, more rarely, newspapers or newsletters. If you're selling first serial rights, the excerpt must be published before your book comes out; after your book is published, you can sell second serial rights. Syndicates sometimes pick up serial rights for book excerpts and provide the excerpts to several publications at once.

Electronic Rights

With the advent of the Internet and technology that allows "print-on-demand" publishing, electronic rights are becoming a core element of copyright grants, rather than the side issue they were a few years ago. Unfortunately, many "standard" electronic rights clauses in publishing contracts are still unsuitably vague, with no clear definition about what the clause covers. Electronic rights can include posting excerpts of your book on an Internet site, distributing an e-book from an Internet site, digitally storing your book for print-on-demand services, and even burning your text onto a CD-ROM. An overly broad or vague grant of electronic rights can have important ramifications down the road, so make sure you know exactly what the clause in your contract covers.

ALERT!

Print-on-demand technology is changing the definition of "in print," which in turn affects your rights to reclaim your copyright. Most contracts allow the copyright to revert to the author when the book is no longer considered in print. Your contract should include a specific definition of "in print," whether by a threshold of annual sales or a clarification about digitally stored books.

Licensing and Merchandising

Licensing and merchandising rights, also known as commercial rights, can be more lucrative for the author than the initial publishing contract, especially if your book becomes a bestseller. The Harry Potter books, for instance, have spawned all kinds of merchandise spinoffs, from action figures and calendars to Christmas ornaments and Halloween costumes. Clothing, coffee mugs, games, toys, even bumper stickers—nearly any commodity can be converted into a derivative of your book, fiction or nonfiction. In most cases, it will be in your best interests to retain all commercial rights in your work.

Other Rights

Your copyright covers rights you may not even think of. Film rights, foreign rights, recordings for audio books, even rights to create large-type and Braille editions of your book are all under the umbrella of your copyright. A typical publishing contract includes a clause stating that you keep any rights you haven't specifically granted to the publisher. This kind of clause is more convenient for both you and the publisher. Dealing with every potential circumstance in legal language would make publishing contracts even more complex than they are now.

FACT

Thanks in part to technological advances and in part to the prevalence of litigation in our society, publishing contracts have gotten longer and more complex than ever. According to a report published by the Authors Guild, the standard contract for Random House was four pages long in 1974; by 1998, the standard contract was eleven pages long. Some contracts today are more than thirty pages long.

Advances and Royalties

The bottom line in any publishing contract is how much you'll get paid and when. Most contracts offer two types of payments: advances and royalties. But there can be quite a bit of variety among publishers in both the amounts and the payment policies.

The Advance

It used to be that publishers paid the author his full advance upon signing the contract. That's the exception more than the rule these days. Publishers now routinely split the advance into two or more payments, based on various criteria. The worst deal for the author is when the final advance payment is scheduled on publication of the book, rather than on delivery of the full manuscript. Even after the final edits are done on the manuscript and it's sent off to the printer, it takes several months for the actual book to be produced and distributed to stores. That means you could wait for a year or more before you receive your final advance payment.

The more common practice is for the publisher to give the first advance payment after the contract has been signed and the final advance payment upon acceptance of the full manuscript. You still have to wait for the actual book to be produced, but at least you don't have to wait for the money. Many publishers split the advance in half, but some split it into thirds or even fourths. The middle payments usually are tied to delivery of a specific percentage of the manuscript.

FACT

For every author who gets a seven-figure advance on his next block-buster, there are dozens who can't even make a decent living off book sales. According to a 1981 study for the Authors Guild Foundation, the median annual income (from books) for an American author was about $5,000. Most observers believe that figure has remained relatively static over the past quarter-century.

Royalty Payments

Royalties are a percentage of the sale of each copy of your book. The percentage can be based on the list price of the book (what it sells for in the stores) or on the wholesale price (what the publisher got for it). List-price percentages usually are lower than wholesale-price percentages. Say the list price on a hardcover book is $30, and your royalty rate is 8 percent. That means you get $2.40 for every copy sold at $30. If the wholesale price on the same book is $15, your royalty rate would have to be 16 percent in order for you to earn the same $2.40 per copy. An 8 percent royalty rate on the whole-sale price would yield only $1.20 per copy.

Royalty rates usually increase with the number of copies sold. You might get 8 percent on the first 5,000 copies, for example, then 10 percent on copies 5,001 through 15,000, and 12.5 percent on every copy sold after that. Royalty rates also can change depending on the format of your book; hardcover rates might be different from trade paperback rates, and trade paperback rates might be different from mass-market paperback rates.

Most publishers report sales and royalty earnings twice a year. A typical royalty statement will show how many copies of your book have been sold to booksellers, the retail or wholesale price, the royalty rate, and the total earnings. The publisher can take up to ninety days after the end of a reporting period to issue the royalty statement, which will be accompanied by a check if any payment is due you. Remember that your book has to earn back its advance before you can expect any royalty checks.

QUESTION?

What is an unearned advance?
Advances are upfront payments against royalties, and the author doesn't receive any more money from the publisher until the royalties on sales exceed the advance. An advance that exceeds the royalties that would be due the author based on actual sales is called an "unearned" advance.

Warranties and Representations

The "warranties and representations" clause is an essential part of your publishing contract. This is where you promise the publisher that the work you submit is your own original creation and that your work doesn't violate another's copyright, right of privacy, libel, or other laws. You also are promising that, as the proper owner of your material and its copyright, you are free to grant your rights to the publisher.

The whole purpose of the warranties clause is to protect the publisher against plagiarism. This has become an increasingly vexing problem in all fields, from academia to journalism to business. Publishers no longer can assume that your work is your own; they want a legally binding assurance that it is. Some even include warnings in their contracts that they use special software or other methods to detect plagiarism from any source, including the Internet.

The dire consequences of submitting plagiarized work cannot be overstated. At the very least, you'll severely cripple your reputation and any future you might have as a book author. You also run the risk of financial ruin, from which you may never recover. Your best protection is to be obsessively meticulous about your work to ensure that it does not violate anyone's intellectual or civil rights.

Delivery Dates

One of the key promises in any publishing contract is when you'll deliver the complete manuscript to the publisher. The time frame can range from three months to a year, depending on the publisher and on how hot your topic is. Sometimes publishers who normally grant six months for completing a manuscript may ask you to finish in four months if they want to try to cash in on a swelling trend. The delivery date also can vary according to whether you're writing a fiction book or a nonfiction book. Since you have to have the manuscript virtually completed to sell your first novel, the publisher may ask for final delivery in four or six weeks, giving you enough time to polish but not much time to make significant alterations.

ALERT!

Most contracts give the publisher the right to cancel your book—and require you to return any money you've received—if you fail to meet your delivery date. Usually there's a mechanism that calls for formal notification of tardiness from the publisher before this clause kicks in. This is another reason why meeting deadlines is so critical in this business.

Acceptability Standards

Virtually every contract will require you to deliver a manuscript that the publisher deems acceptable or satisfactory. This clause usually is not negotiable. It has become standard practice because too many publishers have found themselves in possession of a manuscript that is far from what they expected when they made the deal.

The "acceptable manuscript" clause typically includes a definite process for fixing problems. The publisher has to notify the author, usually in writing and usually within thirty days of final delivery, that the manuscript is unacceptable, citing specific things that need to be changed. The author then is given a set period, usually another thirty days, to fix the manuscript to the publisher's satisfaction. If you fail to make the necessary changes, or if the changes aren't satisfactory, the publisher then has the right to cancel your contract or hire someone else to fix the manuscript. The expense of hiring the other writer will be charged against your advance and/or royalties.

For most writers, this clause sounds a lot more sinister than it really is. It isn't meant to foster disputes over minor issues; it doesn't even come into play unless there are major problems or major misunderstandings with the book as it was proposed versus the final manuscript. But it does illustrate the importance of making sure you and your editor share the same general vision for your book.

Obligation to Publish

The promise that the publisher makes to you in a contract is that your work will be published. But in the last few years, many publishers have inserted clauses that relieve them of this obligation. The reasons are mainly economic: Book sales might plummet before your book is ready to go to print; a publishing house may run into financial difficulties unrelated to your specific project; or the publisher may feel that the market won't be as receptive to your book as was anticipated when the contract was signed.

The issue for writers in this case is what happens to your book rights if the publisher decides not to issue your book. If there are no guarantees in the contract that your book will be published, you end up in a sort of legal limbo, unable to move forward with either your book or the rest of your career.

You can avoid this by negotiating a time limit for publication. Specify in the contract that the publisher has so many months—usually between one and two years—to publish your book, and that, if the publisher fails to do so, all rights in the material revert to you. That way, you can at least shop your book to another publisher after the time limit expires.

If the publisher accepts your manuscript as satisfactory but decides not to publish your book for other reasons, you usually will not have to repay any advance you've already received. However, the contract may stipulate that the publisher is not obligated to make future advance payments under these circumstances.

Returns and Remainders

Publishers contract with booksellers to order a certain number of copies of a given title, generally at a significant discount off the list price. Typically, the contract includes a provision that allows the bookseller to return unsold copies; stores often will return that unsold inventory when the publisher's invoice comes due, usually ninety days after the books are shipped. In an average year, bookstores return about 30 percent of their books to publishers. Large discount outlets such as Wal-Mart and Price Club, which got into the bookselling business relatively recently, might send back as much as 40 percent of the copies they order from publishers.

Some publishers give booksellers a slightly better discount if the bookseller waives its right to return unsold copies, but few booksellers accept the additional discount because it makes better financial sense to get rid of titles that aren't selling.

Reserve Against Returns

Because of the industry policy of accepting returned books for a full refund, most publishers will place a "hold" on part of your royalties—that is, they'll keep a portion of your royalties from the first six-month reporting period until after the next reporting period. This is called "reserve against returns" and it can be up to 25 percent or more of your earned royalties. Publishers do this because if they overpay an author, it's very difficult for them to recoup the money.

Your publisher's reserve won't necessarily show up on your royalty statement. The statement may indicate that you earned $800 in royalties and that the publisher is holding $200 in additional royalties as its reserve. If the next reporting period shows less than $200 in returns, the difference will be added to your next check, minus the reserve for that reporting period.

Remainders

Remainders are deeply discounted sales of copies that haven't sold. Many contracts specify when a publisher can "remainder" its stock of your book, how and when the publisher has to notify you that it intends to do so, and what royalties, if any, the publisher will pay on remaindered stock. A typical remainder clause prohibits the publisher from offering its stock at remainder prices for two years after your book is first published. After that, if there is a significant overstock and the book is not selling well, the publisher can offer its stock to booksellers for as much as 70 percent (or even more) off the regular discount price. If the discount drops the price below the publisher's cost per copy, you probably won't receive any royalties. However, you may have the option to buy the overstock at the remaindered price.

Publishers usually won't issue royalty checks for small amounts, though the threshold can vary. If your book only earns $85 in royalties (after the advance is deducted), for example, the publisher usually will wait until the next reporting period and add the $85 to that next royalty payment.

Future Projects

Publishers often include a provision in their contracts that gives them the first right of refusal on an author's next book. There are several reasons for this. One is that it takes a tremendous investment of time and money to launch a new author's career. Your first book might generate only enough sales to cover the advance and maybe a little more, but your second, or even your third, might be a bestseller, and that success will make the investment in your first book worthwhile. In general, publishers like to establish long-term relationships with authors because they know that the profits are more likely to come later rather than sooner.

Authors who are looking to build careers also tend to look for a publishing home, because there are both tangible and intangible benefits to working with the same house on a series of projects. For one thing, you're a known author now, rather than one of the many unknown; it's easier to market your next project to a publisher that already likes your work and is enthusiastic about producing and selling it. Your relationships with editors and even the publicity department get stronger over time, which in turn helps build your career.

Your Next Project

In most cases, your publisher won't even want to look at your next book until it has some sales figures for your first. That usually means you'll have to wait at least three months after your first book hits the store shelves before submitting your next proposal or manuscript. Sometimes the publisher will want to wait six months. This can be frustrating for authors who are anxious to get on with their careers, but it is a sound business practice from the publisher's point of view.

There are a couple of tricky points in the "future projects" clause. One is the issue of genre. Suppose your publisher specializes in nonfiction trade paperbacks, but you want to write a novel next. Does your "future projects" clause prevent you from shopping your novel to fiction publishers? If the clause isn't specific enough, you might have to get the publisher's permission to market your novel elsewhere, even though you know the publisher isn't interested in it.

Another gray area arises when the book you've sold is actually the second book you've written, but the first you've had published. If you have your proposal or manuscript for the other book all done up and ready to be marketed, do you have to wait the three or six months before submitting it to your publisher? What if your publisher already rejected that first proposal during your first round of marketing? What if you get a belated offer from a different publisher after you've signed the contract for your first book?

The answers to these questions all depend on the wording of the "future projects" clause. If these situations apply to you, make sure you point them out to your agent or, if you don't have an agent, raise them during the contract negotiations. Although it can be tedious trying to get the wording of the contract just right, it will save you enormous headaches later on.

Matching Offers

The "future projects" clause usually gives the publisher a finite period to consider your next proposal or manuscript. Often the publisher gets thirty days to decide; if the publisher doesn't make you an offer by the end of the thirty days, you're free to approach other publishers. However, many times the contract will include a clause that gives your publisher the right to snap up your next project by matching the terms of any other publisher who might be interested.

This is a bad deal for authors. The first thing other publishers will ask you is whether your current contract has a "matching offer" clause; if it does, other publishers likely won't be interested. The reason is simple: Publishing is a highly competitive business, and publishers can't afford to waste their resources going after a project that may be yanked from them at the last minute. If at all possible, make sure your contract eliminates the troublesome "matching offer" clause.

Other Options

There are countless other clauses in publishing contracts, which can range from how many free copies the publisher will give you to what happens if the publisher declares bankruptcy. Many of these clauses are part of a publishing house's standard contract, and generally you don't need to worry too much about them. However, there are two increasingly common provisions you need to be aware of: noncompete clauses and work-for-hire agreements.

Noncompete Clauses

Almost all publishers include a noncompete clause in their contracts, because they don't want their authors writing new books that could hurt the sales of their first book. If you've written a book about do-it-yourself kitchen remodeling, your publisher will want to make sure that your future books—at least for the term of the contract—don't focus solely or substantially on kitchen remodeling. A typical noncompete clause prohibits you from selling another work that either competes directly with your book or is likely to "diminish its sale or diminish the value of any rights granted" in your contract.

FACT

If you have an agent, she should be well versed in all the terms and industry standards for publishing contracts; your agent also will know which items are negotiable and which aren't. If you don't have an agent, you might want to consider hiring an attorney who specializes in copyright law or publishing to look over your contract before you sign it.

Sometimes noncompete clauses can be overly strict, and you'll want to negotiate more reasonable concessions. No noncompete agreement should extend beyond the term of the contract, nor should it bar you from including a chapter in your next book that is related to your current book's topic. It also should not prevent you from doing other types of work on the same topic; you should be free to write magazine articles about kitchen remodeling, for instance.

Work for Hire

As recently as ten years ago, work-for-hire arrangements were considered to be terrible deals for authors. When you write a work for hire, the publisher owns the copyright and the myriad rights that go with it, while you get a comparatively small flat fee and, sometimes, not even credit for your work. You don't participate in any future earnings from the book, and you can't exploit other rights like merchandising.

Work-for-hire arrangements still make many authors—and their advocates, like the Authors Guild—cringe. But they have become far more acceptable and more common as publishing has become more competitive. Importantly, many work-for-hire arrangements today give you credit as author of the work, which is a distinct advantage for new authors who are looking for that first book credit to launch their career.

There are several factors to weigh when deciding whether to accept a work-for-hire contract. Most critical for beginning authors—even more critical than the money—is whether you'll be credited on the book cover. If so, this kind of project can help you break into publishing. If not, you'll still be considered an unpublished author, so it won't help your career. Other factors to consider include the following:

- Is the fee fair for the amount of work you'll have to do?
- Is the publisher established and respected?
- Are the topic and angle reasonable?
- Is the topic something you're interested in?
- Does the timeline for the book suit you and your schedule?

Because it is so difficult for newcomers to break into publishing, you should give a fair amount of thought to work-for-hire opportunities before declining them. As long as you get author's credit, a work-for-hire book carries just as much weight with other publishers as a royalty-based book. The right work-for-hire project can be the springboard for your book-writing career.

Chapter 20

E Once You Get the Contract

All the negotiations are complete. You've signed the contract with the publisher; maybe you've even photocopied your advance check for framing. You're floating through the unique euphoria that comes from realizing that someone is paying you to write a book. But eventually the euphoria fades, and then the truth smacks you like a wet fish between the eyes: You have to actually *write the whole book*. Don't panic; just as you took one step at a time to land the contract, writing your manuscript is a one-step-at-a-time process.

Getting Organized

It's easy to feel overwhelmed when you're faced with writing 100,000 words in four months. It's the same feeling you got at the beginning of the school year, when your social studies teacher handed out a syllabus for the semester showing reading assignments, papers, tests, and special projects. Most of us suffer a deer-in-the-headlights brain freeze when we see all the things that have to be done; it takes a while to realize that it doesn't all have to be done right now.

Still, the magnitude of the work requires organization if it is to be finished on time. That means, first, breaking down the work into smaller, more manageable pieces. When you created your proposal, you organized your book into chapters or sections, and you've already written at least two or three of the chapters for your proposal, so that lightens your workload significantly. Now you have to figure out what to do next.

Make a List

Whether your book is fiction or nonfiction, it's often helpful to make a list of what you have and what you still need to complete the work. New fiction authors almost always must have their manuscripts completed before they're offered a contract; this may be required even for your second or third novel. However, if you haven't finished your manuscript, you have an outline or synopsis of your plot; you also probably have bios for your main characters, and you have at least a couple of chapters finished. You might need to collect details for your setting, or you might need to double-check facts. Perhaps you don't have a firm handle on one of your primary character's motivations and need to spend some time fleshing that out. If you've written most of your novel already, you may need to go through it to strengthen weak passages, eliminate scenes that get in the way of the story, or punch up the ending.

In nonfiction, your needs will be different. You might have to do more research before you can write certain chapters, or you might have to go through the research you already have to pick out the key points. You might need to arrange and conduct interviews with sources, or you might need to create a more detailed outline of each chapter to help you stay focused.

FACT

After you've made a list of what you need for your manuscript, figure out what you need first, or what is most critical, in order for you to continue your work. It's frustrating and time-consuming to dive into work and find that you have to stop because some crucial piece is missing, and you risk losing the rare rhythm of a good writing session.

Get Files in Order

You don't have to be neat to be organized. Lots of people have unkempt stacks of papers, books, and files piled in apparently haphazard fashion around their writing space, but these people invariably know where everything is and can lay their hands on a needed document or folder in seconds. For our purposes, then, that's the definition of getting your files in order: Know where your notes, research, and so on are, and make sure they're within easy reach while you're writing. This is less disruptive to the creative process, which makes your writing time more efficient and more productive.

Setting a Schedule

Once the contract is signed, you are legally bound to meet the deadlines specified in the contract, but no one will be watching over your shoulder to make sure you're getting the work done. You'll have to use your own self-discipline and knowledge about how you work to establish a viable schedule. Some writers prefer to set aside blocks of time; they know from experience that they can write a chapter, say, in six hours. Others prefer to set their schedule in terms of words-per-day; you might decide you can comfortably write 2,500 words each day, for example, so you would need forty working days to write 100,000 words. Still others pace themselves by chapters per week rather than setting daily writing times or word-count goals.

Whatever method you use to set your work schedule, make sure you build in time for relaxation and unforeseen glitches. This won't always be possible, as publishers sometimes need extraordinarily fast delivery dates to meet their printing and distribution schedules. If you have only three months to write a 100,000-word manuscript, you can't count on a lot of down time during that period. However, if you have six months to do the same amount of work, you can adjust your work pace to allow for the occasional day or weekend off.

The Publisher's Deadlines

Publishing houses differ in their policies about deadlines. Some give you only a final delivery date and expect the complete manuscript to be delivered by that date. Others have interim deadlines with a certain percentage of the manuscript due at more or less evenly spaced times before the final due date. From the writer's point of view, there are advantages and disadvantages to both kinds of deadlines.

One final due date gives you the freedom to work at your own pace and in your own style, as long as you meet the deadline. But it can pose perils, especially for writers who have a hard time getting motivated to finish their work until a deadline is imminent. Interim deadlines tend to make you structure your work time more consistently because you know the editor is expecting to see at least some of your material relatively soon; they also force you to break your manuscript into smaller pieces so you can meet those interim deadlines. However, interim deadlines can be perceived as putting more pressure on you, which might interfere with doing your best writing.

Just as you expect your editor to accommodate your circumstances, you should make a good-faith attempt to understand your editor's needs and accommodate them. Don't hold up the process on your end just for the sake of taking more time; even if a time crunch isn't your doing, do your best to minimize its impact on the larger schedule.

Your Own Deadlines

No matter what kind of deadlines your publisher sets, it's good practice to establish your own deadlines. Ideally, your personal deadline should be a few days before the publisher's deadline; that gives you a cushion in case something comes up to prevent you from meeting your own goal. If you have interim deadlines every thirty days, for example, set your personal deadlines at twenty-five day intervals. If you are able to meet your own deadline, you'll have five days to relax before beginning the next round of work, or five extra days to work on the next batch of material. If you don't meet your deadline, for whatever reason, you still have time to meet the publisher's deadline.

Setting your own deadlines can be more critical when the publisher has only given you a final delivery date. It's easy to procrastinate when you don't have to produce your manuscript until six months from now, but giving in to that temptation can put you in a tough spot down the road. If you set your own goal of finishing 20 percent of your manuscript every month, you'll be on a good pace to meet your publisher's deadline and still have plenty of time to polish your prose.

A Good Writer-Editor Relationship

Contrary to a popular perception among writers, editors are not the enemy. In fact, a good editor has nearly as high a stake in your work as you do: If your book does well, your editor looks good to his superiors, because he's the one who recognized your talent and potential. He's your ally in the publishing house, first convincing the pub board your work is worth the publisher's investment and then taking care of the innumerable details involved in seeing a manuscript from acquisition to publication. Anything you can do to foster a good relationship with your editor is well worth doing—as long as you don't make a pest of yourself.

"Meeting" Your Editor

More often than not, you'll never meet your editor in person. Most of your communication will take place over the telephone or via e-mail. When you first sign the contract, your editor will usually call or e-mail you to introduce herself and to talk briefly about your book. If you have any questions about how the process works, this will be the time to ask them. Don't worry about appearing to be naïve or uninformed; if this is your first book, your editor is aware of that, and she'll be happy to give you a little insight into how things work.

Keep in mind that your editor, like your agent, will want to hear from you about important things, but she won't have time to indulge in idle chitchat. When important things do come up, e-mail is a convenient communication tool; it also provides a record of what was discussed should questions arise later. Most e-mail programs allow you to sort and archive your e-mail in folders, and it's a good idea to create a folder where you keep copies of all communications between you and your editor.

Creating Buzz

An editor who is enthusiastic about your book and enthusiastic about working with you can do wonders for your career by creating "buzz" about you and your book. Buzz starts in-house with an editor whose excitement about your work and its potential spreads among the rest of the staff. Maybe he's gotten positive feedback from the sales staff, or from key book buyers who like your book so much that they increase their orders. The news gets around the publishing house, and the publicity department starts paying attention, eventually deciding to invest part of their precious budget in promoting your work with ads or media interviews, which leads to out-of-house buzz, which further promotes you and your book. Before you know it, you might find your book has gotten endorsements from prominent people or great critical reviews, and suddenly you're climbing the bestseller lists. And it all starts with an enthusiastic editor.

Communicate, Communicate, Communicate!

It's important to keep in touch with your agent or editor during the writing process. You don't have to alert him every time you sneeze, but it's a good idea to send brief, periodic updates (usually easiest to do via e-mail, and less intrusive for the agent or editor) as you reach important markers in your manuscript. A one- or two-line e-mail saying you've finished the first third of your book is sufficient.

You should let your agent or editor know if you'll be out of town or otherwise unavailable for more than, say, one business day. This is especially important after you've turned in your manuscript. Issues may come up during editing that need your attention, and your editor (and agent) will appreciate knowing in advance that you'll be on vacation until next Tuesday.

Finally, should any crises or major problems arise during your writing, be sure to let your agent and editor know as soon as possible. There might be a sudden illness or accident; your coauthor might encounter a problem that pushes back your planned schedule; a computer virus may wreak havoc with your hard drive; a massive power outage two days before one of your interim deadlines may prevent you from finishing the chapter you were working on. When the agent or editor is aware of the situation, she's more willing to work with you to make adjustments.

If you have an agent, tell her first about any problems that come up, and let her work with the editor to find a solution. Editors don't have time to listen to a litany of personal problems; they need to know when the author can meet his obligations. Your agent is the best person to keep this discussion on a professional level while still making sure everyone's needs are addressed.

Working Through Writer's Block

Every writer experiences times when words take on the less pleasant attributes of a class of fourth-graders. They are raucous and unruly, and despite your best attempts to wrangle them into some semblance of order, they keep breaking out of formation and taking off in the wrong direction, or even dozens of different directions. The pressure of time can add to your rising distress, and that only makes things worse; like fourth-graders facing a substitute teacher, it sometimes seems as though words can smell fear in those who would try to control them. Fortunately, there are several techniques to help you scale the wall of writer's block, or even skirt it.

Take a Break

Creative energy is an incredible force, but it can burn itself out, especially when you're fatigued or stressed. Sometimes the most effective way to help your writing is to take a break from it and do something else for a while. Psychological rest is just as critical as physical rest, especially when you're working on a long-term project like writing a book.

It doesn't matter what you do instead of writing while you're taking your break. What does matter is that you don't give in to feelings of guilt for indulging in that break. If you're convinced that you should be writing instead of taking a walk, going to a movie, having lunch with friends, and so on, you're adding another layer to the blanket of pressure you already feel, and that just makes writer's block more intractable. Walking away from your writing for a few hours—or even a day or two—is a legitimate and essential aspect of the successful writing life.

ALERT!

Some writers take so many breaks from their writing work that they end up falling behind schedule, and that additional time pressure can in turn feed writer's block. You shouldn't feel guilty about taking breaks, but make sure breaks don't take over your writing time.

If you can't get over feeling guilty about taking a break, try looking back at what you've done so far. When you realize how much work you've completed already, you might find it easier to recognize that you've earned a respite.

Change Your Assignment

Sometimes you can get hung up on minute details in a specific chapter or plot point, and that can bring the entire project to a grinding halt. If possible, put the portion that's causing problems aside and focus on a different part of your manuscript. While you're working on that new section, your subconscious mind can gnaw away at the original problem and may have it solved by the time you're ready to return to it.

This technique may be easier to use with nonfiction projects than with fiction. Chapters in nonfiction books often resemble related, but stand-alone, magazine articles, while chapters in fiction usually interlock more closely; it may be more difficult to jump from Chapter 2 to Chapter 10 to Chapter 6 in your novel. If you feel that you can't leap back and forth in your fiction, try taking a fresh look at your synopsis or outline again. These are your road maps for your story, showing how each chapter leads into the next. If you're having difficulty with the way Chapter 5 is shaping up, your synopsis or outline reminds you where you need to be in Chapter 6; that reminder may be enough to get Chapter 5 back on track.

In fiction, it sometimes helps to retype the last few pages, or even the entire previous chapter, leading up to the part you're stuck on. Doing this can help you recapture your writing voice and your focus, which in turn helps build up your momentum.

Write Through It

One surprisingly effective technique for punching through writer's block is to write about it. Pouring out your frustrations and fears on paper can help you identify the obstacles that keep you from getting the words right. Writers who use this technique often find that it helps them clear away the detritus that builds up during the creative process. It's like cleaning a showerhead that has become caked with lime; when the lime is removed, the water flows freely again.

This technique works best when you're honest with yourself and your emotions as they relate to your writing. Remember that no one will read your thoughts on your writer's block, so you have the freedom to be frank. It may take you a few paragraphs or a few pages to get through your particular block; you'll know your therapy has been successful when you're ready to stop writing about your writer's block and start working on your manuscript again.

The "write through it" technique saves time because it forces you to confront the issues that are holding you back instead of passively waiting for your subconscious mind to deal with them. This is especially important when you're up against a tight deadline and don't have the luxury of waiting for things to fall back into place.

Alternatively, you can decide just to write, even if what you turn out is bad. Giving yourself permission to write poorly removes the pressure of "getting it right" the first time through. You can always fix it later, or throw it out entirely. Often, getting the bad writing out of your system creates a bridge to great new material.

The Rewrite

Most writers heave an enormous sigh of relief when their manuscript is finally finished and sent off to the editor. There's a satisfying sense of accomplishment to be savored, worthy of a grand celebration. There also is the sometimes complacent anticipation of enjoying a well-earned rest from your labors, knowing that, after weeks or months of being tied to your computer, you're finally free. Then you get the notes from your editor.

This can be quite disconcerting for first-time authors. Everyone knows that editors will have feedback to offer, but in practice such feedback, even if tactful and diplomatic, can sting like a whip, especially when you're still feeling drained from your initial effort. Far from being free and able to relax, you are being forced to go back to work, whether you want to or not. Very often, you won't want to; even when you know your manuscript is good, you can become heartily sick of it by the time you're done with it, and an editor asking you to make changes can be akin to a zookeeper asking you to hold a poisonous snake.

The good news is that the negative emotional reaction usually passes in a day or so, if you know how to deal with it. You still have to work with your editor on the rewrite, and you probably will have a very limited time in which to make the changes. But your reward this time is a better manuscript and a more complete sense of accomplishment.

Stay Professional

Feedback on your final manuscript can feel just as hurtful as a rejection, and it can dredge up the same feelings of inadequacy and anger. Give yourself time to recover from those feelings before you respond to feedback; your perspective can change greatly in just twenty-four hours. Comments that seemed devastating when you first read them almost never look quite so menacing after a night's sleep.

After you've had a chance to step back from the natural reaction to feedback, look at the comments from the editor's point of view. Remember that the editor's job is to help make your manuscript the best it can be. Even if the editor's tone or approach grates on you, which sometimes happens, the intent behind the comments always is to improve the final copy. Your responsibility as the author is to work with the editor toward that common goal in a professional manner.

Choose Your Battles

Some writers feel they have to fight every suggestion for changing their copy, even if it's minor. Egos and bad impressions aside, the bottom-line truth is that not every word is worth fighting for. Your integrity isn't at risk if the editor wants to replace the word "eczema" with "rash." You might think it's a silly change, but it's not worth arguing about.

FACT

There's an old two-part joke that aptly illustrates the difference between editors and writers:

Q. How many editors does it take to change a light bulb? A. Does it have to be a light bulb?

Q. How many writers does it take to change a light bulb? A. Does it have to be changed?

Keep this in mind next time you see notes from your editor, and approach the suggestions with a smile.

As a professional author, you have to make a conscious effort to separate the genuinely important battles from the skirmishes that don't matter in the long run. This can be difficult to do, but it's essential to the success of your career. If you challenge every little suggestion from your editor, you'll quickly earn a reputation for being difficult to deal with at best and an egotistical prima donna at worst. If you reserve your energies for the things that really matter, on the other hand, the editor will know when an issue really is important to you, and your objection will carry more weight.

Negotiate Deadlines

The publishing business is full of impossible, or at least wildly improbable, deadlines, and this holds true for revisions as well. Sometimes a hitch on the publisher's end will delay the editor in getting your manuscript back to you with her notes, and that will put extra pressure on the original design and printing schedule. The result may be that your editor will ask you to make changes or corrections incredibly quickly.

Sometimes that fast turnaround is feasible; sometimes it's not. Much depends on how extensive the corrections or changes are and whether they require substantial rewriting or additional research. Another factor is your own schedule. If you need more time than the editor has offered to make changes, let her know—politely and professionally, of course—what your situation is and try to work out a reasonable arrangement. Don't make excuses; calmly discuss what schedule is realistic for you, and do your best to accommodate the editor's needs. As noted earlier, open lines of communication are most effective in eliminating or at least diminishing potential areas of conflict, and most editors will work with you to find a compromise if they understand the circumstances.

If your editor doesn't give you a deadline for finishing the revisions, ask her when she would like to have them. Establishing a due date on revisions helps both of you stay on course. You know how much time you have to do your work, and the editor knows when to expect the final draft.

The Final Product

The details involved in converting a manuscript to book form are endless. It's tempting to think you're finished when the final revisions are completed, but there is more to be done. Your editor likely will ask for "front matter"—the industry term for the dedication, acknowledgments, and so on—which wasn't even included in your original manuscript.

Some books, like this one, feature the author's signature in the front matter, and you'll have to supply a sample for reproduction in the book. There may be issues regarding the design, illustrations, or permissions that you'll be asked to weigh in on.

ESSENTIAL

When you're writing your acknowledgments, include your agent, if you have one, and your editor. They've worked hard to help you turn your book from dream to reality, and their jobs often involve little recognition and less thanks. Let them and the world know that you appreciate their efforts on your behalf.

Page Proofs

With most royalty-paying publishers, you'll get a final chance to make corrections or minor changes with the proofs. Usually, the proof pages are laid out as they will look in the book, but they have extra-wide margins and are not bound in a book covering. You'll be asked to read the proofs to check for typos and factual errors. You are not expected—and probably won't be permitted—to make any substantial changes to the text at this point.

Your editor will expect a quick turnaround on the proofs; usually he will need them back on his desk within ten days to two weeks. This is the final step before the book is sent for printing, so the schedule usually is fairly tight. In most cases, you can mark your changes in any color ink except black, but it's best to use something that will stand out clearly on the page.

FACT

The term "galley proof" or "galley" dates from the days of hand-set lead type; a galley is the tray in which the typesetter laid out the individual letters. Virtually all printing today is done with computers, but the term "galley proof" has been slow to die out. Today, it is generally taken to mean the uncorrected layout of the book text.

It's a Book!

You'll see the catalog blurb for your book long before you ever hold an actual copy in your hands. Chances are you'll even be deep into writing your next book before your first one shows up in the bookstores. But, no matter what the intervening months bring, there is no feeling on earth that compares with finally seeing your name on the cover of the genuine article, printed and bound and available to the entire reading public. If you're like most first-time authors, you'll hand out your free copies left and right, graciously accede to requests from friends and relatives for a personalized signature, and make regular stops at the local bookstore to see how many copies are on the shelf.

Christopher Morley, an American journalist and author who plied his trade in the first half of the twentieth century, once said, "When you sell a man a book, you don't sell him twelve ounces of paper and ink and glue—you sell him a whole new life." For writers, seeing our work published and for sale in book form gives us a new life as well—one that we not only have the privilege of sharing with our contemporaries but one that will live on to be shared with others long after we depart.

Appendix A

Resources for Writers

Books

Books on Writing

Complete Guide to Self-Publishing, 4th Edition by Tom and Marilyn Ross, F&W Publications, 2002.

How Fiction Works by Oakley Hall, Writer's Digest Books, 2004.

How to Write a Children's Book and Get It Published by Barbara Seuling, John Wiley & Sons, 1991.

On Writing by Stephen King, Pocket Books, 2002.

On Writing Well, 25th Anniversary: The Classic Guide to Writing Nonfiction by William K. Zinsser, HarperResource, 2001.

Techniques of the Selling Writer by Dwight V. Swain, University of Oklahoma Press, 1982.

The Writer's Guide to Character Traits by Linda Edelstein, Writer's Digest Books, 2004.

The Writer's Guide to Crafting Stories for Children by Nancy Lamb, Writer's Digest Books, 2001.

The Writer's Idea Book by Jack Heffron, Writer's Digest Books, 2002.

Writing Creative Nonfiction, edited by Carolyn Forché and Philip Gerard, Story Press, 2001.

Writing Down the Bones by Natalie Goldberg, Shambhala, 1986.

Writing Mysteries, 2nd Edition, edited by Sue Grafton, Writer's Digest Books, 2002.

You Can Write a Romance by Rita Clay Estrada and Rita Gallagher, Writer's Digest Books, 1999.

Useful Reference Books for Writers

1001 Ways to Market Your Books, 5th Edition by John Kremer, Open Horizons, 2000.

The Birth Order Effect: How to Better Understand Yourself and Others by Cliff Isaacson and Kris Radish, Adams Media Corp., 2002.

Chicago Manual of Style, 15th Edition by University of Chicago Press Staff, University of Chicago Press, 2003.

Children's Writer's & Illustrator's Market (updated annually), Writer's Digest Books.

Deadly Doses: A Writer's Guide to Poisons by Serita Deborah Stevens and Anne Klarner, Writer's Digest Books, 1990.

Elements of Style, 4th Edition by William Strunk Jr., E.B. White, Roger Angell, Pearson Higher Education, 2000.

Everyday Life Among the American Indians by Candy Moulton, Writer's Digest Books, 2001.

Everyday Life in the 1800s: A Guide for Writers, Students & Historians by Marc McCutcheon, Writer's Digest Books, 2001.

Guide to Literary Agents: 600+ Agents Who Sell What You Write (updated annually), Writer's Digest Books.

Howdunit: How Crimes are Committed and Solved, edited by John Boertlein, Writer's Digest Books, 2000.

Just the Facts, Ma'am: A Writer's Guide to Investigators and Investigative Techniques by Greg Fallis, Writer's Digest Books, 1998.

The New Dictionary of Cultural Literacy, edited by James Trefil, Joseph F. Kett, E.D. Hirsch, Houghton Mifflin Company, 2002.

Novel & Short Story Writer's Market (updated annually), Writer's Digest Books.

Roget's II: The New Thesaurus, 3rd Edition, Berkeley Publishing Group, 1997.

Roget's Descriptive Word Finder: A Dictionary/Thesaurus of Adjectives and Adverbs, edited by Barbara Ann Kipfer, Writer's Digest Books, 2003.

The Writer's Complete Fantasy Reference: An Indispensable Compendium of Myth and Magic by the editors of Writer's Digest Books, Writer's Digest Books, 2000.

Writer's Market (updated annually), Writer's Digest Books.

Writer's Market FAQs by Peter Rubie, F&W Publications, 2002.

Writer's Online Marketplace by Debbie Ridpath Ohi, Writer's Digest Books, 2001.

Useful Internet Sites for Writers

AllExperts
www.allexperts.com
Free Q&A archive on broad range of topics; writers can send e-mail questions to experts they choose.

Amazon.com
www.amazon.com
Information about books in print and upcoming books; publisher information; book descriptions; sometimes provides excerpts.

American Booksellers Association
www.bookweb.org
Information about the bookselling industry; research and statistics; lists of book reviews and other features.

Association of Author's Representatives
www.aar-online.org
Information about literary agents; canon of ethics for members; member database.

Barnes & Noble Booksellers

✍ *www.bn.com*

Information about books in print and upcoming books; publisher information; book descriptions.

B.J. Doyen

✍ *www.barbaradoyen.com*

Information for writers seeking representation or publication; FAQs; information about seminars, speaking engagements, etc.

Book Industry Study Group

✍ *www.bisg.org*

Information on the publishing industry, including market research and buying trends.

Fiction Factor

✍ *www.fictionfactor.com*

Online magazine for fiction writers; articles about the craft and business of writing; interviews; book reviews; contests; market listings.

How Stuff Works

✍ *www.howstuffworks.com*

Useful information on broad range of topics, from the mundane (changing a tire) to the exotic (how hypnosis works).

Ipsos Book Trends

✍ *www.ipsos-insight.com/books.cfm*

Information and research about the book industry.

Meg Schneider

✍ *www.megschneider.com*

Q&A and information for aspiring writers; sample proposal elements; information about seminars, speaking engagements, etc.

ProfNet

✍ *www.profnet.com*

Service of PR Newswire, connecting reporters and writers with experts in all fields; includes scholarly experts and sources from business, government, and not-for-profits.

Publish Lawyer

✍ *www.publishlawyer.com*

Legal information for writers and artists.

Publishers Weekly

✍ *www.publishersweekly.com*

Information and articles about the publishing industry.

Society of Children's Book Writers and Illustrators

✍ *www.scbwi.org*

Information and articles about the children's book market.

Truth or Fiction

✍ *www.truthorfiction.com*

Identifies hoaxes and urban legends.

U.S. Copyright Office

✍ *www.loc.gov/copyright*

Searchable database of copyright status for books, music, movies, and computer software.

Writer's Digest

✍ *www.writersdigest.com*

Articles from *Writer's Digest* magazine; bookstore; FAQs; market tips; online workshops; editing services.

Writer's Resource Center

✍ *www.poewar.com*

Articles about writing and the business of writing.

Writing-World.com

✍ *www.writing-world.com*

Tips on writing; avoiding scams; contests; links.

Appendix B

Writers' Organizations

American Society of Journalists and Authors (ASJA)

New York, NY

✍ *www.asja.org*

Organization for published freelancers and nonfiction book authors.

Associated Writing Programs

Fairfax, VA

✍ *www.awpwriter.org*

Nonprofit group for supporting writers, writing programs, and writing teachers; open to beginning writers.

Authors Guild

New York, NY

✍ *www.authorsguild.org*

Largest U.S. organization of published authors; associate membership available to unpublished authors with contracts from royalty-paying publishers.

Canadian Authors Association

✍ *www.canauthors.org*

National writing association for Canada; professional and associate memberships available.

Christian Writers Fellowship International

Clinton, SC

✍ *www.cwfi-online.org*

Provides newsletter and other services to writers.

Editorial Freelancers Association

New York, NY

✎ *www.the-efa.org*

Nonprofit organization of full- and part-time freelancers in publishing.

Heartland Writers Guild

Kennett, MO

✎ *www.heartlandwriters.org*

Provides conferences and other services to published and unpublished writers.

Horror Writers Association

Palo Alto, CA

✎ *www.horror.org*

Organization specializing in horror and dark fantasy genres; affiliate membership available to unpublished writers.

Mystery Writers of America

New York, NY

✎ *www.mysterywriters.org*

Organization specializing in mystery genres; affiliate membership available to unpublished writers.

National Writers Association

✎ *www.nationalwriters.com*

Offers several services to writers and holds several annual contests that are open to nonmembers.

National Writers Union

New York, NY

✐ *www.nwu.org*

Trade union for freelance writers of all genres; membership open to published and unpublished writers.

Novelists Inc.

✐ *www.ninc.com*

Organization aimed at writers who have published at least two novels.

PEN American Center

✐ *www.pen.org*

Organization aimed primarily at literary novelists; "friend of PEN" membership available.

Poets & Writers Inc.

New York, NY

✐ *www.pw.org*

Nonprofit service organization for various artists, including fiction and literary nonfiction authors; various membership levels available.

Romance Writers of America

Spring, TX

✐ *www.rwanational.org*

Nonprofit organization supporting published and unpublished romance writers.

Science Fiction and Fantasy Writers of America Inc.

Chestertown, MD

www.sfwa.org

Organization devoted to helping science fiction/fantasy authors deal with publishing professionals; open to published book and short story authors.

Sisters in Crime

Lawrence, KS

www.sistersincrime.org

Organization supporting mystery and crime authors, especially women; open to unpublished authors.

Small Publishers, Artists and Writers Network (SPAWN)

Ojai, CA

www.spawn.org

Organization promoting exchange of ideas and information across publishing; open to unpublished authors.

Society of Children's Book Writers and Illustrators

Los Angeles, CA

www.scbwi.org

Organization focusing on children's literature; open to published and unpublished authors.

Western Writers of America

Cheyenne, WY

www.westernwriters.org

Organization promoting Western literature; open to published writers of Western books and magazine stories.

E Index

The EVERYTHING Series!

BUSINESS & PERSONAL FINANCE

Everything® Budgeting Book
Everything® Business Planning Book
Everything® Coaching and Mentoring Book
Everything® Fundraising Book
Everything® Get Out of Debt Book
Everything® Grant Writing Book
Everything® Homebuying Book, 2nd Ed.
Everything® Homeselling Book
Everything® Home-Based Business Book
Everything® Investing Book
Everything® Landlording Book
Everything® Leadership Book
Everything® Managing People Book
Everything® Negotiating Book
Everything® Online Business Book
Everything® Personal Finance Book
Everything® Personal Finance in Your
    20s & 30s Book
Everything® Project Management Book
Everything® Real Estate Investing Book
Everything® Robert's Rules Book, $7.95
Everything® Selling Book
Everything® Start Your Own Business Book
Everything® Time Management Book
Everything® Wills & Estate Planning Book

COOKING

Everything® Barbecue Cookbook
Everything® Bartender's Book, $9.95
Everything® Chinese Cookbook
Everything® Chocolate Cookbook
Everything® College Cookbook
Everything® Cookbook
Everything® Dessert Cookbook
Everything® Diabetes Cookbook
Everything® Easy Gourmet Cookbook
Everything® Fondue Cookbook
Everything® Grilling Cookbook

Everything® Healthy Meals in Minutes
    Cookbook
Everything® Holiday Cookbook
Everything® Indian Cookbook
Everything® Low-Carb Cookbook
Everything® Low-Fat High-Flavor Cookbook
Everything® Low-Salt Cookbook
Everything® Meals for a Month Cookbook
Everything® Mediterranean Cookbook
Everything® Mexican Cookbook
Everything® One-Pot Cookbook
Everything® Pasta Cookbook
Everything® Quick Meals Cookbook
Everything® Slow Cooker Cookbook
Everything® Soup Cookbook
Everything® Thai Cookbook
Everything® Vegetarian Cookbook
Everything® Wine Book

HEALTH

Everything® Alzheimer's Book
Everything® Anti-Aging Book
Everything® Diabetes Book
Everything® Hypnosis Book
Everything® Low Cholesterol Book
Everything® Massage Book
Everything® Menopause Book
Everything® Nutrition Book
Everything® Reflexology Book
Everything® Stress Management Book

HISTORY

Everything® American Government Book
Everything® American History Book
Everything® Civil War Book
Everything® Irish History & Heritage Book
Everything® Middle East Book

HOBBIES & GAMES

Everything® Blackjack Strategy Book
Everything® Brain Strain Book, $9.95
Everything® Bridge Book
Everything® Candlemaking Book
Everything® Card Games Book
Everything® Cartooning Book
Everything® Casino Gambling Book, 2nd Ed.
Everything® Chess Basics Book
Everything® Crossword and Puzzle Book
Everything® Crossword Challenge Book
Everything® Cryptograms Book, $9.95
Everything® Digital Photography Book
Everything® Drawing Book
Everything® Easy Crosswords Book
Everything® Family Tree Book
Everything® Games Book, 2nd Ed.
Everything® Knitting Book
Everything® Knots Book
Everything® Motorcycle Book
Everything® Online Genealogy Book
Everything® Photography Book
Everything® Poker Strategy Book
Everything® Pool & Billiards Book
Everything® Quilting Book
Everything® Scrapbooking Book
Everything® Sewing Book
Everything® Woodworking Book
Everything® Word Games Challenge Book

HOME IMPROVEMENT

Everything® Feng Shui Book
Everything® Feng Shui Decluttering Book, $9.95
Everything® Fix-It Book
Everything® Homebuilding Book
Everything® Landscaping Book
Everything® Lawn Care Book
Everything® Organize Your Home Book

All Everything® books are priced at $12.95 or $14.95, unless otherwise stated. Prices subject to change without notice.

EVERYTHING® *KIDS'* BOOKS

All titles are $6.95

Everything® Kids' Animal Puzzle & Activity Book
Everything® Kids' Baseball Book, 3rd Ed.
Everything® Kids' Bible Trivia Book
Everything® Kids' Bugs Book
Everything® Kids' Christmas Puzzle & Activity Book
Everything® Kids' Cookbook
Everything® Kids' Halloween Puzzle & Activity Book
Everything® Kids' Hidden Pictures Book
Everything® Kids' Joke Book
Everything® Kids' Knock Knock Book
Everything® Kids' Math Puzzles Book
Everything® Kids' Mazes Book
Everything® Kids' Money Book
Everything® Kids' Monsters Book
Everything® Kids' Nature Book
Everything® Kids' Puzzle Book
Everything® Kids' Riddles & Brain Teasers Book
Everything® Kids' Science Experiments Book
Everything® Kids' Sharks Book
Everything® Kids' Soccer Book
Everything® Kids' Travel Activity Book

KIDS' STORY BOOKS

Everything® Bedtime Story Book
Everything® Bible Stories Book
Everything® Fairy Tales Book

LANGUAGE

Everything® Conversational Japanese Book (with CD), $19.95
Everything® French Phrase Book, $9.95
Everything® French Verb Book, $9.95
Everything® Inglés Book
Everything® Learning French Book
Everything® Learning German Book
Everything® Learning Italian Book
Everything® Learning Latin Book
Everything® Learning Spanish Book
Everything® Sign Language Book
Everything® Spanish Grammar Book
Everything® Spanish Phrase Book, $9.95
Everything® Spanish Verb Book, $9.95

MUSIC

Everything® Drums Book (with CD), $19.95
Everything® Guitar Book
Everything® Home Recording Book
Everything® Playing Piano and Keyboards Book
Everything® Reading Music Book (with CD), $19.95
Everything® Rock & Blues Guitar Book (with CD), $19.95
Everything® Songwriting Book

NEW AGE

Everything® Astrology Book
Everything® Dreams Book, 2nd Ed.
Everything® Ghost Book
Everything® Love Signs Book, $9.95
Everything® Meditation Book
Everything® Numerology Book
Everything® Paganism Book
Everything® Palmistry Book
Everything® Psychic Book
Everything® Reiki Book
Everything® Spells & Charms Book
Everything® Tarot Book
Everything® Wicca and Witchcraft Book

PARENTING

Everything® Baby Names Book
Everything® Baby Shower Book
Everything® Baby's First Food Book
Everything® Baby's First Year Book
Everything® Birthing Book
Everything® Breastfeeding Book
Everything® Father-to-Be Book
Everything® Father's First Year Book
Everything® Get Ready for Baby Book
Everything® Getting Pregnant Book
Everything® Homeschooling Book
Everything® Parent's Guide to Children with ADD/ADHD
Everything® Parent's Guide to Children with Asperger's Syndrome
Everything® Parent's Guide to Children with Autism
Everything® Parent's Guide to Children with Dyslexia
Everything® Parent's Guide to Positive Discipline

Everything® Parent's Guide to Raising a Successful Child
Everything® Parent's Guide to Tantrums
Everything® Parent's Guide to the Overweight Child
Everything® Parenting a Teenager Book
Everything® Potty Training Book, $9.95
Everything® Pregnancy Book, 2nd Ed.
Everything® Pregnancy Fitness Book
Everything® Pregnancy Nutrition Book
Everything® Pregnancy Organizer, $15.00
Everything® Toddler Book
Everything® Tween Book
Everything® Twins, Triplets, and More Book

PETS

Everything® Cat Book
Everything® Dachshund Book, $12.95
Everything® Dog Book
Everything® Dog Health Book
Everything® Dog Training and Tricks Book
Everything® Golden Retriever Book, $12.95
Everything® Horse Book
Everything® Labrador Retriever Book, $12.95
Everything® Poodle Book, $12.95
Everything® Pug Book, $12.95
Everything® Puppy Book
Everything® Rottweiler Book, $12.95
Everything® Tropical Fish Book

REFERENCE

Everything® Car Care Book
Everything® Classical Mythology Book
Everything® Computer Book
Everything® Divorce Book
Everything® Einstein Book
Everything® Etiquette Book
Everything® Great Thinkers Book
Everything® Mafia Book
Everything® Philosophy Book
Everything® Psychology Book
Everything® Shakespeare Book

RELIGION

Everything® Angels Book
Everything® Bible Book
Everything® Buddhism Book
Everything® Catholicism Book

All Everything® books are priced at $12.95 or $14.95, unless otherwise stated. Prices subject to change without notice.

Everything® Christianity Book
Everything® Jewish History & Heritage Book
Everything® Judaism Book
Everything® Koran Book
Everything® Prayer Book
Everything® Saints Book
Everything® Torah Book
Everything® Understanding Islam Book
Everything® World's Religions Book
Everything® Zen Book

SCHOOL & CAREERS

Everything® After College Book
Everything® Alternative Careers Book
Everything® College Survival Book, 2nd Ed.
Everything® Cover Letter Book, 2nd Ed.
Everything® Get-a-Job Book
Everything® Job Interview Book
Everything® New Teacher Book
Everything® Online Job Search Book
Everything® Paying for College Book
Everything® Practice Interview Book
Everything® Resume Book, 2nd Ed.
Everything® Study Book

SELF-HELP

Everything® Dating Book
Everything® Great Sex Book
Everything® Kama Sutra Book
Everything® Self-Esteem Book

SPORTS & FITNESS

Everything® Fishing Book
Everything® Fly-Fishing Book
Everything® Golf Instruction Book
Everything® Pilates Book
Everything® Running Book
Everything® Total Fitness Book
Everything® Weight Training Book
Everything® Yoga Book

TRAVEL

Everything® Family Guide to Hawaii
Everything® Family Guide to New York City, 2nd Ed.
Everything® Family Guide to RV Travel & Campgrounds
Everything® Family Guide to the Walt Disney World Resort®, Universal Studios®, and Greater Orlando, 4th Ed.
Everything® Family Guide to Washington D.C., 2nd Ed.

Everything® Bachelorette Party Book, $9.95
Everything® Bridesmaid Book, $9.95
Everything® Creative Wedding Ideas Book, $9.95
Everything® Elopement Book, $9.95
Everything® Father of the Bride Book, $9.95
Everything® Groom Book, $9.95
Everything® Mother of the Bride Book, $9.95
Everything® Wedding Book, 3rd Ed.
Everything® Wedding Checklist, $9.95
Everything® Wedding Etiquette Book, $7.95
Everything® Wedding Organizer, $15.00
Everything® Wedding Shower Book, $7.95
Everything® Wedding Vows Book, $9.95
Everything® Weddings on a Budget Book, $9.95

WRITING

Everything® Creative Writing Book
Everything® Get Published Book
Everything® Grammar and Style Book
Everything® Guide to Writing a Book Proposal
Everything® Guide to Writing a Novel
Everything® Guide to Writing Children's Books
Everything® Screenwriting Book
Everything® Writing Poetry Book
Everything® Writing Well Book